Blockchain Essentials

Ramchandra Sharad Mangrulkar • Pallavi Vijay Chavan

Blockchain Essentials

Core Concepts and Implementations

Apress®

Ramchandra Sharad Mangrulkar
Mumbai, Maharashtra, India

Pallavi Vijay Chavan
Mumbai, Maharashtra, India

ISBN-13 (pbk): 978-1-4842-9974-6   ISBN-13 (electronic): 978-1-4842-9975-3
https://doi.org/10.1007/978-1-4842-9975-3

Managing Director, Apress Media LLC: Welmoed Spahr
Acquisitions Editor: Smriti Srivastava
Development Editor: Laura Berendson
Coordinating Editor: Shaul Elson

Cover designed by eStudioCalamar

Cover image by Sketchepedia@freepik.com

Distributed to the book trade worldwide by Apress Media, LLC, 1 New York Plaza, New York, NY 10004, U.S.A. Phone 1-800-SPRINGER, fax (201) 348-4505, e-mail orders-ny@springer-sbm.com, or visit www.springeronline.com. Apress Media, LLC is a California LLC and the sole member (owner) is Springer Science + Business Media Finance Inc (SSBM Finance Inc). SSBM Finance Inc is a **Delaware** corporation.

For information on translations, please e-mail booktranslations@springernature.com; for reprint, paperback, or audio rights, please e-mail bookpermissions@springernature.com.

Apress titles may be purchased in bulk for academic, corporate, or promotional use. eBook versions and licenses are also available for most titles. For more information, reference our Print and eBook Bulk Sales web page at http://www.apress.com/bulk-sales.

Any source code or other supplementary material referenced by the author in this book is available to readers on GitHub (https://github.com/Apress). For more detailed information, please visit https://www.apress.com/gp/services/source-code.

Paper in this product is recyclable

To our cherished daughter, Mansi:
Your unwavering support, encouragement, and constant
sympathy were invaluable during the creation of this book.
Without you, it would have been completed in half the time.

Contents

About the Authors

Dr. Ramchandra Mangrulkar is a Professor in the Department of Information Technology in the Dwarkadas J. Sanghvi College of Engineering in Mumbai, India. He holds various memberships in professional organizations such as IEEE, ISTE, ACM, and IACSIT. He completed his Doctor of Philosophy (Ph.D.) in Computer Science and Engineering from S.G.B. Amravati University in Maharashtra and Master of Technology (MTech) in Computer Science and Engineering from the National Institute of Technology, Rourkela. Dr. Mangrulkar is proficient in several technologies and tools, including Microsoft's Power BI, Power Automate, Power Query, and Power Virtual Agents, Google's Dialog Flow, and Overleaf. With over 22 years of combined teaching and administrative experience, Dr. Mangrulkar has established himself as a knowledgeable and skilled professional in his field. He has also obtained certifications like Certified Network Security Specialist International CyberSecurity Institute (ICSI) – Certified Network Security Specialist (CNSS) from ICSI, UK. Dr. Mangrulkar has an extensive publication record, with 95 publications including refereed/peer-reviewed international journal publications, book chapters with international publishers (including ones indexed in Scopus), and international conference publications.

Dr. Pallavi Vijay Chavan is Associate Professor at Ramrao Adik Institute of Technology, D. Y. Patil "Deemed-to-be-University," Navi Mumbai, MH, India. She has been in academia for the past 17 years working in the area of computing theory, data science, and network security. In her academic journey, she has published research in data science and security with reputable publishers such as Springer, Elsevier, CRC Press, and Inderscience. She has published 2 books, over 7 book chapters, more than 10 international journal papers, and over 30 international conference papers. Presently she serves as advisor to five Ph.D. research scholars in related fields. She completed her Ph.D. at Rashtrasant Tukadoji Maharaj Nagpur University, Nagpur, MH, India, in 2017. In 2003, she earned the first merit position at Nagpur University for a B.E. in Computer Engineering. She is the recipient of research grants from University Grants Commission (UGC), Council of Scientific & Industrial Research (CSIR), and University of Mumbai. She serves as a reviewer for Elsevier and Inderscience journals. Her motto is "Teaching is a mission."

About the Technical Reviewer

Dr. Parikshit Mahalle is a senior member of the Institute of Electrical and Electronics Engineers and Professor, Dean of Research and Development and -Chair of the Department of Artificial Intelligence and Data Science at Vishwakarma Institute of Information Technology, Pune, India. He completed his Ph.D. at Aalborg University, Denmark, and continued as a postdoctoral researcher at Communication, Media & Information Technologies, Copenhagen, Denmark. He has over 23 years of teaching and research experience. He is a former member of the Board of Studies in Computer Engineering and former chairman of the Department of Information Technology at Savitribai Phule Pune University and various universities and autonomous colleges throughout India. He owns 15 patents, has published over 200 research studies and papers (2950+ Google Scholar, 1550+ H index-25 and Scopus citations, 438 H index-8, Web of Science, and H index-10 citations), and has authored/edited 56 books with Springer, CRC Press, Cambridge University Press, and others. He is editor in chief for IGI Global's *International Journal of Rough Sets and Data Analysis* and Inderscience's *International Journal of Grid and Utility Computing*, is a member of the editorial review board for IGI Global's *International Journal of Ambient Computing and Intelligence*, and serves as a reviewer for various reputable journals and conferences. His research interests include machine learning, data science, algorithms, Internet of Things, identity management, and security. He currently advises eight Ph.D. students in the areas of IoT and machine learning, and six students have successfully defended their Ph.D. under his supervision from Savitribai Phule Pune University. He is also the recipient of the Best Faculty Award by Sinhgad Institutes and Cognizant Technology Solutions. He has delivered over 200 lectures at the national and international levels.

Preface

Blockchain has become the buzzword of the day. Developers are focusing on more user-friendly applications with the help of blockchain, achieving decentralization and a trustless environment without third-party involvement. This includes diverse concepts and tools that play major roles in developing crypto-based applications in various programming languages. The distributed ledger and smart contracts involved reveal the importance of blockchain in creating immutable and transparent, cryptographically secure record-keeping of transactions. The programming approach helps to shed light on the core concepts of blockchain and relevant applications in easy steps. This helps to motivate learners to become part of the solution to most of the applications demanding trustless and independent autonomous systems. The identification and examination of blockchain technology beyond cryptocurrency will help to investigate alternative solutions using many blockchain-supportive tools.

The main purpose of this book is to present the difficult concepts of blockchain technology in very accessible and easy-to-understand language using a programming approach so that learners can easily grasp the key concepts arising from the emerging notion of blockchain technology. Another purpose of this book is to make available the experience of academia and industry to the target audience through hands-on programming.

This book presents the concepts of blockchain technology in a concise manner with clear and easy examples using trending blockchain programming languages. The book fills a gap of address issues surrounding the practical implementation of blockchain concepts using case studies. The book also highlights the usefulness of blockchain technology beyond its current applications.

Mumbai, India
September 2023

Ramchandra Sharad Mangrulkar
Pallavi Vijay Chavan

Acknowledgements

We extend our sincere gratitude to the dedicated contributors and accomplished researchers in the field of blockchain for their invaluable contributions and pioneering work.

Introduction to Blockchain

1

Readers of this book are likely to have some knowledge and basic idea about the enormous potential of the trending, decentralizing, and trustworthy technology called blockchain. This technology represents an innovation in the digital ecosystem that has significantly impacted trusted computing activities, resulting in an enhanced level of protection from cyber security threats.

This chapter lays out the fundamentals of blockchain technology, presenting its theoretical background, historical milestones, and present growth trends. Further, the conceptual view of a block in blockchain and the types of blockchain are described. The chapter discusses the basic skill set and libraries required to start doing "blockchain programming," which is a key objective of this book. The chapter ends with a few examples and their implementation in Python.

1.1 Prerequisites

The prerequisites for blockchain technology include:

- Understanding of cryptography: Cryptography is the foundation of blockchain technology. A basic understanding of cryptographic concepts, such as hashing, public-key encryption, and digital signatures, is necessary.
- Distributed systems: Blockchain is a distributed system that runs on multiple nodes. Therefore, it is essential to have a good understanding of distributed systems to build and deploy blockchain applications.
- Data structures and algorithms: Blockchain technology relies on complex data structures such as Merkle trees and algorithms such as consensus algorithms. Understanding of these concepts is crucial for building a robust blockchain system.
- Networking and security: Blockchain technology requires a good understanding of networking protocols, such as TCP/IP, HTTP, and HTTPS. Additionally, a solid understanding of security concepts, such as firewalls, encryption, and authentication, is necessary to develop secure blockchain applications.
- Smart contracts: Smart contracts are self-executing contracts with the terms of the agreement between buyer and seller directly written into lines of code. Knowledge of smart contract programming languages, such as Solidity, is necessary for building decentralized applications.

© The Author(s), under exclusive license to APress Media, LLC, part of Springer Nature 2024
R. S. Mangrulkar, P. Vijay Chavan, *Blockchain Essentials*,
https://doi.org/10.1007/978-1-4842-9975-3_1

- Business and economics: Blockchain technology is disrupting traditional business models and creating new opportunities. Understanding the economics of blockchain and how it can be applied to business is essential for leveraging its potential.
- Legal and regulatory dimensions: Blockchain technology operates in a regulatory gray area in many countries, and regulations are constantly evolving. Understanding the legal and regulatory environment in which blockchain operates is critical for creating compliant and successful blockchain applications.

1.2   Blockchain Myths

Blockchain is an emerging technology. The following list dispels some of the myths surrounding blockchain:

- Blockchain is the same thing as Bitcoin (or any other cryptocurrency)
  There is a misleading idea that if you learn blockchain technology, you will become a good trader! This is untrue. Blockchain is not equivalent to any cryptocurrency, whether Bitcoin or any other currencies on the market like Altcoins. In fact, blockchain is a technology, whereas Bitcoin is a cryptocurrency that makes use of blockchain technology. Blockchain has many applications outside the crypto world. Blockchain technology provides a full support system for developing cryptocurrencies, whereas Bitcoin is a fundamental application that builds on this emerging blockchain technology.
- Blockchain can solve all security issues
  Blockchain cannot be used to definitively eliminate corruption or fraudulent activities. Blockchain's many applications have been developed by players in the various models governing economies around the world. Blockchain cannot all issues related to security. Solving all societal issues using blockchain is a formidable challenge. Thus, careful consideration needs to be given as to which societal issues should be addressed using blockchain.
- Blockchain is the only possible technology
  Blockchain is not necessarily the best technology for solving your problems; they might be better solved employing technology that does not use blockchain. It is possible that many different existing technologies would yield better results in terms of security without the use of blockchain.
- Blockchain and distributed databases are similar technologies
  Blockchain and distributed databases are different technologies. Blockchain is not a distributed databases. Blockchain is not designed to store and secure data. Blockchain and distributed databases are two different technologies, each with its own merits and demerits and different potential to solve different problems. Both are essential, and one cannot easily replace the other.

1.3   Blockchain and Decentralization

Blockchain technology emerged to solve most of the issues in decentralization. Decentralization refers to the distribution of power or authority away from a single central entity to multiple individuals or groups. In the context of technology, it refers to systems or networks that operate without a central authority controlling them. Figure 1-1 gives an overview of centralized and decentralized systems.

Decentralization is required to address trust issues, that is, the different parties involved do not trust each other, but they should cooperate. The network of different entities such as businesses, individuals, government, private- and public-sector organizations, with their own interests, can come

Centralized   **Decentralized**

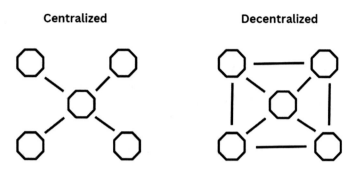

Figure 1-1 Overview: centralized and decentralized systems

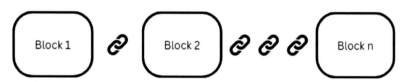

Figure 1-2 Blocks and chain in blockchain

together and cooperate with each other to solve societal issues. Decentralization and blockchain work together to create a secure, transparent, and tamper-proof system that operates without the need for a central authority.

1.4   What Is Blockchain?

Blockchain is an append-only, immutable, never-ending chain of data where data, once added, cannot be deleted or modified, achieving a tamper-proof system. The immutable property of blockchain means no one can change it. Its append-only nature ensures that no one can erase data once they are written in the blockchain. This append-only nature of blockchain makes it a never-ending but fully traceable system. Figure 1-2 shows the basic idea of blocks and chain in blockchain.

Every individual player maintains a copy of the blockchain, removing the need for central administration or centralization. The addition of information to the existing blockchain happens in the form of a new block appended at the end while at the same time ensuring that all copies of the local blockchain available to the different network players must also be updated in the same order. This will ensure data consistency in the blockchain, and all copies will be the same. This doubtlessly will require an additional authentication and validation mechanism, but at a superficial level, everyone will have an updated copy of the blockchain.

The data structure in blockchain consists of a chain of blocks linked together with the help of current and previous pointers. These two fields store the hashed data of the contents of the block, the previous pointer stores the hashed data of the previous block, and the current pointer stores the hashed data of the current block.

The data are stored in the blockchain in a transparent way and are available to everyone, allowing anyone to validate and verify the data as and when required.

Definition 1.1 Blockchain is a decentralized, immutable, append-only public ledger.

1.5   Disruptive Technology

Clayton Christensen introduced the idea of disruptive technologies in a 1995 *Harvard Business Review* article. Disruptive technology refers to any innovation that disrupts an existing market or industry, displacing established products or services and creating new markets and opportunities. These technologies often have a transformative effect on society, leading to changes in business models, consumer behavior, and even cultural norms.

Not all innovations are disruptive technologies. It is the process rather than product or services. Blockchain is a sustaining innovation rather than a disruptive innovation in the financial sector.

Disruptive technologies typically emerge from unexpected sources and are often initially dismissed as inferior or irrelevant by established players in the market. However, as they gain momentum and become more widely adopted, they can completely change the competitive landscape and reshape entire industries.

The following are examples of disruptive technologies:

- Ecommerce: The rise of ecommerce in the 2000s disrupted traditional brick-and-mortar retail, creating new opportunities for businesses to sell products and services online.
- Personal computers: The development of personal computers in the 1970s and 1980s disrupted the established mainframe computer industry, creating new markets and opportunities for businesses and individuals.
- Social media: The emergence of social media in the 2010s disrupted traditional media and advertising industries, leading to the rise of new platforms for content creation and distribution.
- Digital photography: The advent of digital photography in the 1990s disrupted the traditional film photography industry, leading to the demise of many established companies and the emergence of new players in the market.

Blockchain is considered a disruptive technology for several reasons:

- Decentralization: One of the key features of blockchain technology is its ability to operate in a decentralized manner, without the need for intermediaries such as banks or government institutions. This eliminates the need for trust in centralized institutions, which can be slow, expensive, and prone to corruption.
- Immutable and transparent: Blockchain technology is immutable and transparent, meaning that once data are added to a blockchain, it cannot be modified or deleted. This creates a high degree of trust in the data stored on the blockchain and eliminates the need for intermediaries to verify data.
- Security: Blockchain technology is secured by cryptographic algorithms that make it virtually impossible to tamper with the data stored on the blockchain. This creates a high degree of security for transactions and other data stored on the blockchain.
- Smart contracts: Smart contracts are self-executing contracts with the terms of the agreement between buyer and seller being directly written into lines of code. This eliminates the need for intermediaries to execute and enforce contracts, which can be slow, expensive, and prone to errors.
- Tokenization: Blockchain technology enables the creation and exchange of digital assets, or tokens, which can represent anything of value, such as currency, property, or ownership rights. This creates new opportunities for businesses to generate value and disrupt traditional business models.

1.6 History

Blockchain, a technology with the potential to become the foundation of global record-keeping systems, was introduced a mere decade ago by anonymous individuals associated with the digital currency Bitcoin, under the pseudonym Satoshi Nakamoto. Despite its relatively recent inception, blockchain has quickly gained recognition as a transformative innovation, poised to revolutionize various industries through its decentralized and secure nature.

1.6.1 Milestones in Blockchain Development

The subsection discusses some of the significant milestones in the development of blockchain technology (Figure 1-3).

1. 2008 – The publication of Bitcoin's whitepaper by Satoshi Nakamoto marked the groundbreaking introduction of the cryptocurrency. This event revolutionized the financial landscape, ushering in a new era of decentralized digital currency. The whitepaper laid the foundation for a peer-to-peer electronic cash system that would eventually disrupt traditional monetary systems worldwide.
2. 2009 – The inaugural Bitcoin transaction between Satoshi Nakamoto and Hal Finney stands as a significant milestone in cryptocurrency history. This historic event symbolized the practical application and transferability of Bitcoin as a digital currency. The transaction showcased the

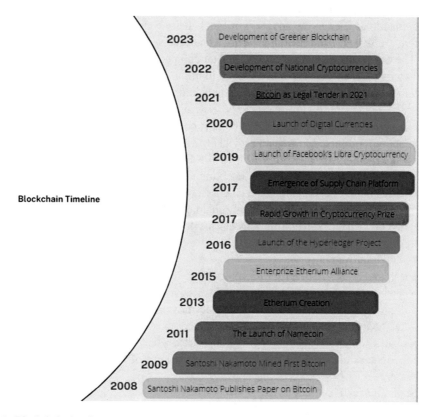

Figure 1-3 Blockchain timeline

potential of Bitcoin as a decentralized payment system, setting the stage for its widespread adoption and subsequent impact on the financial industry.

3. 2011 – Namecoin's launch marked a groundbreaking moment as it became the first alternative cryptocurrency to utilize blockchain technology. This pioneering step opened the door for a multitude of innovative blockchain-based digital assets. Namecoin's introduction demonstrated the potential for decentralized systems beyond traditional currencies, paving the way for the development of various blockchain applications and cryptocurrencies.

4. 2013 – Vitalik Buterin's creation of Ethereum unleashed a revolutionary platform enabling the creation of smart contracts and decentralized applications (dApps). Ethereum's emergence introduced a new paradigm in blockchain technology, empowering developers to build complex applications on a decentralized network. Buterin's vision laid the foundation for a vibrant ecosystem of dApps, fueling innovation and transforming industries through the power of decentralized computing.

5. 2015 – The formation of the Enterprise Ethereum Alliance united leading corporations and blockchain startups, fostering collaboration in the advancement of blockchain technology. This alliance served as a catalyst for exploring the potential of Ethereum in various industries and promoting blockchain adoption on a global scale. The Enterprise Ethereum Alliance aimed to accelerate innovation, establish industry standards, and drive the mainstream integration of blockchain solutions across sectors.

6. 2016 – The Hyperledger Project, initiated by the Linux Foundation, set out to develop open-source blockchain software specifically tailored to enterprise applications. This strategic launch brought together industry leaders and technologists to collaborate on building scalable and interoperable blockchain solutions. By providing a collaborative platform, the Hyperledger Project aimed to accelerate the adoption of blockchain technology among businesses, fostering transparency, efficiency, and trust in enterprise operations.

7. 2017 – The cryptocurrency market witnessed an unprecedented surge in value, primarily led by Bitcoin, accompanied by an explosive growth in initial coin offerings (ICOs). This phenomenon resulted in widespread frenzy and speculation, attracting investors seeking to capitalize on the potential returns of digital assets. The soaring value of cryptocurrencies and the ICO boom reshaped the financial landscape, bringing both opportunities and risks while fueling the development of innovative blockchain projects worldwide.

8. 2018 – Blockchain-based platforms like IBM's Food Trust have emerged as transformative solutions for supply chain management, enabling enhanced transparency and traceability within the food industry. By leveraging blockchain technology, these platforms offer a secure and immutable record of every step in the supply chain, promoting accountability and reducing fraud. The adoption of such blockchain solutions has the potential to revolutionize the way we track and verify the origins, quality, and safety of food products, ensuring consumer confidence and driving industry-wide improvements.

9. 2019 – Facebook's launch of the Libra cryptocurrency encountered substantial regulatory scrutiny and widespread resistance from governments worldwide. The ambitious project aimed to create a global digital currency, but concerns over data privacy, monetary sovereignty, and potential risks to the financial system led to intense pushback. The Libra initiative highlighted the complex challenges and regulatory hurdles that arise when tech giants venture into the realm of cryptocurrencies and sparked discussions on the future of digital currencies in a regulated environment.

10. 2020 – Major financial institutions like JP Morgan and Goldman Sachs have embraced blockchain technology, recognizing its potential for efficiency and security in financial operations. Simultaneously, numerous countries have launched their own central bank digital currencies (CBDCs),

aiming to leverage the benefits of blockchain and enhance their monetary systems. This combined trend showcases the growing acceptance and integration of blockchain technology within the traditional financial sector, paving the way to transformative changes in how transactions and currencies are managed globally.

11. 2021 – In a historic move, El Salvador became the first country to officially adopt Bitcoin as legal tender in 2021. This decision enabled businesses to utilize Bitcoin for paying employee salaries and established its acceptance as a valid payment method throughout the country. El Salvador's embrace of Bitcoin as a form of currency marked a significant milestone in the mainstream acceptance and integration of cryptocurrencies into national economies.

12. 2022 – The year 2022 witnessed notable blockchain growth, particularly in the emergence of national cryptocurrencies. This concept revolved around the idea of CBDCs, where central banks opted to develop their own digital coins instead of relying on decentralized cryptocurrencies. This trend highlighted a shift toward more centralized control over digital currencies, with central banks exploring the benefits and challenges of issuing their own blockchain-based currencies.

13. 2023 – The year 2023 has witnessed a notable focus on environmentally friendly blockchains, facilitated by carbon offsetting practices and energy-conscious network architectures. The adoption of greener blockchains will be made more feasible through the utilization of eco-friendly algorithms like proof of stake. These developments signify a growing commitment to reducing the environmental impact of blockchain technology and promoting sustainable practices within the industry.

1.7   Features of Blockchain

The remarkable attention and interest surrounding blockchain technology can be attributed to several key factors (Figure 1-4).

1. Immutable

   Immutability lies at the core of blockchain technology, rendering it an unchangeable and enduring network. By operating through a network of nodes, the blockchain ensures that once a transaction is recorded, it becomes permanent and resistant to modification. This immutability characteristic establishes the blockchain as a secure and trustworthy ledger, bolstering confidence in its integrity and authenticity.

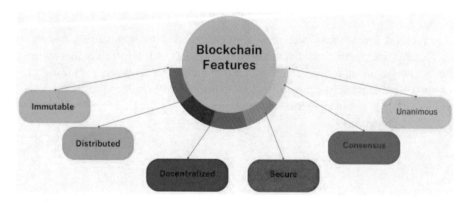

Figure 1-4 Features of blockchain

2. Distributed

Transparency is a fundamental feature of blockchain technology, as all network participants possess a copy of the ledger, ensuring complete visibility. By employing a public ledger, the blockchain offers comprehensive information regarding participants and transactions. The distributed computational power across multiple computers enhances the efficiency and reliability of the network, leading to improved outcomes in terms of security and consensus.

3. Decentralized

Blockchain technology operates as a decentralized system, devoid of a central authority, whereby numerous nodes collaborate to authenticate and validate transactions. Every node within a blockchain network possesses an identical copy of the ledger, ensuring consistency and eliminating the need for a central point of control. This decentralized architecture enhances the security, resilience, and transparency of the network, making it resistant to single points of failure or manipulation.

4. Secure

In a blockchain, each record undergoes individual encryption, bolstering the overall security of the network. The absence of a central authority does not grant unrestricted access to add, update, or delete data on the network. Cryptographic hashing assigns a unique identity to every piece of information on the blockchain, ensuring the integrity and immutability of the data. Each block contains a distinctive hash along with the hash of the preceding block, creating cryptographic links between blocks. Modifying the data would require changing all the hash IDs, an exceedingly challenging and practically infeasible task.

5. Consensus

Consensus plays a vital role in blockchain networks by enabling efficient and impartial decision-making. It involves the use of algorithms that allow a group of active nodes to reach swift and reliable agreements, ensuring the smooth operation of the system. Although nodes may lack trust in one another, they rely on the consensus algorithm at the heart of the network to facilitate consensus. Various consensus algorithms exist, each with its own advantages and disadvantages. A consensus algorithm is essential for any blockchain to maintain its value and integrity.

6. Unanimous

In a blockchain network, agreement on the validity of records is crucial before their inclusion. When a node intends to add a block, it requires majority consensus through voting, ensuring that the block can be added to the network. Unauthorized addition, modification, or deletion of information is prevented. Updates to records occur simultaneously, rapidly propagating throughout the network. Therefore, any changes without the consent of the majority of nodes are practically impossible due to the stringent consensus requirements in place.

7. Smart Contract

Smart contracts are agreements whose provisions are encoded in computer code and automatically execute. Without intermediaries, they automate, facilitate, and enforce contractual agreements. Smart contracts augment a blockchain with programmable capabilities, allowing actions and transactions to be activated automatically when predefined conditions are met. This function improves the efficacy and independence of blockchain applications, such as financial services and supply chain management.

1.8   Present Growth

The growth of blockchain technology has continued to accelerate in recent years. Here are some examples of its present growth:

- Investment: According to a report by CB Insights, global investment in blockchain startups has increased steadily, with over USD 8.2 billion raised across 342 deals in 2021 alone.
- Enterprise adoption: Major corporations, including IBM, Walmart, and Visa, are investing in and implementing blockchain technology for supply chain management, payment processing, and other applications.
- Cryptocurrency adoption: Cryptocurrencies such as Bitcoin and Ethereum have seen significant increases in adoption and investment. In 2021, the total market capitalization of all cryptocurrencies surpassed USD 2 *trillion*.
- Government interest: Several governments around the world are exploring the use of blockchain technology for various applications, including the development of CBDCs and voting systems.
- NFTs: The emergence of nonfungible tokens (NFTs) on blockchain platforms has created a new market for digital assets and has the potential to revolutionize the art, music, and gaming industries.
- Increased scalability: The development of new blockchain technologies, such as sharding and layer-2 solutions, is addressing the issue of scalability, making it possible to process more transactions per second and enabling more widespread adoption.

1.9   Predicted Market

The market for blockchain technology is expected to continue to grow in the coming years. The market size of blockchain technology globally was valued at USD 10.02 billion in 2022. It is projected to experience significant growth at a compound annual growth rate (CAGR) of 87.7% from 2023 to 2030. This growth can be attributed to the rising venture capital funding in companies involved in blockchain technology.

- Etherium will dominate
  In 2023, Ethereum is poised to become the leading blockchain platform, driven by updates such as the Merge and the Shanghai upgrade. These enhancements will enhance usability, performance, and scalability, particularly with the implementation of proto-danksharding. As a result, Ethereum will solidify its position as the preeminent player in the blockchain industry.
- Ethereum Staking
  In 2023, Ethereum has emerged as the leading platform for staking, with over $20 billion staked, driving innovation in this field. EigenLayer, a notable project, offers "security as a service" to other blockchain platforms, leveraging Ethereum's staked security to enhance their own. EigenLayer's upcoming EigenDA protocol aims to introduce a restaking mechanism in 2023, further advancing staking innovation. With growing demand for ETH staking and the development of new solutions, Ethereum will solidify its role as a global settlement layer for the Web3 ecosystem.
- Evolution of NFTs In the coming year, NFTs will expand beyond digital art, driven by major brands like Starbucks. NFT rewards programs will inspire other commercial leaders to follow suit. The fusion of physical and digital experiences will fuel NFT adoption. Projects lacking adaptation and utility may fail, while recognized ones like CryptoPunks could thrive. The widespread commercial use of NFTs will shape their future.
- Future of Tech Crypto

Cryptocurrency enables trading and investment, while "tech crypto" prioritizes peer-to-peer networks and global software for transactions. The shift toward tech crypto includes decentralized finance and nonfinancial decentralized applications. Growing adoption of tech crypto will bolster its importance, paving the way to the next bull market and providing stability amid market fluctuations.

- Reputation Management in Web3
  Decentralized identity and reputation systems will be vital for Web3 transactions in 2023, allowing reputation transfer and holistic identity views. Projects like Intuition are leading the way by leveraging attested data for a deeper understanding of identity. These systems will be fundamental to Web3, enabling global decentralized coordination and supporting diverse interactions and transactions.

- Bitcoin's Market Challenges
  Bitcoin's market share is likely to be challenged in the coming year due to various factors. The lack of daily utility compared to other tokens and ecosystems with higher commercial use diminishes Bitcoin's appeal. Criticism related to environmental concerns and the energy-intensive proof-of-work system adds to the challenges. Bitcoin's failure to serve as a risk-off digital gold hedge may hinder its progress, creating an opportunity for a more utility-driven layer 1 asset in the next bull run.

- Web 3.0 Gaming
  In 2023, Web 3.0 gaming is set to overcome its early flaws and integrate Web3 utility and gaming aesthetics more seamlessly. The industry's focus will shift toward gameplay-centered studios, moving away from token-centric projects. Game projects will leverage advanced technologies to enhance gameplay experiences and drive growth in the Web 3.0 gaming market. The upcoming year holds promise for Web 3.0 gaming to engage the global gaming community of three billion players and reshape its negative reputation.

1.10   Blockchain Types

Blockchain is a digital ledger technology that provides a secure and transparent way of storing and sharing data. There are different types of blockchain, each with its unique features and characteristics (Figure 1-5).

Some of the blockchain types are categorized into permissioned and permissionless; they overlap is illustrated in Figure 1-6.

The following subsections present the characteristics of various categories of blockchain and provides examples of each.

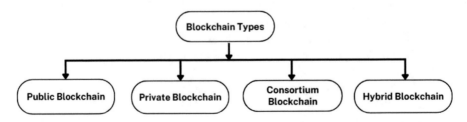

Figure 1-5 Types of blockchain

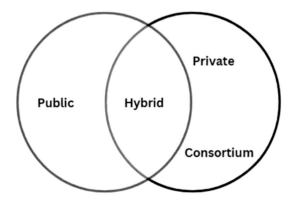

Figure 1-6 *Permissionless vs. permissioned blockchain*

1.10.1 Public

A public blockchain is a type of blockchain technology that is open to anyone, and anyone with Internet facilities is eligible to participate. It operates in a decentralized manner, allowing participants to validate blocks and send transactions without the need for permission from a central authority. Public blockchains often use two major consensus algorithms: proof of work (PoW) and proof of stake (PoS).

They are characterized by their openness, transparency, and lack of central authority. Nodes can join and leave a network freely, and all nodes can verify new data added to the blockchain.

Public blockchains employ incentive mechanisms to ensure the correct operation of the system. They are permissionless, meaning anyone can access the blockchain without requiring permission, and the ledger is shared and transparent. Participants in a public blockchain can remain anonymous, as real names and identities are not necessary. Public blockchains offer users greater freedom and flexibility in how they use the platform, without the limitations imposed by regulations.

Characteristics of Public Blockchain

- Permissionless and open to all
- Cooperation among all nodes to verify data
- Use of incentive mechanism-based protocols
- Shared and transparent ledger
- Secure with 51% rule
- Anonymous and hidden user identity
- Absence of regulations or limitations on participant
- No way to track transactions

Examples of Public Blockchain

Examples of public blockchains include Bitcoin (BTC), Ethereum (ETH), Ripple (XRP), Litecoin (LTC), Cardano (ADA), and Stellar (XLM) are examples of public blockchains.

1.10.2 Private

Private blockchains are blockchain networks that are permissioned and accessible only to a specific group of people or organizations. Unlike public blockchains, where anyone can participate in the network, private blockchains are designed to restrict access to certain authorized users. Private blockchains are often used by organizations to build secure and private networks that can improve efficiency and reduce costs.

Characteristics of Private Blockchain

- Private blockchains operate in a closed network and have permissions managed by an organization.
- They are suitable for specific use cases where organizations want to exert control over access and network parameters.
- The advantages of private blockchains include faster transaction speeds, better scalability, and customization options.
- However, private blockchains go against decentralization and distributed ledger principles. They rely on centralized nodes, which can create challenges in establishing trust and compromise security.
- Use cases for private blockchains include supply chain management, asset ownership verification, and internal voting systems.
- Private blockchains provide organizations with control and customization but may sacrifice the decentralization and security offered by public blockchains.

Examples of Private Blockchain

Hyperledger Fabric, Corda, Quorum, Multichain, and R3 Corda Enterprise are examples of private blockchains.

1.10.3 Federated

A federated blockchain is a type of blockchain network that operates under a federated consensus model. It involves a consortium of organizations or nodes that work together to validate transactions and maintain the blockchain. Federated blockchains are permissioned, meaning access and participation are restricted to authorized entities within the consortium.

In a federated blockchain, the consensus mechanism is typically based on a select group of nodes that form the federation. These nodes are responsible for validating transactions and reaching consensus on the state of the blockchain. Unlike public blockchains, federated blockchains are more centralized as the decision-making power lies with the participating entities.

Federated blockchains offer advantages such as improved scalability, faster transaction speeds, and enhanced privacy and security compared to public blockchains. They are suitable for use cases where a consortium of organizations needs to collaborate and share data while maintaining control and privacy.

Characteristics of Federated Blockchain

- Permissioned and accessible only to authorized entities within a consortium
- Consensus achieved through a select group of nodes forming the federation
- Improved scalability and faster transaction speeds compared to public blockchains
- Enhanced privacy and security features
- More centralized decision-making compared to public blockchains
- Suitable for consortium-based collaborations and data sharing

Examples of Federated Blockchain

IBM Blockchain Platform, Ripple, Quorum (Enterprise Ethereum), Corda Enterprise, and Hyperledger Fabric Consortium Networks are examples of federated blockchains.

1.10.4 Hybrid

A hybrid blockchain is a combination of both public and private blockchains, offering the benefits of both models. It allows for the interoperability of different blockchain networks and enables the exchange of data and assets between them. Hybrid blockchains provide flexibility in terms of transparency, control, and scalability.

In a hybrid blockchain, certain parts of the network are public, allowing for open participation and transparency, while other parts are private, providing restricted access and enhanced privacy. The integration of public and private blockchains enables organizations to leverage the advantages of public networks for certain use cases while maintaining control and privacy for sensitive data or operations.

The hybrid model offers the ability to customize the level of decentralization and privacy based on specific requirements. It provides a balance between transparency and confidentiality, making it suitable for various applications, such as supply chain management, healthcare, finance, and government sectors.

Characteristics of Hybrid Blockchain

- Combination of public and private blockchains
- Flexibility in terms of transparency and control
- Interoperability between different blockchain networks
- Customization of decentralization and privacy
- Suitable for applications with varying requirements

Table 1-1 Comparison of Public and Private Blockchains

Basis of Comparison	Public Blockchain	Private Blockchain
Access	Permissionless	Permissioned
Network actors	Don't know each other	Know each other
Decentralized vs. centralized	Decentralized	More centralized
Order of magnitude	Lower	Higher
Native token	Yes	Not necessary
Speed	Slow	Fast
Transactions per second	Fewer	More
Security	More secure	Less secure
Energy consumption	More	Less
Consensus algorithms	Proof of work, proof of stake, etc.	Proof of elapsed time, raft, etc.
Attacks	Risk of collision or 51% attack	No minor collision, known validators
Effects	Disrupt current business models	Reduce transaction costs and data redundancies
Examples	Bitcoin, Ethereum, etc.	R3, EWF, B3i, Corda

Examples of Hybrid Blockchain

Dragonchain, Ardor, Wanchain, XinFin, and MultiChain are examples of hybrid blockchain platforms.

1.10.5 Difference Between Public and Private Blockchains

Let us differentiate between public and private blockchains with respect to a few criteria as given in Table 1-1.

1.11   Blockchain Framework

A blockchain framework is a set of protocols, rules, and standards that define the structure and operations of a blockchain network. A blockchain framework has the following five major layers (Figure 1-7).

1.11.1 Hardware/Infrastructure Layer

The bottom-most layer of the blockchain is the hardware or infrastructure layer. It involves servers hosted in data centers that store the content of the blockchain. These servers provide the necessary resources for the blockchain network to function effectively. Some important features of this layer are as follows:

- The top layer of the blockchain is the hardware or infrastructure layer, consisting of servers hosted in data centers.
- The servers store the content of the blockchain and provide necessary resources.
- Client–server architecture is different from blockchain's peer-to-peer (P2P) network.

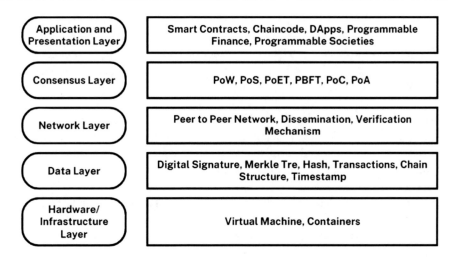

Figure 1-7 Blockchain framework

- Blockchain utilizes a P2P network of computers to calculate, validate, and record transactions in a shared ledger.
- Transactions are organized into blocks in an ordered format.
- The end result is a distributed database that tracks all data, transactions, and relevant information.
- Nodes, which are computers in the P2P network, play a crucial role in the blockchain.
- Nodes verify transactions, group them into blocks, and roadcast them to the network.
- Once consensus is reached, nodes update their local copies of the ledger and commit the block to the blockchain network.
- Any device that connects to the blockchain network becomes a node and contributes to the network's functioning.

1.11.2 Data Layer

By combining the use of linked lists, Merkle trees, and digital signatures, blockchain technology establishes a secure and transparent structure for storing and verifying data. Some of the important features of the data layer are as follows:

- The blockchain's data structure relies on a linked list, which consists of blocks with transactions and pointers to previous blocks.
- Pointers in the linked list refer to the location of other variables and maintain the sequential order of blocks.
- The blockchain employs a Merkle tree, a binary tree of hashes, to ensure security, integrity, and immutability.
- The Merkle tree holds important information such as the hash of the previous block, date, nonce, block version number, and current difficulty goal.
- Transactions on the blockchain are digitally signed, providing authentication and integrity.
- The digital signature allows anyone with the corresponding public key to verify the authenticity of a transaction.
- Data encryption further enhances security and protects the sender's or owner's identity.
- The structure of a block on the blockchain is determined by the data layer.

1.11.3 Network Layer

The network layer, also known as the P2P layer, is responsible for facilitating communication between nodes in a blockchain network. It enables transactions, block propagation, and discovery among the nodes. Some important features of the network layer are as follows:

- The network layer focuses on maintaining the validity of the blockchain network's current state by enabling effective communication, synchronization, and information propagation between nodes.
- In a P2P network, distributed nodes collaborate to achieve a common goal, and in the context of blockchain, they perform tasks related to transactions and contribute to the overall functioning of the network.
- There are two types of nodes: full nodes and light nodes. Full nodes handle crucial functions such as mining, enforcing consensus rules, and validating transactions. Light nodes, on the other hand, have limited capabilities and primarily store the blockchain headers, allowing them to send transactions but with fewer responsibilities compared to full nodes.

1.11.4 Consensus Layer

The consensus layer is a critical component of blockchain platforms like Ethereum, Hyperledger, and others. It plays a fundamental role in the functioning of these platforms. Some of the notable feature of the consensus layer are as follows:

- The consensus layer validates blocks, ensures correct ordering, and achieves agreement among participants.
- In a distributed P2P network, the consensus layer establishes essential agreements and rules for maintaining integrity and security.
- Consensus ensures agreement on the validity and order of transactions, preventing manipulation and maintaining fairness.
- The consensus layer maintains power distribution and decentralization, preventing a single entity from controlling the blockchain.
- It enables collective decision-making and agreements among network participants.

1.11.5 Application and Presentation Layer

This is the nearest layer from user perspective. Some of the important features of this layer are:

- The application and presentation layer is the user-facing part of the blockchain that provides a graphical user interface (GUI) and allows users to interact with the network.
- It includes execution layer and application layer protocols, such as smart contracts, scripts, and frameworks.
- Users can communicate with the blockchain network through various applications like wallets, social media apps, browsers, and NFT platforms.
- These applications interact with the blockchain network using application programming interfaces (APIs).
- The semantic layer within this layer is where transaction validations and executions take place, ensuring the integrity and accuracy of transactions.

- One key characteristic of these applications is their decentralized data storage, which sets them apart from traditional applications.
- Decentralized data storage provides secure and tamper-proof storage of data, enhancing the overall security and trustworthiness of the blockchain network.
- Users can access and manage their data securely within these applications, knowing that their information is stored in a decentralized and immutable manner.

1.12   A Block and Its Structure

A block is an essential component of a blockchain, typically comprising a collection of transactions. Its structure consists of a preamble that stores metadata such as a timestamp and reference to the previous block (known as the parent block) and a body that contains the actual transaction data. The unique cryptographic hash of each block ensures the chain's integrity. Blocks are chained together in chronological order to create a secure and immutable ledger.

1.12.1 A Block

A blockchain block is a fundamental component of a blockchain database that serves as a data structure for permanently recording transaction data in a cryptocurrency blockchain. It contains a collection of the most recent transactions that have not yet been validated by the network. Once the data within a block are validated, the block is considered closed, and a new block is created to accommodate and validate new transactions.

The significance of a block lies in its role as a secure and immutable storage unit. Once information is written into a block, it becomes a permanent part of the blockchain and cannot be altered or removed without detection.

1.12.2 Block Structure

The structure of a block in a blockchain can vary depending on the specific implementation and type of blockchain. However, in general, a block typically consists of several components (Figure 1-8).

- Block header: The block header contains metadata about the block, including the block number, timestamp, and the hash of the previous block in the chain.
- Nonce: A nonce is a random number generated by miners in order to solve the cryptographic puzzle required to add a block to a blockchain.
- Transaction data: The transaction data section contains the actual data that are being added to the blockchain. This can include information such as the sender and recipient addresses, the amount of cryptocurrency being transferred, and any additional data related to the transaction.
- Block hash: The block hash is a unique identifier that represents the contents of the block. It is generated by hashing the block header and transaction data using a specific cryptographic algorithm.
- Merkle tree: The Merkle tree is a data structure used to efficiently store and verify large amounts of transaction data. The transactions are hashed and combined in pairs to form a series of hashes, which are then combined until a single root hash is produced.

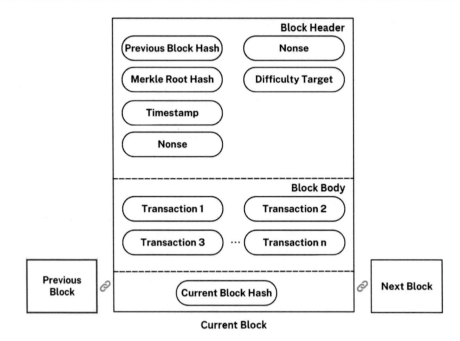

Figure 1-8 Block structure

1.12.3 Ledger

In the context of blockchain, a ledger is a digital record-keeping system that records all transactions made on the network. The ledger maintains a permanent and tamper-proof record of all transactions. Since a blockchains commonly track transactions, they are often referred to as ledgers or some times distributed ledgers.

The ledger is decentralized; no central authority controls it. Instead, all nodes on the network have a copy of the ledger. The copy is updated in real time as long as new transactions are made. All nodes can view the transactions and their associated data.

The ledger is usually maintained using cryptographic algorithms, such as hashing, ensuring the integrity and security of the data. Each block on the blockchain contains a hash of the previous block, creating a chain of blocks that are linked together. This creates an immutable ledger that cannot be altered or tampered with without the consensus of the network. To say that anyone can operate a node means the blockchain can be stored in a distributed manner called a distributed ledger. This makes it very difficult for an attacker, who must make changes to a number of copies across the network. This causes the prevention of a denial-of-service (DoS) attack, since there is no single point of failure.

The ledger can also be permissioned or permissionless. In a permissioned blockchain, access to the ledger is restricted to authorized participants, whereas in a permissionless blockchain, anyone can participate in the network and view the ledger.

The ledger provides a transparent, secure, and tamper-proof record of all transactions made on the network.

1.12.4 Distributed

Distributed refers to the way in which data are stored and processed across a network of computers or nodes. The workload is shared across multiple nodes, rather than being centralized in a single location.

Allowing anyone to operate a node means the blockchain can be stored in a distributed manner. Each node has a copy of the entire blockchain, and each node is responsible for verifying transactions and maintaining the integrity of the network. Distributed architecture provides several benefits, including the following:

- Resource sharing:
  In a distributed system, computers connect and share resources like software and hardware. Resource sharing involves remote access to components, reducing costs and improving convenience. Data sharing ensures consistency and facilitates information exchange.
- Heterogeneity:
  Distributed systems are diverse, with varying hardware, programming languages, networks, and implementations, all working together efficiently.
- Scalability:
  Scalability in distributed systems involves accommodating more users and computers, without altering components but designing them to handle growth effectively.
- Concurrency:
  The concurrency property of distributed systems enables simultaneous execution of multiple activities across different machines, managed by a common system, allowing for parallel processing.
- Fault tolerance:
  Distributed systems enhance fault tolerance and availability through software recovery and hardware redundancy, ensuring reliable operation despite failures.
- Openness:
  Openness in distributed systems refers to their capability to adapt and enhance hardware and software components as needed, enabling seamless integration of new components through standardized interfaces. This ensures compatibility and allows for resource sharing services.

1.12.5 Transparency

Transparency refers to the ability of anyone on a network to view and verify transactions and other data on the blockchain.

In a blockchain network, transactions are public and visible to all nodes on the network. This means that anyone can view the transaction data, including the sender, receiver, amount, and all other relevant details.

The transparency of the blockchain provides several benefits, as follows:

- Trust:
  The transparency of blockchain instills trust by allowing anyone to verify the validity and proper execution of transactions.
- Accountability:
  The public nature of blockchain ensures accountability for all participants' actions on the network.

- Fraud prevention:
  The transparency of blockchain makes it more difficult for bad actors to commit fraud or engage in other malicious activities on a network.
- Efficiency: The transparency of blockchain improves network efficiency by eliminating intermediaries and reducing transaction costs.

1.12.6 Confirmation

Block confirmation refers to the process of validating and adding transactions to a blockchain. This verification involves solving mathematical puzzles, ensuring transaction integrity, and preventing double-spending. Nodes compete to solve these puzzles, and the first node to succeed is rewarded for its efforts. Validated transactions are added to a block, which is then appended to the blockchain through the process of mining.

Block confirmation is crucial for maintaining the integrity and security of the blockchain. Once a transaction is confirmed and added to the blockchain, it becomes permanent and cannot be altered. This process eliminates the need for intermediaries, enhances network efficiency, and reduces transaction costs. Confirmation helps prevent fraudulent activities and ensures trust within the blockchain network.

1.12.7 Proof of Work

Proof of work (PoW) is a consensus algorithm used in most cryptocurrencies to prevent double-spending. It requires users to solve complex mathematical puzzles to validate transactions and add them to the blockchain. PoW ensures transaction integrity and prevents fraud, making it necessary for maintaining a secure and trustworthy network.

In PoW, transactions are grouped into blocks, and miners use computing power to hash block data and find solutions to puzzles. The hashing process creates a unique fingerprint for each block, making it impossible to reverse-engineer the original data. Miners play a guessing game, modifying a nonce value until they find a hash that meets protocol conditions. Successful miners are rewarded with cryptocurrency and can broadcast the new block to the network, where other participants update their blockchains accordingly.

The difficulty of finding valid hashes increases with network hash rate, ensuring a controlled block discovery rate. While mining can be computationally expensive, the potential rewards incentivize miners to contribute their resources to secure the blockchain.

1.12.8 Block Awards

Block rewards, also known as mining rewards, are a type of incentive provided to miners in a blockchain network as compensation for their efforts in verifying transactions and adding new blocks to the blockchain.

The block reward consists of newly generated coins and transaction fees given to miners for securing the network. As an example, the current reward is 6.25 coins per block, which undergoes a halving event every four years to limit the total supply. While the block reward remains stable, transaction fees can fluctuate. Transactions are initiated through a wallet and transmitted to a decentralized network of nodes, which validate and authenticate the transaction details. Nodes play a crucial role in securing blockchain networks, and mining nodes assemble validated transactions into candidate blocks. Miners are rewarded with a block reward for solving the PoW algorithm and providing confirmed financial settlement.

1.12.9 Transactions and UTXOs

Transactions are the fundamental building blocks that represent the transfer of cryptocurrency or other digital assets from one user to another. A transaction typically includes information such as the sender's address, the recipient's address, the amount of cryptocurrency being transferred, and a transaction fee.

Nodes validate transactions before adding them to the blockchain. Unspent transaction outputs (UTXOs) are created with each transaction, representing unspent outputs associated with specific addresses. UTXOs enhance privacy and security by making it difficult to trace cryptocurrency flow and preventing theft from unauthorized addresses.

In a UTXO-based blockchain, each transaction creates one or more UTXOs, which represent unspent outputs of a transaction. Each UTXO is associated with a specific address and can only be spent by the owner of that address.

For example, suppose Alice wants to send 1 Bitcoin to Bob. Alice would create a transaction that includes the details of the transfer, including Bob's address and the amount being transferred. The transaction would create a new UTXO associated with Bob's address for the amount of Bitcoin being transferred. Alice's UTXO associated with her address would also be created, but it would be marked as spent.

When Bob wants to spend the Bitcoin he received from Alice, he creates a new transaction that includes the details of the transfer, including the recipient's address and the amount being transferred. The transaction would reference the UTXO associated with Bob's address that was created when he received the Bitcoin from Alice. The UTXO associated with Alice's address would still be marked as spent. It is more difficult for a malicious actor to steal cryptocurrency from another user's address.

Examples

- Consider Alice's desire to make a purchase from an online store that accepts cryptocurrency. She initiates a transaction by sending the requisite cryptocurrency amount to the store's wallet address. The transaction details include the wallet address of the recipient, the payment amount, and a transaction fee. Once confirmed and added to the blockchain, this transaction establishes a UTXO associated with the store's address that represents the payment received. This UTXO can now be spent at the store.
- Imagine a decentralized application (DApp) that rewards ecosystem participation with a native token. When a user interacts with a decentralized application and earns tokens, a transaction is generated to transmit the tokens to the user's wallet address. This transaction establishes a UTXO representing the received tokens that is linked to the user's address. Whenever the user wishes to use these tokens within the DApp or transmit them to another user, they can reference the UTXO associated with their address in a subsequent transaction. This mechanism ensures that token transfers within the DApp's ecosystem are secure and traceable.

Nodes

In a blockchain network, a node is a computer or device that is connected to the network and participates in the validation and propagation of transactions and blocks. Nodes play a critical role in the security and decentralization of a blockchain network.

There are several different types of nodes, as described in what follows.

A blockchain network contains different types of nodes with distinct roles:

- Full nodes: These maintain a complete copy of the blockchain, validate transactions and blocks, and propagate information to other nodes.
- Mining nodes: These nodes solve complex mathematical problems to add new blocks to the blockchain and receive rewards for their work.
- Light nodes: Also known as thin clients, they rely on full nodes to validate transactions and blocks, without maintaining a complete copy of the blockchain.
- Master nodes: Found in some networks, these nodes perform additional functions like network governance, enhanced security, and enabling advanced features.

Nodes play a crucial role in blockchain networks by facilitating communication and validation through a P2P network. They contribute to the security and decentralization of the network without the need for a centralized authority. Additionally, nodes can participate in governance processes, such as voting on network changes. By acting as nodes, users actively support the overall integrity and functioning of blockchain networks.

1.12.10 Consensus

Consensus refers to the process by which participants on a blockchain network agree on the state of the ledger. In a decentralized network, there is no central authority to make decisions. Instead, participants on the network must come to a consensus on which transactions are valid and which blocks should be added to the chain. Consensus mechanisms, such as proof of work or proof of stake, are used to ensure that all nodes on a network agree on the state of the ledger.

1.12.10.1 Types of Consensus

In a blockchain network, consensus refers to the process of achieving agreement among network participants about the state of the blockchain. Consensus is critical for the security and integrity of the network as it ensures that all nodes have a consistent view of the blockchain and prevents double-spending and other types of fraudulent activity.

Blockchain networks use several different mechanisms to achieve consensus, including:

PoW: This is the most widely known consensus mechanism used by networks such as Bitcoin and Ethereum. In a PoW system, miners compete to solve complex mathematical problems in order to add new blocks to the blockchain. The first miner to solve the problem and add the block is rewarded with newly created cryptocurrency and transaction fees. The difficulty of the problem adjusts over time to maintain a consistent rate of block creation.

Proof of stake (PoS): In a PoS system, network participants "stake" their cryptocurrency as collateral to be selected to validate new blocks. Validators are chosen based on the amount of cryptocurrency they have staked and are rewarded with transaction fees for adding new blocks to the blockchain. The idea behind PoS is that it is less resource-intensive than PoW as it does not require miners to solve complex mathematical problems.

Delegated proof of stake (DPoS): DPoS is a variant of PoS used by networks such as EOS and BitShares. In a DPoS system, token holders vote to elect a smaller group of validators (known as "delegates") to validate transactions and add new blocks to the blockchain. The delegates are rewarded with transaction fees, and token holders can vote to replace delegates that are not performing their duties satisfactorily.

Byzantine fault tolerance (BFT): BFT is a consensus mechanism that is used in some blockchain networks, such as Hyperledger Fabric. In a BFT system, network participants communicate with each other to reach agreement on the state of the blockchain. The system is designed to tolerate a certain degree of malicious behavior (known as the "Byzantine fault"), such as nodes intentionally trying to disrupt the network.

1.13 Scaling Blockchain

Scalability in blockchain refers to expanding the transaction capacity of a network while maintaining security, speed, and decentralization. Overcoming this challenge is crucial as most existing blockchain networks have limitations in transaction throughput.

There are various approaches to scaling blockchain, which include

- Segregated Witness (SegWit): This protocol upgrade separates signature data from transaction data, thereby increasing the capacity of a blockchain network.
- Sharding: Through sharding, a blockchain network is divided into smaller subsets called shards, enabling independent transaction processing and enhancing overall network capacity.
- Layer 2 solutions: These solutions build upon existing blockchain networks to boost transaction throughput without requiring changes to the underlying blockchain protocol. Examples include Lightning Network and Plasma.
- PoS: This is an alternative consensus mechanism to the traditional PoW used by most blockchain networks. PoS reduces the computational power needed for mining and thus increases transaction throughput.
- Off-chain transactions: These transactions occur outside a blockchain network, reducing the load on the network and increasing transaction throughput.
- Sidechains: Sidechains are separate blockchain networks connected to a main blockchain. They enhance transaction throughput by independently processing transactions and then settling them on the main blockchain.

1.13.1 Issues in Scaling

Scaling blockchain is a complex and ongoing challenge that involves addressing technical and nontechnical issues. Here are some of the key concerns:

- Decentralization: Maintaining decentralization is crucial while scaling a network since centralizing it for higher transaction throughput could compromise security and trust.
- Security: Scaling blockchain networks can introduce security risks, as larger networks become more vulnerable to attacks. It is vital to maintain network security during capacity expansion.
- Interoperability: With the emergence of multiple blockchain networks, ensuring interoperability among them is important. Interoperability provides opportunities for scaling blockchain networks, but coordination between different networks is necessary.

- Governance: Governance plays a critical role in the success of blockchain networks, and it becomes more complex as networks scale. Establishing clear governance structures ensures a secure, decentralized, and efficient network.
- Energy consumption: Blockchain networks consume significant computational power for transaction validation and block creation. Scaling a network could lead to increased energy consumption, which is not sustainable in the long run.
- Adoption: Adoption is vital for blockchain networks, and scaling can present adoption barriers. As a network expands, it becomes more complex and challenging for new users to navigate.
- Regulations: Different jurisdictions have varying regulations for blockchain technology, which can hinder scaling efforts. Implementing clear regulatory frameworks is essential for the legal and efficient operation of a network.

Addressing these issues requires collaboration among blockchain developers, industry leaders, and regulators to ensure the long-term viability and success of blockchain technology.

1.13.2 Off-Chain Computation

Off-chain computation involves conducting computations outside a blockchain network using separate computational resources or infrastructure. Its benefits include reducing the load on the blockchain network, increasing transaction throughput, and reducing transaction fees.

Several techniques facilitate off-chain computation in blockchain:

- State channels: State channels are off-chain payment channels that allow multiple transactions between two parties without recording them on the blockchain. They enhance transaction throughput and reduce fees by enabling direct transactions.
- Sidechains: Sidechains are separate blockchain networks connected to the main blockchain. They provide a space for developers to experiment with new features and functionalities without compromising the security or performance of the main network.
- Plasma: Plasma is a framework for creating scalable blockchain networks by using a treelike structure of sidechains. Plasma allows for off-chain computation by enabling developers to create customized sidechains that can process transactions independently of the main network.
- Trusted execution environments (TEEs): TEEs are secure computing environments that can run code in isolation from the rest of the system. TEEs can be used to perform off-chain computations securely and efficiently.

Off-chain computation in blockchain offers benefits such as higher transaction throughput, lower transaction fees, and improved scalability. However, it comes with challenges regarding security, interoperability, and governance. Striking a balance between on-chain and off-chain computation is crucial to ensuring the long-term viability and success of blockchain technology.

1.13.3 Sharding in Blockchain

Sharding is a technique used to scale blockchain networks by dividing them into smaller subsets called shards. Each shard operates independently and processes its own transactions, leading to increased overall transaction throughput. Sharding addresses scalability issues by distributing the transaction load among different shards.

Implementing sharding involves partitioning a network and assigning transactions to specific shards based on certain criteria. Coordination between shards is crucial to maintaining network security and decentralization. Communication and synchronization mechanisms are necessary to ensure consistent views and propagate changes across shards.

Although sharding offers benefits, it also introduces challenges. Security and consistency can be more difficult to maintain as each shard operates independently. Governance and interoperability issues may arise due to varying rules and regulations among shards.

Sharding is a promising approach to scaling blockchain networks, but it requires careful planning and execution.

1.14   Blockchain DApps and Usecases

Blockchain DApps are applications that run on a blockchain network, typically using smart contracts to execute code and perform actions on the network. DApps are decentralized, meaning they are not controlled by a central authority or organization, and they are transparent, meaning that their code and data are publicly visible and auditable.

There are several use cases for blockchain DApps, including the following:

- Financial applications: Blockchain DApps can be used for a wide range of financial applications, such as payment systems, remittances, lending platforms, and asset tokenization.
- Supply chain management: Blockchain DApps can be used to track and manage supply chains, providing greater transparency and accountability in the movement of goods and products.
- Identity verification: Blockchain DApps can be used for identity verification and authentication, creating a secure and decentralized system for managing personal data and credentials.
- Voting systems: Blockchain DApps can be used for secure and transparent voting systems, ensuring that votes are recorded and counted accurately.
- Gaming and entertainment: Blockchain DApps can be used for gaming and entertainment applications, such as decentralized marketplaces for in-game items and virtual assets.
- Healthcare: Blockchain DApps can be used for managing healthcare data and records, providing a secure and transparent system for storing and sharing sensitive medical information.

Blockchain DApps have the potential to transform a wide range of industries and applications, providing greater security, transparency, and efficiency. However, developing and deploying DApps on blockchain networks can be complex and challenging, requiring specialized skills and expertise. As the technology continues to evolve, it is likely that we will see even more innovative use cases for blockchain DApps in the future.

1.15   Laboratory Work

This section presents the implementation of basic concepts in blockchain using Python.

1.15.1 Program for Implementing Blockchain in Python

```python
# Program 1: Program for Implementing Blockchain in Python
# Define the block structure
import hashlib

class Block:
    def __init__(self, data, previous_hash):
        self.data = data
        self.previous_hash = previous_hash
        self.nonce = 0
        self.hash = self.calculate_hash()

    # Calculate the SHA256 hash of the block
    def calculate_hash(self):
        hash_string = str(self.data)+str(self.previous_hash)+str(self.nonce)
        return hashlib.sha256(hash_string.encode()).hexdigest()

    # Proof of work algorithm
    def mine_block(self, difficulty):
        while self.hash[0:difficulty] != '0' * difficulty:
            self.nonce += 1
            self.hash = self.calculate_hash()

# Define the blockchain structure
class Blockchain:
    def __init__(self):
        self.chain = [self.create_genesis_block()]
        self.difficulty = 2

    # Create the first (genesis) block
    def create_genesis_block(self):
        return Block("Genesis Block", "0")

    # Get the last block in the blockchain
    def get_last_block(self):
        return self.chain[-1]

    # Add a new block to the blockchain
    def add_block(self, new_block):
        new_block.previous_hash = self.get_last_block().hash
        new_block.mine_block(self.difficulty)
        self.chain.append(new_block)

# Test the blockchain
blockchain = Blockchain()
blockchain.add_block(Block("Block 1", ""))
blockchain.add_block(Block("Block 2", ""))
blockchain.add_block(Block("Block 3", ""))

# Print the blockchain
for block in blockchain.chain:
    print("Block data: ", block.data)
    print("Block hash: ", block.hash)
```

Sample Output

```
 1  Block data:   Genesis Block
 2  Block hash:    8d59df74150242faafaaba4d1632c6e31
 3  e4e470c175c2c90c168ec6a4500fc3e
 4  Block data:   Block 1
 5  Block hash:    000ed2983b9272d8536e07beba4678ffb
 6  a9ac7b3a62d55e31e1843da25144efa
 7  Block data:   Block 2
 8  Block hash:    00172655ca0210f6bf693a27363c99a0c
 9  3108ad9257c0fc3fc14dd01e481d34e
10  Block data:   Block 3
11  Block hash:    007eb6b94b1874d4bfbeef92412df242b
12  b835183d9860c80750791e99ac3be60
```

Explanation of Code

1. A `Block` class is defined to represent a block in a blockchain. Each block has the following attributes:
   - `data`: The data or payload that the block contains.
   - `previous_hash`: The hash of the previous block in the blockchain.
   - `nonce`: A value that is incremented during the mining process.
   - `hash`: The hash of the current block.
2. The `calculate_hash` method in the `Block` class is used to calculate the SHA256 hash of a block. It concatenates the `data`, `previous_hash`, and `nonce` and then encodes and hashes the resulting string using the SHA256 algorithm.
3. The `mine_block` method implements a simple PoW algorithm. It increments the `nonce` value and recalculates the hash until the hash of the block satisfies the difficulty requirement. The difficulty requirement is defined as a certain number of leading zeros in a hash.
4. The `Blockchain` class is defined to represent the entire blockchain. It has the following attributes:
   - `chain`: A list that holds all the blocks in a blockchain.
   - `difficulty`: The difficulty level for mining new blocks; it specifies the number of leading zeros required in a block's hash.
5. The `create_genesis_block` method creates the first block in a blockchain, often called the genesis block. It is a special block with no previous hash.
6. The `get_last_block` method returns the last block in a blockchain.
7. The `add_block` method adds a new block to a blockchain. It takes a `new_block` as input, sets the previous hash of the new block to the hash of the last block in the chain, and then initiates the mining process by calling `mine_block`.
8. A `Blockchain` instance named `blockchain` is created.
9. Three blocks are added to the blockchain using the `add_block` method, each with its own data.
10. Finally, the contents of the blockchain are printed by iterating over each block in the chain and displaying the block's data and hash.

1.15.2 Program for Mining a New Block in Blockchain and Printing It

```
import datetime

class BlockNode:
    def __init__(self, data, timestamp=None):
        self.data = data
        self.timestamp = timestamp or datetime.datetime.now()
        self.next = None


class Blockchain:
    def __init__(self):
        self.head = None

    def add_block(self, data):
        new_block = BlockNode(data)
        if self.head is None:
            self.head = new_block
        else:
            current_block = self.head
            while current_block.next:
                current_block = current_block.next
            current_block.next = new_block

    def mine_block(self, data):
        new_block = BlockNode(data)
        new_block.next = self.head
        self.head = new_block

    def traverse(self):
        current_block = self.head
        while current_block:
            print(f"Block Data: {current_block.data}")
            print(f"Timestamp: {current_block.timestamp}")
            print()
            current_block = current_block.next


# Create a new blockchain
blockchain = Blockchain()

# Add blocks to the chain
blockchain.add_block("Block 1")
blockchain.add_block("Block 2")
blockchain.add_block("Block 3")

# Traverse the blockchain and print the data
print("Blockchain before mining new block:")
blockchain.traverse()

# Mine a new block and add it to the chain
blockchain.mine_block("Block 4")

# Traverse the blockchain again after mining new block
print("Blockchain after mining new block:")
blockchain.traverse()
```

Sample Output

```
1  Blockchain before mining new block:
2  Block Data: Block 1
3  Timestamp: 2023-05-15 13:25:15.586847
4
5  Block Data: Block 2
6  Timestamp: 2023-05-15 13:25:15.586873
7
8  Block Data: Block 3
9  Timestamp: 2023-05-15 13:25:15.586879
10
11 Blockchain after mining new block:
12 Block Data: Block 4
13 Timestamp: 2023-05-15 13:25:15.586926
14
15 Block Data: Block 1
16 Timestamp: 2023-05-15 13:25:15.586847
17
18 Block Data: Block 2
19 Timestamp: 2023-05-15 13:25:15.586873
20
21 Block Data: Block 3
22 Timestamp: 2023-05-15 13:25:15.586879
```

Explanation of Code

The given code implements a basic blockchain using a linked list data structure. It defines two classes: `BlockNode` and `Blockchain`.

The `BlockNode` class represents a block in the blockchain. It has three attributes:

- `data`: The data stored in the block.
- `timestamp`: The timestamp of the block creation, which defaults to the current date and time.
- `next`: A reference to the next block in the chain.

The `Blockchain` class represents the entire blockchain and has the following methods:

- `__init__()`: The constructor initializes an empty blockchain by setting the `head` attribute to None.
- `add_block(data)`: This method adds a new block to the blockchain. It creates a new `BlockNode` object with the given data. If the blockchain is empty (i.e., `self.head` is None), the new block becomes the head. Otherwise, it traverses to the last block using the `next` pointers and appends the new block at the end.
- `mine_block(data)`: This method mines a new block and adds it to the blockchain. It creates a new `BlockNode` object with the given data and sets its `next` pointer to the current head of the blockchain. The new block then becomes the new head of the blockchain.
- `traverse()`: This method traverses the blockchain and prints the data of each block. It starts from the head of the blockchain and iterates through the blocks using the `next` pointers until it reaches the end.

The code demonstrates the use of the blockchain by performing the following steps:

1. Create a new instance of the `Blockchain` class.
2. Add three blocks ("Block 1," "Block 2," and "Block 3") to the blockchain using the `add_block()` method.
3. Print the data of each block in the blockchain by calling the `traverse()` method.
4. Mine a new block with the data "Block 4" using the `mine_block()` method and add it to the blockchain.
5. Print the updated blockchain by calling the `traverse()` method again.

1.15.3 Program for Creating Four Blocks in Blockchian and Printing and Traversing

```
1  import hashlib
2  import datetime
3
4  class Block:
5      def __init__(self, data, previous_hash):
6          self.timestamp = datetime.datetime.now()
7          self.data = data
8          self.previous_hash = previous_hash
9          self.hash = self.calculate_hash()
10
11     def calculate_hash(self):
12         data_string = str(self.timestamp) + str(self.data) + str(self.previous_hash)
13         return hashlib.sha256(data_string.encode('utf-8')).hexdigest()
14
15 class Blockchain:
16     def __init__(self):
17         self.chain = [self.create_genesis_block()]
18
19     def create_genesis_block(self):
20         return Block("Genesis Block", "0")
21
22     def add_block(self, new_block):
23         new_block.previous_hash = self.chain[-1].hash
24         self.chain.append(new_block)
25
26     def traverse_chain(self):
27         for block in self.chain:
28             print("Timestamp:", block.timestamp)
29             print("Data:", block.data)
30             print("Previous Hash:", block.previous_hash)
31             print("Hash:", block.hash)
32             print("")
33
34 # Create a new blockchain
35 my_blockchain = Blockchain()
36
37 # Add four blocks to the blockchain
38 my_blockchain.add_block(Block("Transaction 1", ""))
39 my_blockchain.add_block(Block("Transaction 2", ""))
40 my_blockchain.add_block(Block("Transaction 3", ""))
41 my_blockchain.add_block(Block("Transaction 4", ""))
```

```
42
43 # Traverse the blockchain and print the contents of each block
44 my_blockchain.traverse_chain()
```

Sample Output

```
 1 Timestamp: 2023-05-12 12:21:53.769642
 2 Data: Genesis Block
 3 Previous Hash: 0
 4 Hash: d6aac92c2473dfd315eb3e56de81e7
 5 9ea0c27fc3597a77015727f7121b3b5a6f
 6
 7 Timestamp: 2023-05-12 12:21:53.769642
 8 Data: Transaction 1
 9 Previous Hash: d6aac92c2473dfd315eb3
10 e56de81e79ea0c27fc3597a77015727f7121
11 b3b5a6f
12 Hash: ca4c4a003c999931620ffeee202d8b
13 7d440892220531e42ad9b5365122d4817d
14
15 Timestamp: 2023-05-12 12:21:53.769642
16 Data: Transaction 2
17 Previous Hash: ca4c4a003c999931620ffe
18 ee202d8b7d440892220531e42ad9b5365122d
19 4817d
20 Hash: 8e3632909658df4f899250c076140a1
21 2a9ebc10cb260f505d43810fdfb07782e
22
23 Timestamp: 2023-05-12 12:21:53.769642
24 Data: Transaction 3
25 Previous Hash: 8e3632909658df4f899250
26 c076140a12a9ebc10cb260f505d43810fdfb0
27 7782e
28 Hash: 5aca49067dd6ddf963dba2b304d93d6
29 c1227990d0e95c196f0bf36a82a5f75d2
30
31 Timestamp: 2023-05-12 12:21:53.769642
32 Data: Transaction 4
33 Previous Hash: 5aca49067dd6ddf963dba2b
34 304d93d6c1227990d0e95c196f0bf36a82a5f7
35 5d2
36 Hash: 6ad5e7293db8109fcfe21585e4946e61
37 41958bf1f911bd50b3ad3f3e0d0abe06
```

Explanation of Code

The code imports the necessary modules: hashlib for calculating hashes and datetime for timestamping the blocks.

The `Block` class is defined, representing a block in the blockchain. Each block has the following attributes:

- `timestamp`: Timestamp indicating when block was created.
- `data`: Data or payload the block contains.
- `previous_hash`: Hash of previous block in blockchain.
- `hash`: Hash of current block, calculated using `calculate_hash` method.

The `calculate_hash` method in the `Block` class calculates the SHA256 hash of the block. It concatenates the timestamp, data, and previous hash, encodes the resulting string using UTF-8, and then calculates the hash using `hashlib.sha256`.

The `Blockchain` class is defined to represent the entire blockchain. It has a single attribute:

- `chain`: A list that holds all blocks in the blockchain. The initial block in the chain is the genesis block, created using the `create_genesis_block` method.

The `create_genesis_block` method creates the genesis block, which is a special block with no previous hash. It returns a new `Block` instance with the data "Genesis Block" and an empty string as the previous hash.

The `add_block` method adds a new block to the blockchain. It takes a `new_block` as input, sets the previous hash of the new block to the hash of the last block in the chain (`self.chain[-1].hash`), and then appends the new block to the chain.

The `traverse_chain` method traverses the blockchain and prints the contents of each block. It iterates over each block in `self.chain` and displays the timestamp, data, previous hash, and hash of each block.

An instance of the `Blockchain` class named `my_blockchain` is created.

Four blocks are added to the blockchain using the `add_block` method. Each block has its own data, while the previous hash for the first block is an empty string.

The `traverse_chain` method is called to print the contents of each block in the blockchain.

This program demonstrates the creation of a blockchain, adding blocks with transaction data and traversing the blockchain to display the details of each block.

1.15.4 Implementing Blockchain and Printing All Fields as per Etherscan.io

```
1  import hashlib
2  import datetime
3
4  class Block:
5      def __init__(self, block_number, transactions, previous_hash,
       gas_limit, gas_used, miner):
6          self.block_number = block_number
7          self.timestamp = datetime.datetime.now()
8          self.transactions = transactions
9          self.previous_hash = previous_hash
10         self.gas_limit = gas_limit
11         self.gas_used = gas_used
12         self.miner = miner
13         self.hash = self.calculate_hash()
14
```

```python
    def calculate_hash(self):
        data_string = (
            str(self.block_number)
            + str(self.timestamp)
            + str(self.transactions)
            + str(self.previous_hash)
            + str(self.gas_limit)
            + str(self.gas_used)
            + str(self.miner)
        )
        return hashlib.sha256(data_string.encode('utf-8')).hexdigest()

class Blockchain:
    def __init__(self):
        self.chain = [self.create_genesis_block()]

    def create_genesis_block(self):
        return Block(0, "Genesis Block", "0", 0, 0, "Genesis Miner")

    def add_block(self, new_block):
        new_block.previous_hash = self.chain[-1].hash
        self.chain.append(new_block)

    def print_block(self, block):
        print("Block Number:", block.block_number)
        print("Timestamp:", block.timestamp)
        print("Transactions:", block.transactions)
        print("Previous Hash:", block.previous_hash)
        print("Gas Limit:", block.gas_limit)
        print("Gas Used:", block.gas_used)
        print("Miner:", block.miner)
        print("Hash:", block.hash)
        print("")

    def traverse_chain(self):
        for block in self.chain:
            self.print_block(block)

# Create a new blockchain
my_blockchain = Blockchain()

# Add three blocks to the blockchain
my_blockchain.add_block(Block(1, "Transaction 1", "", 1000000, 500000, "
    Miner 1"))
my_blockchain.add_block(Block(2, "Transaction 2", "", 2000000, 1500000, "
    Miner 2"))
my_blockchain.add_block(Block(3, "Transaction 3", "", 3000000, 2500000, "
    Miner 3"))

# Traverse the blockchain and print all the fields of each block
my_blockchain.traverse_chain()
```

Sample Output

```
 1 Block Number: 0
 2 Timestamp: 2023-05-12 12:36:20.943472
 3 Transactions: Genesis Block
 4 Previous Hash: 0
 5 Gas Limit: 0
 6 Gas Used: 0
 7 Miner: Genesis Miner
 8 Hash: 505122533e78651228391d8357d3fa60adad9e7ba4d73a53b73def3
 9 438104cc0
10
11 Block Number: 1
12 Timestamp: 2023-05-12 12:36:20.943472
13 Transactions: Transaction 1
14 Previous Hash: 505122533e78651228391d8357d3fa60adad9e7ba4d73a5
15 3b73def3438104cc0
16 Gas Limit: 1000000
17 Gas Used: 500000
18 Miner: Miner 1
19 Hash: 5503bc24259e86f01c597c3e577cb930729f0e55f5cbf3209c47c6c5
20 a737e775
21
22 Block Number: 2
23 Timestamp: 2023-05-12 12:36:20.943472
24 Transactions: Transaction 2
25 Previous Hash: 5503bc24259e86f01c597c3e577cb930729f0e55f5cbf32
26 09c47c6c5a737e775
27 Gas Limit: 2000000
28 Gas Used: 1500000
29 Miner: Miner 2
30 Hash: f11ff8690ec58119d0cdb67b11186e382ee3e1ec07731eb5a14f6a94
31 f649e723
32
33 Block Number: 3
34 Timestamp: 2023-05-12 12:36:20.943472
35 Transactions: Transaction 3
36 Previous Hash: f11ff8690ec58119d0cdb67b11186e382ee3e1ec07731eb
37 5a14f6a94f649e723
38 Gas Limit: 3000000
39 Gas Used: 2500000
40 Miner: Miner 3
41 Hash: a44c347b1d328e2f3cec5d2abd3d5f39a47d73402b9218967b53c21f
42 43f4e086
```

Explanation of Code

The code begins by importing the necessary modules, `hashlib` and `datetime`.

The `Block` class is defined to represent a block in the blockchain. Each block has the following attributes:

- `block_number`: Number assigned to block.
- `timestamp`: Timestamp indicating when block was created.
- `transactions`: Transactions or data included in block.

- `previous_hash`: Hash of previous block in blockchain.
- `gas_limit` and `gas_used`: Attributes related to gas in a blockchain (specific to the application).
- `miner`: Miner responsible for mining the block.
- `hash`: Hash of current block, calculated using `calculate_hash` method.

The `calculate_hash` method in the `Block` class calculates the SHA256 hash of the block. It concatenates the various attributes of the block into a single string and then encodes and hashes the resulting string using the SHA256 algorithm from `hashlib`.

The `Blockchain` class is defined to represent the entire blockchain. It has a single attribute:

- `chain`: A list that holds all the blocks in the blockchain. The initial block in the chain is the genesis block, created using the `create_genesis_block` method.

The `create_genesis_block` method creates the genesis block, which is a special block with no previous hash. It returns a new `Block` instance with predefined values for the block number, data, previous hash, gas limit, gas used, and miner.

The `add_block` method adds a new block to the blockchain. It takes a `new_block` as input, sets the previous hash of the new block to the hash of the last block in the chain (`self.chain[-1].hash`), and then appends the new block to the chain.

The `print_block` method prints the contents of a block, including its block number, timestamp, transactions, previous hash, gas limit, gas used, miner, and hash.

The `traverse_chain` method traverses the blockchain and calls the `print_block` method for each block in the chain, effectively printing the contents of each block.

An instance of the `Blockchain` class named `my_blockchain` is created.

Three blocks are added to the blockchain using the `add_block` method. Each block has its own block number, transactions, gas limit, gas used, and miner. The previous hash for each block is initially set to an empty string.

The `traverse_chain` method is called to print the contents of each block in the blockchain.

1.15.5 Implementing Blockchain and UTXo in Python

```python
# Importing required libraries
import hashlib

# Defining the UTXO class
class UTXO:
    def __init__(self, txid, index, value):
        self.txid = txid
        self.index = index
        self.value = value

    def __str__(self):
        return f"UTXO ({self.txid}:{self.index}) with value {self.value}"

# Defining the transaction class
class Transaction:
    def __init__(self, inputs, outputs):
        self.inputs = inputs
        self.outputs = outputs
```

```
19
20      def __str__(self):
21          return f"Transaction with {len(self.inputs)} inputs and {len(self.
        outputs)} outputs"
22
23      def hash(self):
24          # Generating a hash for the transaction
25          tx_input = ''.join([str(inp.txid) + str(inp.index)
26          for inp in self.inputs])
27          tx_output = ''.join([str(out.value) for out in
28          self.outputs])
29          tx_data = tx_input + tx_output
30          return hashlib.sha256(tx_data.encode('utf-8')).hexdigest()
31
32 # Defining the sample UTXOs and transactions
33 utxo1 = UTXO('txid1', 0, 10)
34 utxo2 = UTXO('txid2', 1, 20)
35
36 input1 = [utxo1]
37 output1 = [UTXO('txid3', 0, 25), UTXO('txid3', 1, 5)]
38 tx1 = Transaction(input1, output1)
39
40 input2 = [utxo2]
41 output2 = [UTXO('txid4', 0, 15), UTXO('txid4', 1, 5)]
42 tx2 = Transaction(input2, output2)
43
44 # Printing the UTXOs and transactions
45 print(utxo1)
46 print(utxo2)
47 print(tx1)
48 print(tx2)
49
50 # Generating hashes for the transactions
51 print(tx1.hash())
52 print(tx2.hash())
```

Sample Output

```
1 UTXO (txid1:0) with value 10
2 UTXO (txid2:1) with value 20
3 Transaction with 1 inputs and 2 outputs
4 Transaction with 1 inputs and 2 outputs
5 fe3230fe9ee48b845306422ff3c8ae3423fe87ea0cffde0f898813
6 ee6adddd4e
7 d0b5cddfc541febacd6188b4f15947cc3234e2f590bc3f7cd5a619
8 aa644aa070
```

1.15.6 Explanation of Code

The code begins by importing the required libraries, `hashlib`.

The `UTXO` class is defined to represent an unspent transaction output. Each UTXO has the following attributes:

- `txid`: Transaction ID that UTXO belongs to.
- `index`: Index of output in transaction.
- `value`: Value of output.

The `__str__` method is defined to provide a string representation of the UTXO.

The `Transaction` class is defined to represent a transaction. Each transaction has the following attributes:

- `inputs`: List of UTXOs being spent as inputs.
- `outputs`: List of new UTXOs created as outputs.

The `__str__` method is defined to provide a string representation of a transaction.

The `hash` method generates a hash for the transaction by concatenating the transaction IDs and indices of the input UTXOs and the values of the output UTXOs. It then calculates the SHA256 hash of the resulting string using `hashlib`.

Sample UTXOs and transactions are defined using the `UTXO` and `Transaction` classes.

The UTXOs and transactions are printed using the `print` function.

The hashes for the transactions are generated using the `hash` method and printed.

1.15.7 Implementation of PoW Algorithm in Python

```
1  #Implementation of Proof of Work(PoW) algorithm in Python
2
3  import hashlib
4  import time
5
6  class Block:
7      def __init__(self, data, previous_hash):
8          self.timestamp = time.time()
9          self.data = data
10         self.previous_hash = previous_hash
11         self.nonce = 0
12         self.hash = self.generate_hash()
13
14     def generate_hash(self):
15         block_contents = str(self.timestamp) + str(self.data) + str(self.
       previous_hash) + str(self.nonce)
16         block_hash = hashlib.sha256(block_contents.encode()).hexdigest()
17         return block_hash
18
19     def mine_block(self, difficulty):
20         while self.hash[:difficulty] != '0' * difficulty:
21             self.nonce += 1
22             self.hash = self.generate_hash()
23         print("Block mined: {}".format(self.hash))
```

```python
class Blockchain:
    def __init__(self):
        self.chain = [self.create_genesis_block()]
        self.difficulty = 2

    def create_genesis_block(self):
        return Block("Genesis Block", "0")

    def get_latest_block(self):
        return self.chain[-1]

    def add_block(self, new_block):
        new_block.previous_hash = self.get_latest_block().hash
        new_block.mine_block(self.difficulty)
        self.chain.append(new_block)

    def is_chain_valid(self):
        for i in range(1, len(self.chain)):
            current_block = self.chain[i]
            previous_block = self.chain[i - 1]

            if current_block.hash != current_block.generate_hash():
                return False

            if current_block.previous_hash != previous_block.hash:
                return False

        return True

if __name__ == '__main__':
    blockchain = Blockchain()
    print("Mining block 1...")
    block1 = Block("Transaction 1", "")
    blockchain.add_block(block1)

    print("Mining block 2...")
    block2 = Block("Transaction 2", "")
    blockchain.add_block(block2)

    print("Mining block 3...")
    block3 = Block("Transaction 3", "")
    blockchain.add_block(block3)

    print("Is blockchain valid? {}".format(blockchain.is_chain_valid()))

    # Tamper with blockchain
    blockchain.chain[1].data = "Tampered transaction"

    print("Is blockchain valid after tampering? {}"
    .format(blockchain.is_chain_valid()))
```

Explanation of Code

The code defines two classes: `Block` and `Blockchain`. The `Block` class represents a single block in the blockchain. Each block has several attributes:

- `timestamp`: Stores the time when block was created using `time.time()` function.
- `data`: Represents data or transaction that the block contains.
- `previous_hash`: Stores hash of previous block in chain.
- `nonce`: Number incremented during mining to find a valid hash.
- `hash`: Stores hash of block itself.

The `Block` class also has the following methods:

- `generate_hash()`: This method generates the hash of a block by concatenating the block's attributes and applying the SHA-256 hash function from the `hashlib` module.
- `mine_block(difficulty)`: This method performs the mining process by incrementing the nonce value until a hash is found that meets the difficulty criteria. The difficulty is the number of leading zeros required in the hash.

The `Blockchain` class represents the blockchain itself and manages blocks. It has the following attributes and methods:

- `chain`: List that stores blocks in blockchain.
- `difficulty`: Represents the difficulty level of mining.

The `Blockchain` class also uses the following methods:

- `create_genesis_block()`: This method creates the first block in a blockchain, called the genesis block, with arbitrary data and a previous hash of "0".
- `get_latest_block()`: This method returns the most recently added block in a chain.
- `add_block(new_block)`: This method adds a new block to a chain. It sets the previous hash of new block to the hash of the latest block, mines the new block, and appends it to the chain.
- `is_chain_valid()`: This method checks the validity of a blockchain by verifying the integrity of each block. It iterates through the chain and compares the hash and previous hash values of each block.

The `if __name__ == '__main__'` block at the end of the code is the entry point of the program. It creates an instance of the `Blockchain` class and adds three blocks to the chain. After mining each block, it checks the validity of the blockchain using the `is_chain_valid()` method.

Finally, to demonstrate the tamper-proof nature of the blockchain, the code modifies the data of the second block in the chain (`blockchain.chain[1].data = "Tampered transaction"`). It then rechecks the validity of the blockchain, showing that it detected the tampering.

The output of the code includes information about the mining process and the validity of the blockchain after each step.

Sample Output

```
1 Mining block 1...\\
2 Block mined: 00c79fe980c3cc690ab7c67a8ce27e225624b2e0279a1bb94dc\\33
    fdb413956cc\\
3 Mining block 2...\\
4 Block mined: 00d0385afb7ed1d74678ef52405c9099b7e1cb5672177aa6b96f27\\7
    c8a1354a9\\
5 Mining block 3...\\
6 Block mined: 0090781a61faa4c61d2da85979c4768e05be0aec0f455a043ba948\\7
    c51667dba\\
7 Is blockchain valid? True\\
8 Is blockchain valid after tampering? False\\
```

1.15.8 Implementation of PoS Algorithm in Python

```python
1 import hashlib
2 import time
3
4 class Block:
5     def __init__(self, data, previous_hash):
6         self.timestamp = time.time()
7         self.data = data
8         self.previous_hash = previous_hash
9         self.hash = self.generate_hash()
10
11     def generate_hash(self):
12         block_contents = str(self.timestamp) + str(self.data) + str(self.
    previous_hash)
13         block_hash = hashlib.sha256(block_contents.encode()).hexdigest()
14         return block_hash
15
16 class Blockchain:
17     def __init__(self):
18         self.chain = [self.create_genesis_block()]
19
20     def create_genesis_block(self):
21         return Block("Genesis Block", "0")
22
23     def get_latest_block(self):
24         return self.chain[-1]
25
26     def add_block(self, new_block):
27         new_block.previous_hash = self.get_latest_block().hash
28         new_block.hash = new_block.generate_hash()
29         self.chain.append(new_block)
30
31     def is_chain_valid(self):
32         for i in range(1, len(self.chain)):
33             current_block = self.chain[i]
34             previous_block = self.chain[i - 1]
35
36             if current_block.hash != current_block.generate_hash():
37                 return False
38
```

```
39                if current_block.previous_hash != previous_block.hash:
40                    return False
41
42          return True
43
44 if __name__ == '__main__':
45     blockchain = Blockchain()
46
47     print("Mining block 1...")
48     block1 = Block("Transaction 1", "")
49     blockchain.add_block(block1)
50
51     print("Mining block 2...")
52     block2 = Block("Transaction 2", "")
53     blockchain.add_block(block2)
54
55     print("Mining block 3...")
56     block3 = Block("Transaction 3", "")
57     blockchain.add_block(block3)
58
59     print("Is blockchain valid? {}".format(blockchain.is_chain_valid()))
```

Sample Output

```
1 Mining block 1...
2 Mining block 2...
3 Mining block 3...
4 Is blockchain valid? True
```

Explanation of Code

The Block class represents a single block in a blockchain. It has the following attributes:

- timestamp: Stores current time using time.time().
- data: Represents data or transaction stored in block.
- previous_hash: Stores hash of previous block in blockchain.
- hash: Stores hash of current block, generated by generate_hash() method.

The __init__ method initializes these attributes and generates a hash for the block.

The generate_hash() method concatenates the block's attributes (timestamp, data, and previous_hash) into a single string, encodes it to bytes, and applies the SHA-256 hash function using hashlib.sha256(). The resulting hash is returned as a hexadecimal string.

The Blockchain class manages the blocks in a blockchain. It has the following methods and attributes:

- The __init__ method initializes the chain attribute with a genesis block created by the create_genesis_block() method.
- The create_genesis_block() method creates the first block in a blockchain (genesis block) with the initial data "Genesis Block" and a previous hash of "0."

- The `get_latest_block()` method returns the most recently added block in a chain.
- The `add_block(new_block)` method adds a new block to a chain. It sets the previous hash of the new block to the hash of the latest block, generates a hash for the new block, and appends it to the chain.
- The `is_chain_valid()` method checks the validity of a blockchain by iterating through the chain. It verifies the integrity of each block by comparing its hash with the generated hash and checks whether the previous hash matches the hash of the previous block.

The `if __name__ == '__main__'` block is the entry point of the program. It creates an instance of the `Blockchain` class and performs the following steps:

- Creates a blockchain instance.
- Mines and adds block 1 with data "Transaction 1."
- Mines and adds block 2 with data "Transaction 2."
- Mines and adds block 3 with data "Transaction 3."
- Checks validity of blockchain using `is_chain_valid()` method.

1.15.9 Program to Fetch the Latest Block Information from Ethereum Blockchain Using Etherscan API

```
 1 import requests
 2
 3 def get_latest_block(api_key):
 4     url = "https://api.etherscan.io/api"
 5     params = {
 6         "module": "proxy",
 7         "action": "eth_getBlockByNumber",
 8         "tag": "latest",
 9         "boolean": "true",
10         "apikey": api_key,
11     }
12
13     try:
14         response = requests.get(url, params=params)
15         if response.status_code == 200:
16             data = response.json()
17             return data["result"]
18         else:
19             print("Request failed with status code:", response.status_code
)
20     except requests.RequestException as e:
21         print("Request failed:", str(e))
22
23     return None
24
25 # Replace "YOUR_API_KEY" with your actual API key
26 api_key = "E34342B4IR3B8RI3K61XG4YKEUT7SR54MM"
27
28 latest_block = get_latest_block(api_key)
29 if latest_block is not None:
30     print("Latest block information:")
31     print("Block Number:", int(latest_block["number"], 16))
32     print("Timestamp:", int(latest_block["timestamp"], 16))
```

```
33  print("Miner Address:", latest_block["miner"])
34  print("Difficulty:", int(latest_block["difficulty"], 16))
35  print("Total Difficulty:", int(latest_block["totalDifficulty"], 16))
36  print("Gas Limit:", int(latest_block["gasLimit"], 16))
37  print("Gas Used:", int(latest_block["gasUsed"], 16))
38  print("Transaction Count:", len(latest_block["transactions"]))
39  print("Transactions:")
40  for tx in latest_block["transactions"]:
41      print("Transaction Hash:", tx["hash"])
42      print("From:", tx["from"])
43      print("To:", tx["to"])
44      print("Value (in Wei):", tx["value"])
45      print("\n")  # Add more fields or formatting as per your
        requirements
46  else:
47      print("Failed to fetch the latest block information.")
```

Sample Input and Output

```
1
2  Latest block information:
3  Block Number: 18055231
4  Timestamp: 1693735151
5  Miner Address: 0x95222290dd7278aa3ddd389cc1e1d165cc4bafe5
6  Difficulty: 0
7  Total Difficulty: 58750003716598352816469
8  Gas Limit: 30000000
9  Gas Used: 19479192
10 Transaction Count: 172
11 Transactions:
12 Transaction Hash: 0x3e1bc70cdcfcbe9c176b4cb7470f0e10bc66cec290465e710e33c
13 21b5c44c355
14 From: 0xae2fc483527b8ef99eb5d9b44875f005ba1fae13
15 To: 0x6b75d8af000000e20b7a7ddf000ba900b4009a80
16 Value (in Wei): 0xe00b9c
17
18
19 Transaction Hash: 0x748d79a17e9d826c0dc6dafee9d8aeba78d80693ce661db5252e
20 968f9055c362
21 From: 0xfcf70fc42a0ad021ba4bc6138a60901d9c95bd9f
22 To: 0x00000047bb99ea4d791bb749d970de71ee0b1a34
23 Value (in Wei): 0x58d15e176280000
```

1.15.10 Explanation of Code

The specified Python code retrieves information about the most recent block on the Ethereum blockchain using the Etherscan API. It defines the get_latest_block function, which sends a GET request to the API with the latest block identifier and an API key for authentication. Upon obtaining a successful response, it parses the JSON data to extract essential block information, including block number, timestamp, miner address, difficulty, gas limit, gas used, and transaction count. In addition, it cycles through the block's transactions to display transaction-specific data, such as hash, sender, beneficiary, and value. This code provides a simple and structured method for accessing and displaying real-time Ethereum blockchain data, providing valuable insights into the properties and transactions of the most recent block.

1.16 Summary

This chapter provided a comprehensive introduction to blockchain technology, covering a range of topics from its history and milestones to its framework components, types, and applications. The chapter began by discussing the prerequisites for blockchain, including distributed systems, cryptography, and P2P networks. It explained that blockchain is a disruptive technology that challenges traditional business models and has the potential to revolutionize industries. The history of blockchain was briefly outlined, highlighting its origins in the creation of Bitcoin and its subsequent development into a standalone technology. The chapter also discussed significant milestones in blockchain's evolution, such as the introduction of smart contracts and the creation of alternative cryptocurrencies.

The features of blockchain were then examined, including its decentralization, immutability, and transparency. The chapter also provided an overview of the current growth of blockchain and its predicted market size in the future. Blockchain types were categorized as public, private, federated, and hybrid. The chapter provided a detailed explanation of each type, including their characteristics and use cases. The blockchain framework was discussed in detail, covering components such as a block, block structure, ledger, distributed network, transparency, confirmation, PoW, block awards, transactions, UTXOs, nodes, consensus, and program for implementing consensus mechanisms. The chapter also included laboratory work sections that provide step-by-step instructions on implementing blockchain and related concepts in Python, including UTXO, PoW, and PoS algorithms. Blockchain applications and challenges were examined, including scaling blockchain, off-chain computation, sharding in blockchain, and blockchain DApps, and use cases were discussed. The chapter highlighted the potential of blockchain to transform industries such as finance, healthcare, and supply chain management but also acknowledged the challenges that must be addressed for blockchain to reach its full potential.

1.17 Exercise

This section gives exercise based on topics covered in the chapter.

1.17.1 Multiple Choice Questions

Choose the correct answer from the following options given:

1. What is a main feature of blockchain technology?
   a. Transparency
   b. Immutability
   c. Decentralization
   d. All of the above
2. What are the different types of blockchain?
   a. Public, private, and hybrid
   b. Public, private, and federated

    c. Public, private, hybrid, and federated

    d. None of the above

3. What is the main challenge facing blockchain technology?

    a. Lack of scalability

    b. High energy consumption

    c. Security concerns

    d. All of the above

4. What is the purpose of consensus in blockchain?

    a. To verify transactions

    b. To prevent double-spending

    c. To maintain the integrity of a blockchain

    d. All of the above

5. What is the main benefit of using a private blockchain?

    a. Greater transparency

    b. Lower cost

    c. Greater control

    d. None of the above

6. What is proof of work?

    a. A consensus mechanism used in blockchain

    b. A way to prove ownership of cryptocurrency

    c. A type of blockchain ledger

    d. None of the above

7. What is the main advantage of using off-chain computation in blockchain?

    a. It reduces the size of the blockchain

    b. It increases transaction speed

    c. It improves security

    d. None of the above

8. What is a UTXO?

    a. An unspent transaction output

    b. A type of blockchain node

    c. A consensus mechanism

    d. None of the above

9. What is the main use case of a federated blockchain?

    a. Decentralized finance

    b. Supply chain management

    c. Voting systems

    d. None of the above

10. What is the purpose of block rewards in blockchain?

    a. To incentivize miners to verify transactions

    b. To increase the number of nodes in the network

    c. To fund the development of the blockchain

    d. None of the above

1.17.2 Short Answer Questions

1. What is the difference between a public and a private blockchain?

2. How does proof of stake work in blockchain?

3. What are some real-world applications of blockchain technology?
4. How can blockchain technology help to solve supply chain management problems?
5. What are some of the challenges facing blockchain technology?

1.17.3 Long Answer Questions

1. Describe the basic structure of a block in a blockchain and explain how transactions are verified and added to the blockchain.
2. Discuss the different types of consensus mechanisms used in blockchain, including their advantages and disadvantages.
3. What are the different methods for scaling blockchain technology? Discuss the advantages and disadvantages of each method.

1.17.4 Practical Questions

1. Develop a program in Python that implements a proof-of-work algorithm.
2. Create a presentation that outlines the different types of blockchain (public, private, federated, hybrid) and the benefits and drawbacks of each.
3. Research and identify at least three real-world applications of blockchain technology, and explain how they are being used to solve real-world problems.

1.17.5 Answer Set of MCQ

d. All of the above
c. Public, private, hybrid, and federated
d. All of the above
d. All of the above
c. Greater control
a. A consensus mechanism used in blockchain
b. It increases transaction speed
a. An unspent transaction output
b. Supply chain management
a. To incentivize miners to verify transactions

Essentials of Blockchain Programming

2

2.1   Cryptography Primitives

Blockchain technology is built on top of many cryptographic primitives. These are

- hash functions
- SHA-256
- puzzle friendliness

2.1.1   Hash Function

The hash functions play an important role in connecting various blocks in blockchain. Hash functions usually take variable size input and produced fixed-length output (usually 256 bits in blockchain) in hexadecimal notation called hash value or message digest. If "x" is an arbitrary-length input then h(x) denotes the hash value.

2.2   Hash Functions

Hash functions are mathematical functions that take an input of arbitrary size and produce a fixed-size output known as a hash value or message digest. A simple illustration of the hashing process is given in Figure 2-1.

Hash functions are widely used in cryptography and computer science, especially for verifying data integrity and securing sensitive information.

A hash function takes an input of any length and generates a fixed-size output known as a message digest. The output of a hash function is typically a string of characters that is unique to the input data, and any small change in the input will result in a vastly different hash value. This property is known as the avalanche effect and is crucial in ensuring data integrity and security.

Hash functions are used in a variety of applications, including digital signatures, password authentication, data integrity verification, and indexing data in hash tables. The most common cryptographic hash functions are MD5, SHA-1, SHA-2, and SHA-3, with SHA-256 being the most widely used.

© The Author(s), under exclusive license to APress Media, LLC, part of Springer Nature 2024
R. S. Mangrulkar, P. Vijay Chavan, *Blockchain Essentials*,
https://doi.org/10.1007/978-1-4842-9975-3_2

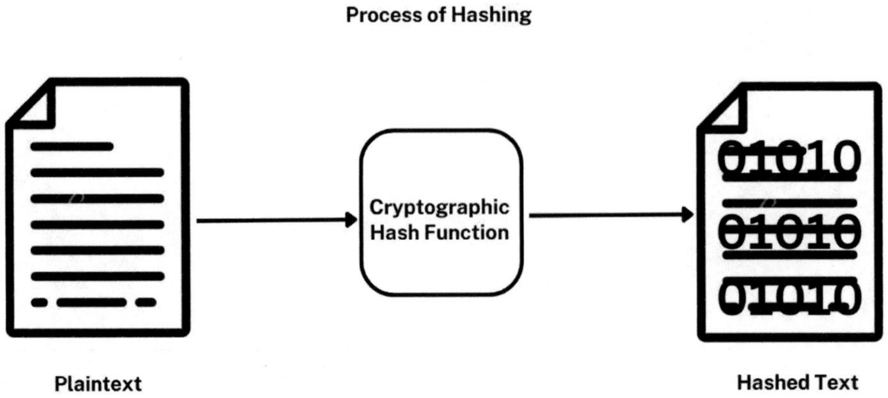

Process of Hashing

Plaintext   Hashed Text

Figure 2-1 Hashing process

2.2.1   Properties of Hash Functions

Hash functions possess several fundamental characteristics, including:

- Deterministic: When given the same input, a hash function will unfailingly produce the same output. This property is crucial in verifying data integrity.
- One way: It should be extremely difficult, computationally speaking, to derive the original input from its corresponding hash value. This property renders hash functions suitable for tasks such as password hashing and digital signatures.
- Fixed output: Regardless of the input size, hash functions generate a fixed-size output. This property enables their effective use in indexing data within hash tables.
- Avalanche effect: A minor alteration in the input should result in a significant alteration in the output. This property guarantees that even slight changes in data will yield substantially different hash values.
- Collision resistance: It should be highly improbable, computationally speaking, to discover two distinct inputs that produce the same hash value. This property ensures that different data elements will be consistently mapped to different hash values.
- Noninvertible: Given only the hash value, it should be exceedingly difficult, computationally speaking, to deduce the original input. This property ensures that hash functions will remain secure against attacks that attempt to reverse-engineer the original input from its hash value.

2.2.2   Hash Pointers and Data Structures

Hash pointers and data structures play a crucial role in the design and implementation of blockchain technology. Hash pointers are essentially references to data stored on a blockchain, and they are created using a combination of a hash function and a pointer to the location of the data, as shown in Figure 2-2.

In blockchain, each block typically contains a set of transactions and a hash pointer to the previous block in the chain. This creates a chain of blocks, with each block containing a cryptographic hash of the previous block's header data, including the hash pointer. This ensures that any tampering with

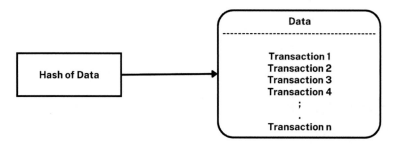

Figure 2-2 Hash pointer

a single block will be immediately detected, as it would cause all subsequent blocks to have invalid hash pointers.

Hash pointers can also be used to create more complex data structures in a blockchain, such as Merkle trees. Merkle trees are binary trees in which each leaf node represents a piece of data, and each nonleaf node represents the hash of its child nodes. This creates a hierarchical structure of hashes, with the root hash representing the entire data set.

Typical transactions in blockchain such as Bitcoins are

$$A- > B : 2BTC,$$

$$A- > C : 3BTC.$$

Figure 2-3 gives a hash obtained using an online tool.[1]

Tampering in a hash is extremely difficult as the hash value generated is unique and follows the principles of diffusion in confusion in cryptography.

2.2.3 Tampering Is Computationally Challenging

Let us take an example showing how tampering in blockchain is computationally challenging. We continue with the example from the previous section:

$$A- > B : 2BTC.$$

Here, party A is sending two BTC (Bitcoin) to B. This is recorded as one of the transactions. Usually, a block in a blockchain has many such transactions. For simplicity, only one transaction is considered using the same tool http://www.blockchain-basics.com/HashPuzzle.html as illustrated in Figure 2-4.

An attempt is made to solve the following puzzle: "To Get Hash Value with Required Leading Zeros."

Similarly, the computation of hash values of the transaction $A- > B : 2BTC$, with various nonces, is shown in Figure 2-5.

A nonce is any random number used together with a transaction to generate a hash value. The puzzle is to get a hash value with the required leading number of zeros. In Figure 2-4, the same tool http://www.blockchain-basics.com/HashPuzzle.html is used with nonce values like "0," "1," "2," "3", which generates hashed values like "6FD8BD96," "76B160BA," "160A6C89," "58121C16". This

---

[1] http://www.blockchain-basics.com/HashFunctions.html.

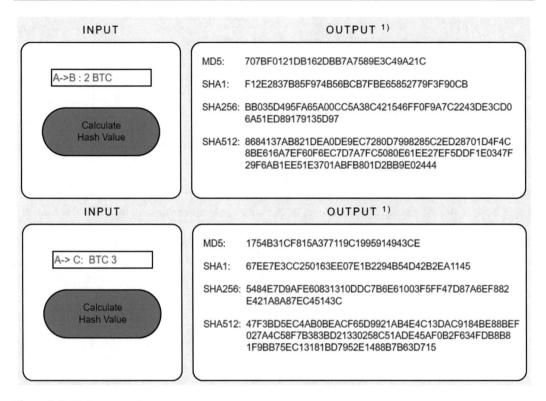

Figure 2-3 Hash computation

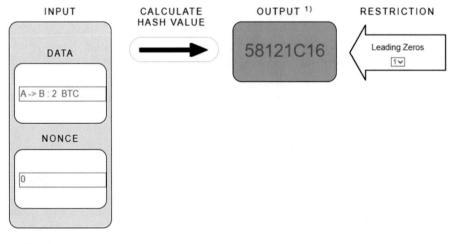

Figure 2-4 Puzzle example

does not solve the puzzle. The puzzle is solved with the nonce value "23" producing the required hash "0E93EC58," (Figure 2-6). Try using the tool to generate a solution to the same transaction with a different number of leading zeros.

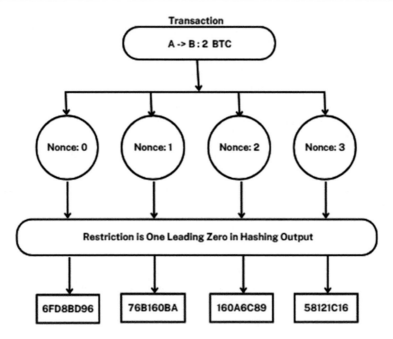

Figure 2-5 Various attempts to solve a puzzle

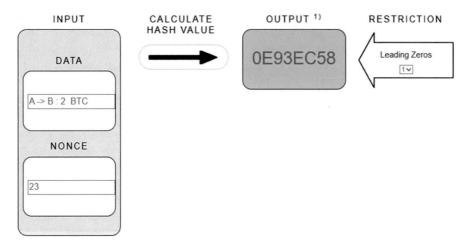

Figure 2-6 Solved puzzle

2.2.4   Role of Hashes in Blockchain

In the context of blockchain, a hash function operates by taking an input of varying length and generating a consistent-length output known as a hash or message digest. This hash serves as a distinct and digital representation of the initial input, akin to a fingerprint.

Here are some key roles of hash functions in blockchain:

- Block validation: Hash functions play a crucial role in validating the integrity of each block within a blockchain. Each block contains a hash of the previous block, forming a chain of interconnected hashes. Any alteration made to the block's data will result in a modified hash, instantly indicating tampering. This ensures that any unauthorized modifications to the blockchain will be easily detected.

- Mining: In proof-of-work blockchains like Bitcoin, miners engage in a competitive process known as mining, wherein they strive to solve a mathematical puzzle by discovering a hash that meets specific criteria. Miners employ their computational power to perform hash computations, with the first miner to find a valid hash being rewarded with newly minted coins. The puzzle's difficulty is adjusted to maintain a predetermined timeframe for the mining process.
- Digital signatures: Hash functions are instrumental in creating digital signatures within a blockchain. Digital signatures serve the purpose of proving that a transaction has been authorized by the owner of a specific private key. The transaction data undergo hashing, and the resulting hash is then signed using the private key. Verification of the signature can be performed by anyone using the corresponding public key.

2.2.4.1 Block Validation

In a blockchain, block validation is the process of verifying the authenticity and validity of a newly created block before adding it to the existing chain. The process of block validation is critical to ensure the security and integrity of the blockchain.

The block validation process involves several steps, as follows:

1. Verification of block header: The first step in block validation is to verify the block header. This includes checking the block's hash, timestamp, nonce, and previous block hash. The hash is generated by applying a cryptographic function to the block's data, including the transactions in the block. The timestamp must be within a certain range to prevent manipulation of the block creation time. The nonce is a random number that is added to the block header to make the hash difficult to compute.
2. Verification of transactions: The next step is to verify the transactions in the block. Each transaction must be valid, meaning that the sender has sufficient funds and the transaction is signed with the correct private key. Additionally, the transaction must not violate any of the blockchain's rules, such as double-spending or spending more than the available balance.
3. Consensus verification: Following verification of the block header and transactions, the block must be validated by the network's consensus mechanism. This ensures that the block will be accepted by the majority of nodes in the network. The consensus mechanism varies depending on the blockchain, but it typically involves proof of work, proof of stake, or a similar algorithm.
4. Block propagation: Once a block has been validated, it is propagated to the network's nodes. Each node will verify the block independently to ensure that it is valid.
5. Block addition: Finally, once the block has been validated by the network's nodes, it is added to the blockchain. The block becomes a permanent part of the chain, and its transactions are considered confirmed.

2.2.4.2 Digital Signatures and Blockchain

Digital signatures play a vital role in the technology of blockchain, ensuring the security and genuineness of transactions. They are created by subjecting a message, like a transaction, to a cryptographic function using the private key of the signer. The resulting signature can be verified using the corresponding public key, enabling the proof that the message was signed by the private key owner while keeping the key itself undisclosed.

In blockchain, transaction data undergo a process called hashing, where a hash function like SHA-256 is applied, generating a fixed-size output known as a hash or digest. This hash is then signed utilizing the sender's private key, producing a digital signature. The signature is attached to the transaction and transmitted across the network.

Upon receiving a transaction, a node within the network can employ the sender's public key to validate the signature. This involves applying the same hash function to the transaction data and comparing the resulting hash with the one signed by the sender. If the two hashes match, the signature is deemed legitimate, and the transaction can be included in the blockchain.

By leveraging digital signatures, blockchain provides a mechanism to establish the ownership and integrity of transactions without relying on a central authority or trusted intermediary. This characteristic ensures that blockchain transactions will remain secure and impervious to tampering, fraud, and other malicious activities.

2.3   Secure Hash Algorithm (SHA)

The SHA-256 algorithm is prominently used in Bitcoin mining to construct a Bitcoin blockchain. SHA-256 generates a 256-bit hex string from variable-length input sometimes also called a message digest.

2.3.1   SHA Algorithm

SHA-256 Algorithm – Preprocessing
- Ensure that the message is extended to a size that is a multiple of 512 through padding.
- Let us assume the length of message M is l, and $l \mod 512 = 0$.
- Add the bit "1" to the end of the message as an appendage.
- Add k zero bits, where k is the smallest nonnegative solution to the equation $1 + 1 + k \equiv 448 \mod 512$.
- Attach a 64-bit block, representing the binary form of the number l.
- The overall length becomes divisible by 512. Partition the message into N blocks of 512 bits each: $M(1), M(2), \ldots, M(N)$.
- Further divide each 512-bit block into 32-bit subblocks: $M_0, M_1, \ldots, M_{15}$.

Message Block Processing
Message blocks are processed one at a time.

Start with a fixed initial hash value $H(0)$.

Sequentially compute $H(i) = C(H(i-1), M(i))$, where C is the SHA-256 compression function and $+$ denotes modular addition modulo 2^{32}.

$H(N)$ represents the hash of the entire message M.

The entire process is summarized in Figure 2-7.

In a blockchain, each block of transactions is hashed using a cryptographic hash function, such as SHA-256 or SHA-3, to create a hash of the block. This hash is then included in the next block, creating a chain of blocks. The hash of each block depends not only on the transactions in that block, but also on the hash of the previous block in the chain. This creates a secure and tamper-proof record of all the transactions that have taken place on the blockchain.

The use of SHA in blockchain provides several key benefits. First, it ensures the integrity of the data stored on the blockchain. Any attempt to tamper with a block would change its hash, which would in turn invalidate the hash of all subsequent blocks in the chain. This makes it virtually impossible to modify the data on a blockchain without being detected.

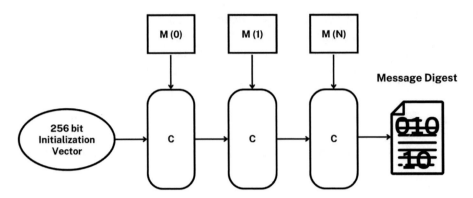

Figure 2-7 SHA-256 overview

Second, SHA provides a high level of security. The cryptographic properties of SHA ensure that it is computationally infeasible to generate the same hash for two different blocks of data. This helps to prevent fraudulent activity and ensures that the data on the blockchain are accurate and reliable.

2.3.2   Hashing Patterns

Hash values are composed of a combination of digits (0–9) and letters (A–F), resulting in a total of 16 possible values represented by 16 bits. These values are known as hexadecimal numbers. Hash functions differ in the length of the hash value they generate, leading to multiple types of hash function. Rather than distinct patterns, these techniques include collision-resistant, cryptographic, message digest, secure, and keyed hash functions.

1. **Independent hashing**: Each input is hashed independently, without any correlation to other inputs.
2. **Repeated hashing**: The output of a hash function is fed back as the input for the next iteration, creating a chain of hashes.
3. **Combined hashing**: Multiple inputs are combined together before applying the hash function.
4. **Sequential hashing**: Multiple hash functions are applied in a specific sequence or order.
5. **Hierarchical hashing**: Hashing is performed in a hierarchical manner, where hashes of subcomponents are combined to form hashes of higher-level components.

2.4   Public Key Cryptography

Basic Concepts of Cryptography
Cryptography is the practice of securing communication by converting information into an unreadable format. There are two fundamental concepts in cryptography: symmetric key cryptography and public key cryptography.

- **Symmetric key cryptography**: In symmetric key cryptography, a single key is utilized for both encrypting and decrypting a message. The sender and receiver must possess a shared secret key that is maintained in confidentiality. The encryption algorithm takes the plaintext and shared key as input, producing the ciphertext, while the decryption algorithm employs the same key to convert the ciphertext back to plaintext. However, the difficulty lies in securely exchanging the key between sender and receiver, ensuring it is not intercepted by unauthorized entities. Moreover, symmetric key cryptography may not adequately address specific needs, such as the secure distribution of keys.

- **Public key cryptography**: Asymmetric cryptography, also referred to as public key cryptography, overcomes the restrictions of symmetric key cryptography. It employs a set of mathematically linked keys: a publicly accessible key for encryption and a confidential key for decryption. The public key is universally disseminated, whereas the private key remains concealed by the proprietor. Any message encoded with the public key can be decoded only using the corresponding private key. Public key cryptography addresses issues such as trustworthy key distribution and empowers features like digital signatures and secure communication over unreliable media. It finds extensive application in technologies like blockchain to guarantee secure transactions and ensure data integrity.

Some important features of public key cryptography are as follows:

Public Key Cryptography
- Public key cryptography: Also referred to as asymmetric cryptography, it involves the use of two different keys, a public key and a private key.
- Key: In this context, a key is a crucial parameter that influences the output of a cryptographic algorithm, determining the encryption or decryption process.
- Encryption: With the use of a public key, a plaintext message is transformed into a ciphertext, denoted by $M' = E(M, k)$.
- Decryption: The private key is used to convert the ciphertext back to its original plaintext form, denoted by $M = D(M', k)$.

Properties of a Cryptographic Key (to Prevent Guessing)
- Generate the key truly randomly so that the attacker cannot guess it.
- The key should be of sufficient length – the longer the key, the more difficult it is to guess.
- The key should contain sufficient entropy; all the bits in the key should be equally random.

2.4.1 Secure Hash Algorithm-3 (Keccak)

SHA-3 is a cryptographic hash function that was selected by the National Institute of Standards and Technology (NIST) in 2012 as the winner of the SHA-3 competition. SHA-3 is based on the Keccak algorithm, which was created by Guido Bertoni, Joan Daemen, Michaël Peeters, and Gilles Van Assche.

The role of SHA-3 in blockchain is to provide a secure and efficient way to create unique digital signatures for transactions and blocks. Hash functions like SHA-3 are used to create a unique digital fingerprint for a block of data. In blockchain, each block contains a hash of the previous block's header, which creates a chain of blocks that cannot be tampered with without invalidating the entire chain.

SHA-3 works by taking an input message and processing it through a series of rounds of operations to produce a fixed-size output, known as a hash or digest. The output is designed to be unique to the input, so even a slight change to the input message will produce a vastly different output. This property makes hash functions useful for verifying the integrity of data and detecting any unauthorized changes.

Here's an example of how SHA-3 works:

Let's say we want to hash the message "Hello, world!" using SHA-3-256 (which produces a 256-bit output). The steps are as follows:

Padding: First, the message is padded so that its length is a multiple of the block size (1600 bits for SHA-3-256). This is done by adding a single 1 bit, followed by as many 0 bits as necessary to reach the desired length.

Absorption: The padded message is divided into 1600-bit blocks, and each block is processed through a series of rounds. In each round, the block is XORed with a 1600-bit state, and then the state is transformed using a nonlinear function.

Squeezing: After all the blocks have been processed, the final state is used to generate the output hash. This is done by repeatedly taking a portion of the state, appending it to the output, and then transforming the state again.

2.5   Merkle Tree

The Merkle tree is a robust data structure employed in computer science and cryptography to efficiently establish the integrity and authenticity of data within expansive datasets.

Constructing a Merkle tree involves recursively hashing pairs of data until only a solitary hash, referred to as the Merkle root, remains. The tree's leaves represent the original data, while each internal node represents the hash of its two child nodes. The entire process is summarized in Figure 2-8.

The Merkle root serves as a means to verify data integrity. A party can substantiate that a specific data element is part of the tree by presenting a path from the leaf node to the root, accompanied by the hashes of each node along the path. The verifier can then compute the root by hashing the provided data and hashes, subsequently comparing it to the expected root.

Merkle trees find widespread application in cryptocurrency systems like Bitcoin and Ethereum to guarantee the integrity of transaction data. They are also instrumental in distributed systems,

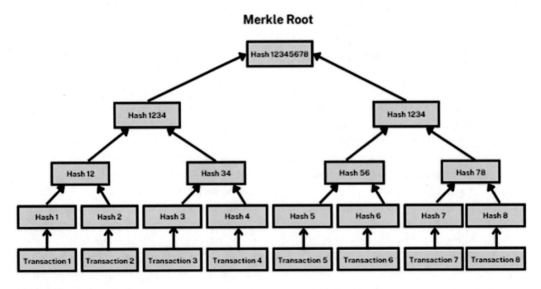

Figure 2-8 Merkle root

data storage systems, and content-addressable storage systems, as they facilitate data consistency verification and thwart data corruption.

2.5.1 Merkle Tree Creation

To create a Merkle tree, follow these steps:

1. Prepare the data: The first step is to prepare the data you want to include in the tree. The data are usually divided into fixed-size blocks, and each block is assigned a unique identifier, such as a hash.
2. Build the bottom layer: In this step, you take each block of data and hash it to create a leaf node. The leaf nodes are then grouped into pairs, and the hash of each pair is calculated to create a new node.
3. Build the next layer: In the next layer, you repeat step 2, but this time you calculate the hash of each pair of nodes from the previous layer. You continue this process until there is only one node left, which is the root of the tree.
4. Store the tree: The Merkle tree can be stored in several ways, such as a flat array or a binary tree. Each node in the tree is assigned a unique identifier, which can be used to verify the authenticity of the data.
5. Verify data: To verify the authenticity of a block of data, you need to provide the leaf node hash, as well as the hashes of all the nodes on the path from the leaf node to the root. The verifier can then recalculate the root hash and compare it to the expected value. If the hashes match, the data are considered authentic.

2.5.2 Role of Merkle Tree in Blockhain

In blockchain, Merkle trees play a crucial role in ensuring the integrity and security of transaction data. This subsection explains how.

When a new block is added to a blockchain, it contains a list of all the transactions that have occurred since the previous block. These transactions are combined and hashed together to create a Merkle tree. The root of the Merkle tree is then included in the block header, along with other important information, such as the timestamp and the previous block hash.

By including the Merkle tree root in the block header, the blockchain can ensure the following:

- Data integrity: The Merkle tree provides a way to verify that all transactions in a block are valid and have not been tampered with. By providing the hash of each transaction in the block, a verifier can easily calculate the Merkle root hash and compare it to the root hash included in the block header. If the hashes match, it can be assumed that all the transactions are valid and have not been modified.
- Scalability: The Merkle tree allows for efficient and scalable verification of transactions. Instead of having to verify each transaction individually, the Merkle tree allows a verifier to quickly verify an entire block by only checking a handful of hashes.
- Tamper resistance: Because a Merkle tree is built using a hash function, it is difficult to modify the transactions in a block without changing the Merkle root hash. This means that once a block has been added to a blockchain, it is extremely difficult to modify or delete any of the transactions in that block.

2.5.3   Structure of Merkle Tree

The Merkle tree is made up of several components, each with its own unique role. Here are the main components of a Merkle tree:

- Leaf nodes: The leaf nodes are the bottom layer of a Merkle tree and represent the individual pieces of data that will be included in the tree. In the context of blockchain, the leaf nodes represent the individual transactions that will be hashed and included in the Merkle tree.
- Hash function: The hash function is used to transform the data in the leaf nodes into fixed-size hashes. A good hash function should be deterministic, meaning that given the same input, it will always produce the same output. It should also be collision-resistant, meaning that it is computationally difficult to find two different inputs that produce the same output.
- Parent nodes: The parent nodes are created by hashing pairs of leaf nodes together. Each parent node represents the hash of its two children, and this process is repeated recursively until there is only one node left – the root node.
- Root node: The root node is the top-level node of a Merkle tree and represents the hash of all the data included in the tree. The root node is included in the block header in the context of blockchain, allowing other nodes in the network to verify the authenticity of the transactions in the block.
- Branch Nodes: The branch nodes are the intermediate nodes between the leaf nodes and the root node. They represent the hash of their two children and are used to verify the authenticity of a particular piece of data in the Merkle tree. To verify a specific piece of data, a node only needs to provide the hashes of the branch nodes on the path from the leaf node to the root.

2.5.4   Merkle Proof

A Merkle proof, also known as a Merkle path or a Merkle authentication path, is a proof that demonstrates the membership or nonmembership of an element in a Merkle tree data structure. Merkle proofs are widely used in distributed systems, such as blockchain technology, to efficiently verify the integrity of data without having to download the entire dataset.

In a Merkle tree, each leaf node represents a piece of data, and each nonleaf node is the hash of its children. The root node of the tree is the hash of all the data in the tree and is called the Merkle root. To prove the membership or nonmembership of an element in the tree, a Merkle proof is generated by providing a list of hashes that allows the verifier to reconstruct the Merkle root, starting with the element in question.

A proof of membership consists of a list of hashes that allows the verifier to reconstruct the Merkle root, starting with the element in question. The proof contains the hashes of all the sibling nodes along the path from the leaf node containing the element to the root node. To verify the proof, the verifier hashes the element and then hashes the result with the first hash in the proof. The verifier then hashes the resulting hash with the next hash in the proof, and so on, until the Merkle root is reconstructed. If the final result matches the known Merkle root, then the proof is valid, and the element is a member of the Merkle tree.

A proof of nonmembership is similar to a proof of membership, except that it contains the hashes of all the sibling nodes along the path from the root node to the closest ancestor node of the element that has a sibling. The proof demonstrates that the element is not present in the Merkle tree by showing that the sibling node that would have existed if the element was present is also not present. To verify the proof of nonmembership, the verifier hashes the element, and then hashes the result with the first hash in the proof. The verifier then hashes the resulting hash with the next hash in the proof, and so on, until the closest ancestor node is reached. If the final result matches the hash of the sibling node, then the proof is valid, and the element is not a member of the Merkle tree.

Merkle proofs are a powerful tool for verifying the integrity of data in a distributed system. They allow verifiers to efficiently verify the membership or nonmembership of an element in a Merkle tree without having to download the entire dataset, making them ideal for use cases such as blockchain technology, where large amounts of data need to be verified quickly and efficiently.

2.5.5   Proof of Membership

To prove membership of a particular transaction in a Merkle tree, a proof must be provided that includes the hash values of the nodes on the path from the transaction to the root of the Merkle tree. What follows is an example of how a proof of membership works in a Merkle tree blockchain:

1. Assume there is a Merkle tree with four transactions, labeled A, B, C, and D, and the root hash of the tree is represented by H.
2. Say we want to prove that transaction C is included in the Merkle tree.
3. To prove this, we need to provide a proof that includes the hash values of the nodes on the path from transaction C to the root of the Merkle tree.
4. In this case, the path from C to the root of the tree includes the hashes of transactions B and D and the root H.
5. The proof of membership for transaction C would therefore include the hashes of transactions B and D, as well as the root hash H.
6. A verifier can then use these hash values to reconstruct the path from transaction C to the root H and verify that the hash of C matches the hash stored in the Merkle tree.
7. If the hash values match, the verifier can be confident that transaction C is included in the Merkle tree and, therefore, in the blockchain.
8. This process of proving membership in a Merkle tree blockchain is secure because any tampering with the transactions in the Merkle tree would result in a different root hash, and the proof would not be valid.

2.5.6   Proof of Nonmembership

1. To prove nonmembership in a Merkle tree blockchain, you need to show that a particular element is not included in the blockchain. Here are the steps you can follow to prove nonmembership in a Merkle tree blockchain:
2. Obtain the Merkle root of the blockchain that you are interested in. This can typically be obtained from a trusted source or by computing it yourself.
3. Compute the hash of the element that you want to prove is not a member of the blockchain.
4. Traverse the Merkle tree from the root to the leaf node corresponding to the hash of the element. Along the way, you need to compute the hash of the sibling of each node that you encounter.
5. If you reach a leaf node that matches the hash of the element, then the element is a member of the blockchain. If you reach a leaf node that does not match the hash of the element, then the element is not a member of the blockchain.
6. To prove nonmembership, you can provide the hash of the sibling of the leaf node that you reached in step 4. This proves that the hash of the element could not have been constructed from the hashes in the Merkle tree, so it is not a member of the blockchain.

2.5.7   Advantages of Merkle Trees

Merkle trees have several advantages, including:

– Data verification is quick and easy due to the structured data, requiring minimal memory and reduced computing power.
– Merkle trees solve the challenges of memory space and computing power in validating blockchain data.
– Merkle trees hash every entry, separating data from supporting evidence and reducing the amount of data needed for verification.
– Merkle trees enable faster processing speed by distributing transactions among validators.
– Crypto wallets, or light-client nodes, can use Simple Payment Verification (SPV) to confirm transactions without downloading the entire blockchain.
– Miners can easily detect tampering with transactions through the hash structure.
– Each block's distinct hash value, generated by the Merkle root, ensures immutability and prevents double-spending.
– Double-spent transactions are rejected if their hash matches existing records on the blockchain.

2.5.8   Applications of Merkle Trees

What follows are a few examples of how Merkle trees are commonly used:

1. Cryptocurrencies: Cryptocurrencies such as Bitcoin and Ethereum use Merkle trees to verify the validity of transactions. Each block in the blockchain contains a Merkle tree of all the transactions in a block, and the root of the tree is included in the block header. This allows nodes in the network to easily verify the authenticity of the transactions in a block.
2. Content-addressable storage: Content-addressable storage systems, such as the InterPlanetary File System (IPFS), use Merkle trees to verify the integrity of stored content. Each file is split into chunks, and a Merkle tree is constructed from the hashes of the chunks. The root of the tree is then used as the content's address, allowing the content to be retrieved and verified from any node in the network.
3. Distributed systems: Distributed systems often use Merkle trees to verify the consistency of replicated data across multiple nodes. Each node stores a Merkle tree of the data it holds, and these trees are compared to ensure that all nodes have the same data.
4. Data storage: Merkle trees are also used in data storage systems, such as the ZFS filesystem. ZFS uses Merkle trees to verify the integrity of stored data, allowing it to detect and correct errors in the storage media.

2.5.9   Merkle Tree Proof of Reserves

Merkle trees offer a data verification method that does not require recomputing the entire dataset. They also separate the "proof" of the data from the actual data themselves. By maintaining the mathematical properties of the hashes, Merkle trees ensure tamper-proof integrity. Users can authenticate a dataset using only a portion of the data. The concept of proof of reserve utilizes Merkle trees to demonstrate that deposited cryptocurrency corresponds to the actual account balance. In this scenario, the leaf nodes represent users' account balances, and the Merkle root reflects the sum of all balances in real time. Independent auditors can compare the exchange's claimed reserves with the provided snapshot, using the Merkle tree proof of reserve. Users have the ability to verify their own balances by hashing their unique ID and account balance, searching for them in the tree. Multiple verification rounds guarantee the integrity of the entire tree structure, ensuring satisfaction for third-party auditors.

2.6 Public Key Cryptography

Public key cryptography, also known as asymmetric cryptography, has a rich history. It was first proposed by Diffie and Hellman in their influential paper "New Directions in Cryptography" in 1976. This paper introduced the concepts of public key encryption schemes and key distribution systems.

The Diffie–Hellman key agreement protocol, which allows two parties to establish a shared secret key over an insecure channel, was also presented in the same paper.

Interestingly, the idea of public-key encryption was initially proposed by James Ellis in a classified paper in 1970. However, it wasn't publicly known until 1997, when the British Governmental Communications Headquarters released the paper.

The concept of digital signatures, an important aspect of public key cryptography, can also be attributed to Diffie and Hellman. They contributed to the development of this concept, which ensures the authenticity and integrity of digital documents.

2.6.1 Public and Private Keys

Public key cryptography, also known as PKI or asymmetric cryptography, utilizes a pair of keys – public and private – to provide secure communication. The public key is widely distributed and accessible to everyone, while the private key must be kept confidential. In the context of Bitcoin, the loss of a private key puts the contents of a wallet at risk, with no traceability in case of theft, highlighting the system's anonymity.

PKI serves two key functions: authentication and message privacy through encryption/decryption. Establishing trust between sender and receiver is crucial during message exchange, ensuring the receiver can trust the message source. Blockchain-based messaging systems leverage decentralized networks, making communication highly secure, tamper-proof, and fast. Messages can be sent directly or through public channels, allowing for broad participation. With these advantages, blockchain-based messaging systems offer a secure and efficient alternative to traditional communication methods for both personal and public purposes.

2.6.2 Public Key Encryption Algorithms

Public key encryption algorithms are fundamental to ensuring secure communication in modern cryptography. These algorithms commonly employ either modular arithmetic number theory or elliptic curves.

The RSA algorithm, one of the most widely used public key encryption algorithms, is based on the computational hardness of factoring large numbers. It involves generating a public key and a private key, where the encryption process utilizes the public key and the decryption process relies on the private key.

Another popular algorithm is El Gamal, which is based on the difficulty of solving discrete logarithms. It shares the same underlying concept as the Diffie–Hellman key agreement protocol. El Gamal encryption involves generating a public key and a private key, and the encryption and decryption processes rely on mathematical operations involving modular exponentiation.

Both RSA and El Gamal are examples of public key encryption algorithms that provide a secure means of encrypting and decrypting messages, ensuring confidentiality and data integrity in communication.

2.6.3   Digitally Signed Transaction

Digital signing is a process used to verify the authenticity and integrity of a document sent by the expected sender. It ensures that the document has not been tampered with during transmission. The sender encrypts the message using a private key, and the corresponding public key, previously shared with the receiver, is used to decrypt the message.

In digital signing for blockchain transactions, the private key is used to sign digital transactions, while the corresponding public key authorizes the sender. It should be noted that digital signing focuses on authenticity rather than document security. Therefore, anyone with the sender's public key can decrypt the document.

The process of digital signing involves creating a hash of the document, encrypting the hash with the sender's private key, and sending it along with the document. The receiver decrypts the hash using the sender's public key. The receiver then calculates the hash of the document independently and compares it with the decrypted hash to determine whether the document has been altered during transmission. If the two hashes match, the receiver can confirm the authenticity of the document and ensure it has not been changed by a network intruder.

2.6.4   Digital Signing in Blockchain

Digital signing in blockchain technology serves multiple purposes. It goes beyond just verifying the authenticity of documents and extends to authenticating transactions and ensuring nonrepudiation. This is achieved through the use of digital signatures, which play a crucial role in validating the origin of transactions and preventing false ownership claims.

In a blockchain network, all participants have a unique digital signature or private key associated with their account. When initiating a transaction, senders need to prove their authorization to spend the balance associated with their account. This is done by digitally signing transactions using their private key.

Upon receiving a transaction, each node in the blockchain network verifies the digital signature to confirm its authenticity. This verification process involves checking whether the signature matches the public key associated with the sender's account. By performing this verification, the network participants can authenticate the transaction and the account linked to it.

Digital signatures provide trust and consensus in the blockchain network by preventing unauthorized parties from manipulating transactions or falsely claiming ownership. The use of elliptic curve cryptography, such as the Elliptic Curve Digital Signature Algorithm (ECDSA) in Bitcoin, ensures strong security and efficient key generation. All transactions are digitally signed by the senders using their private key, and this signature is included in the blockchain as proof of authenticity and ownership.

By combining digital signing with blockchain technology, participants can securely authorize transactions, establish the origin of transactions, and maintain the integrity of the network. This ensures that transactions are legitimate, authorized, and cannot be repudiated, contributing to the overall trust and reliability of blockchain systems.

2.7 Laboratory Work

This section shows the implementation of essential concepts in Blockchain using python.

2.7.1 Program in Python that Demonstrates the Use of Hashlib Library to Generate the SHA-3 Hash of a Message

```
import hashlib

# Define the message to be hashed
message = b"Hello, world!"

# Create a SHA-3 hash object with a 256-bit output size
sha3_256 = hashlib.sha3_256()

# Update the hash object with the message
sha3_256.update(message)

# Get the hash digest as a byte string
digest = sha3_256.digest()

# Convert the digest to a hexadecimal string for display
hexdigest = digest.hex()

# Print the hash digest in hexadecimal format
print(hexdigest)
```

```
The output of above program will be:

f5b5d629b3abd90bafacc650d15f2b2d1eeb55a262b41e60a44d42
d95e1d8481
```

Explanation of Code

The provided code demonstrates the usage of the SHA-3 hashing algorithm from the hashlib module in Python. The hashlib module provides access to various hashing algorithms. In this code, a specific message, "Hello, world!", is chosen to be hashed. The hashlib.sha3_256() function creates a SHA-3 hash object with a 256-bit output size. This hash object is then updated with the message using the update() method. The digest() method is called on the hash object to retrieve the hash digest as a byte string. To display the digest in a more readable format, the hexdigest() method is used to convert the byte string to a hexadecimal string. Finally, the hexadecimal representation of the hash digest is printed using the print() function. The output of the code will be the hexadecimal string "f5b5d629b3abd90bafacc650d15f2b2d1eeb55a262b41e60a44d42d95e1d8481", which represents the SHA-3 hash digest of the message "Hello, world!" with a 256-bit output size.

2.7.2   Python Program that Takes a String and the Desired Number of Leading Zeros from the User and Outputs the Input String, the Nonce Value for Which the Leading Zeros Puzzle Is Solved, and the Corresponding Hash Generated

```
 1  import hashlib
 2
 3  def solve_puzzle(string, leading_zeros):
 4      nonce = 0
 5      while True:
 6          nonce_str = str(nonce)
 7          data = string + nonce_str
 8          hash_value = hashlib.sha256(data.encode()).hexdigest()
 9          if hash_value.startswith("0" * leading_zeros):
10              return nonce_str, hash_value
11          nonce += 1
12
13  # Get input from the user
14  input_string = input("Enter the string: ")
15  input_zeros = int(input("Enter the number of leading zeros: "))
16
17  # Solve the puzzle
18  nonce_value, hash_result = solve_puzzle(input_string, input_zeros)
19
20  # Print the results
21  print("Input String:", input_string)
22  print("Nonce value for which the puzzle is solved:", nonce_value)
23  print("Generated Hash:", hash_result)
```

Explanation of Code

The provided code defines a function called `solve_puzzle`, which takes two parameters: `string` and `leading_zeros`. This function aims to find a nonce, represented by an arbitrary number, that, when concatenated with the provided `string`, generates a hash value with a specified number of leading zeros.

Within the `solve_puzzle` function, a variable `nonce` is initialized to 0. The code then enters a loop that continues indefinitely until a solution is found. During each iteration, the current value of `nonce` is converted to a string and combined with the input `string` to create the variable `data`.

Using the `hashlib.sha256()` function, the `data` string is encoded as bytes and hashed using the SHA-256 algorithm. The resulting hash value is then converted to a hexadecimal string representation using the `hexdigest()` method.

To determine whether the generated `hash_value` starts with the specified number of zeros, the code compares it to a string of zeros (`"0" * leading_zeros`). If the condition is met, indicating a successful solution, the current values of `nonce_str` and `hash_value` are returned from the function. Outside the `solve_puzzle` function, the code prompts the user to input a string and the desired number of leading zeros, which are stored in the variables `input_string` and input_zeros, respectively. The solve_puzzle function is then invoked with the user-provided inputs, and the resulting values are assigned to nonce_value and hash_result.

Finally, the code prints the original input string, the nonce value for which the puzzle was solved, and the generated hash value. By executing this code, you can find a nonce value that, when combined with the input string, produces a hash value with the desired number of leading zeros.

Sample Output

```
1
2 Enter the string: Hello World
3 Enter the number of leading zeros: 1
4 Input String: Hello World
5 Nonce value for which the puzzle is solved: 2
6 Generated Hash: 0de69f56365c10550d05e65ae8229dd0686f7
7 894a807830daec8caa879731f4d
```

2.7.3   Program to Create Hash Code from Given Input String

```
1 import hashlib
2 string = "Hello, World!"
3 # create a hash object using the SHA-256 algorithm
4 hash_object = hashlib.sha256()
5 # update the hash object with the string's bytes
6 hash_object.update(string.encode('utf-8'))
7 # get the hash value as a hex string
8 hex_dig = hash_object.hexdigest()
9 print("String: {}".format(string))
10 print("Hash value (SHA-256): {}".format(hex_dig))
```

Explanation of Code

The preceding code starts by importing the hashlib module, which provides access to various hashing algorithms. Next, a variable string is assigned the value "Hello, World!" as the input string to be hashed. A hash object is created using the SHA-256 algorithm by calling hashlib.sha256(). The hash object is then updated with the bytes of the string by calling the update() method, which takes the encoded bytes of the string using the UTF-8 encoding.

To obtain the hash value as a hexadecimal string, the hexdigest() method is called on the hash object, and the resulting value is assigned to the variable hex_dig. Finally, the original input string and the generated hash value (SHA-256) are printed using the print() function, with placeholders used to format the output. By executing this code, the provided string "Hello, World!" is hashed using the SHA-256 algorithm, and the resulting hash value is displayed as a hexadecimal string. The first line imports the hashlib library, which contains various hash algorithms that can be used to create hash values. The second line defines a string variable called string and sets it to the value "Hello, World!." The third line creates a new sha256 hash object using the hashlib.sha256() function.

The fourth line updates the hash object with the bytes of the string variable, encoded as UTF-8. This step is important because hash functions work on bytes, not on strings. The encode('utf-8') method converts the string to a sequence of bytes in UTF-8 encoding, which can be passed to the hash function.

The fifth line gets the hash value as a hex string using the hexdigest() method of the hash object. The resulting hex string represents the hash value of the input string using the SHA-256 algorithm.

The final two lines print out the input string and the resulting hash value in a human-readable format. The curly braces {} are placeholders for the values that will be printed, and the format() method is used to substitute these values into the string. The output of the program is the input string and its hash value.

2.7.4 Program in Python that Demonstrates How to Use the SHA-256 Hash Function and Its Application in a Simple Blockchain

```python
import hashlib
import json
from time import time

class Block:
    def __init__(self, index, timestamp, data, previous_hash):
        self.index = index
        self.timestamp = timestamp
        self.data = data
        self.previous_hash = previous_hash
        self.hash = self.calculate_hash()

    def calculate_hash(self):
        block_string = json.dumps(self.__dict__, sort_keys=True)
        return hashlib.sha256(block_string.encode()).hexdigest()

class Blockchain:
    def __init__(self):
        self.chain = [self.create_genesis_block()]

    def create_genesis_block(self):
        return Block(0, time(), "Genesis Block", "0")

    def add_block(self, data):
        previous_block = self.chain[-1]
        new_block = Block(previous_block.index + 1, time(), data,
        previous_block.hash)
        self.chain.append(new_block)

    def is_chain_valid(self):
        for i in range(1, len(self.chain)):
            current_block = self.chain[i]
            previous_block = self.chain[i-1]

            if current_block.hash != current_block.calculate_hash():
                return False

            if current_block.previous_hash != previous_block.hash:
                return False

        return True

blockchain = Blockchain()
```

```
44
45  blockchain.add_block("Transaction 1")
46  blockchain.add_block("Transaction 2")
47  blockchain.add_block("Transaction 3")
48
49  print("Blockchain is valid: ", blockchain.
50  is_chain_valid())
51
52  # Attempt to tamper with the second block
53  blockchain.chain[1].data = "Tampered Transaction"
54  print("Blockchain is valid: ", blockchain.
55  is_chain_valid())
```

Explanation of Code

The preceding code implements a basic blockchain using the SHA-256 hashing algorithm and JSON serialization. It defines a `Block` class representing a block in the blockchain, with attributes like `index`, `timestamp`, `data`, `previous_hash`, and `hash`. The `calculate_hash` method computes the hash value for a block based on its attributes.

The code also includes a `Blockchain` class that manages the chain of blocks. It initializes with a genesis block and has methods to add new blocks and validate the integrity of the chain. The `is_chain_valid` method checks whether the hash values and previous hash references of each block are consistent.

After defining the classes, an instance of the `Blockchain` class is created. Three blocks with different transaction data are added to the chain. The validity of the blockchain is checked, demonstrating the successful creation and validation of the blockchain.

To demonstrate the tamper-proof nature of the blockchain, the code attempts to modify the data of the second block. This modification is detected when validating the chain, highlighting the blockchain's ability to detect tampering.

Executing this code allows you to observe the creation of a basic blockchain, addition of blocks, and validation of the blockchain's integrity.

2.7.5   Write a Program in Python to Verify Hash Properties

```
1   import hashlib
2
3   # Define a message to hash
4   message = b"Hello, world!"
5
6   # Calculate hash values using different hash functions
7   md5_hash = hashlib.md5(message).hexdigest()
8   sha1_hash = hashlib.sha1(message).hexdigest()
9   sha256_hash = hashlib.sha256(message).hexdigest()
10
11  # Verify hash properties
12  # MD5
13  if md5_hash == hashlib.md5(message).hexdigest():
14      print("MD5 hash is consistent")
15  else:
16      print("MD5 hash is inconsistent")
```

```
17
18 if len(md5_hash) == 32:
19     print("MD5 hash is 32 characters long")
20 else:
21     print("MD5 hash is not 32 characters long")
22
23 # SHA-1
24 if sha1_hash == hashlib.sha1(message).hexdigest():
25     print("SHA-1 hash is consistent")
26 else:
27     print("SHA-1 hash is inconsistent")
28
29 if len(sha1_hash) == 40:
30     print("SHA-1 hash is 40 characters long")
31 else:
32     print("SHA-1 hash is not 40 characters long")
33
34 # SHA-256
35 if sha256_hash == hashlib.sha256(message).hexdigest():
36     print("SHA-256 hash is consistent")
37 else:
38     print("SHA-256 hash is inconsistent")
39
40 if len(sha256_hash) == 64:
41     print("SHA-256 hash is 64 characters long")
42 else:
43     print("SHA-256 hash is not 64 characters long")
```

Explanation of Code

The program imports the hashlib module in Python, which provides various hash functions for secure one-way hashing. A message is defined to hash. In this example, the message is b"Hello, world!," which is a byte string. Three different hash functions are used to calculate hash values for the message: md5, sha1, and sha256. The hexdigest() method is called on the hash objects to obtain a string representation of the hash value. The program then verifies some basic hash properties for each hash function:

For each hash function, the program checks whether the hash value is consistent. This means that hashing the same message should always produce the same hash value.

For each hash function, the program checks whether the hash value has the expected length. This is specific to each hash function, as different hash functions may produce hash values of different lengths.

Finally, the program prints out whether each hash function produced consistent hash values and whether each hash value has the expected length.

2.7.6   Program to Demonstrate a Simple Implementation of a Blockchain Using Hash Codes as a Chain of Blocks

```
1 import hashlib
2 import datetime
3
4 class Block:
```

```
 5      def __init__(self, timestamp, data, previous_hash):
 6          self.timestamp = timestamp
 7          self.data = data
 8          self.previous_hash = previous_hash
 9          self.hash = self.calculate_hash()
10
11      def calculate_hash(self):
12          hash_string = str(self.timestamp) + str(self.data) +
13          str(self.previous_hash)
14          return hashlib.sha256(hash_string.encode()).hexdigest()
15
16  class Blockchain:
17      def __init__(self):
18          self.chain = [self.create_genesis_block()]
19
20      def create_genesis_block(self):
21          return Block(datetime.datetime.now(), "Genesis Block", "0")
22
23      def get_latest_block(self):
24          return self.chain[-1]
25
26      def add_block(self, new_block):
27          new_block.previous_hash = self.get_latest_block().hash
28          new_block.hash = new_block.calculate_hash()
29          self.chain.append(new_block)
30
31      def is_valid(self):
32          for i in range(1, len(self.chain)):
33              current_block = self.chain[i]
34              previous_block = self.chain[i - 1]
35
36              if current_block.hash != current_block.calculate_hash():
37                  return False
38
39              if current_block.previous_hash != previous_block.hash:
40                  return False
41
42          return True
43
44  # Create a blockchain and add blocks
45  blockchain = Blockchain()
46  blockchain.add_block(Block(datetime.datetime.now(), "Block 1", ""))
47  blockchain.add_block(Block(datetime.datetime.now(), "Block 2", ""))
48  blockchain.add_block(Block(datetime.datetime.now(), "Block 3", ""))
49
50  # Check if the blockchain is valid
51  print("Is blockchain valid?", blockchain.is_valid())
52
53  # Manipulating the blockchain (introducing an invalid block)
54  blockchain.chain[1].data = "Modified Block"
55
56  # Check if the manipulated blockchain is valid
57  print("Is manipulated blockchain valid?", blockchain.is_valid())
```

Explanation of Code

In this code, we define two classes: Block and Blockchain. The `Block` class represents each block in the blockchain, while the `Blockchain` class manages the chain of blocks. Each block contains a timestamp, data (which can represent any information you want to store), a hash code, and a reference to the hash code of the previous block. The hash code is calculated using the SHA-256 algorithm, which is a commonly used cryptographic hash function.

The `Blockchain` class initializes with a genesis block (the first block in the chain), and new blocks are added by calculating their hash codes and linking them to the previous block's hash code. The is_valid() method iterates through the chain and checks whether the hash codes and previous hash codes are consistent.

The example demonstrates the addition of three blocks to a blockchain and then checks the validity of the blockchain. Afterward, it modifies the data of the second block to introduce an inconsistency and checks the validity again.

To run the blockchain demo, follow these steps:

1. Save the code in a file named `blockchain_demo.py`.
2. Open a command prompt or terminal and navigate to the directory where `blockchain_demo.py` is located.
3. Run the Python script using the following command:
   ```
   python blockchain_demo.py
   ```
4. The code will execute and display the output in the terminal.
5. You can modify the code to add or manipulate blocks in the blockchain.
6. Rerun the script to see the updated output and check the validity of the modified blockchain.

2.7.7 Program to Demonstrate the Mining Process in Blockchain

```
 1 import hashlib
 2 import time
 3
 4 # define the block header fields
 5 version = 1
 6 previous_block_hash = "000000000000000000007d28e1a9ac3b37760e3b
 7 3fbbd3df2b8f7670a434f18a6"
 8 merkle_root = "9d7d1c2fa42e7f520d33de8e7bb28132586d30ef7c6d9b9
 9 e446e6c12d1f7cf25"
10 timestamp = int(time.time())
11 difficulty = 4  # number of leading zeros required in the hash
12 nonce = 0
13
14 # combine the header fields into a single string
15 header = str(version) + previous_block_hash + merkle_root +
16 str(timestamp) + str(difficulty) + str(nonce)
17
18 # loop until a valid hash is found
19 while True:
20     # add the nonce value to the header
21     header_with_nonce = header + str(nonce)
22
23     # compute the SHA-256 hash of the header with nonce
24     hash = hashlib.sha256(header_with_nonce.encode()).hexdigest()
```

```
25
26      # check if the hash meets the difficulty target
27      if hash[:difficulty] == "0" * difficulty:
28          print("Block mined successfully!")
29          print("Nonce:", nonce)
30          print("Hash:", hash)
31          break
32
33      # increment the nonce and try again
34      nonce += 1
```

Explanation of Code

This is a basic implementation of a proof-of-work algorithm for mining a block in a blockchain. The code uses the SHA-256 hash function from the `hashlib` library and the time library to get the current time.

The code defines the block header fields, including the version, previous_block_hash, merkle_root, timestamp, difficulty, and nonce. The difficulty represents the number of leading zeros that the hash of the block must have to be considered valid. The nonce is a random value that is added to the header to produce a hash that meets the difficulty target.

The header fields are combined into a single string, and then a loop is started to find a valid hash. The loop continues until a hash is found that meets the difficulty target. In each iteration of the loop, the nonce value is added to the header, and the SHA-256 hash of the header with the nonce is computed. If the hash meets the difficulty target, the loop is exited and the hash and nonce value are printed.

If the hash does not meet the difficulty target, the nonce is incremented and the loop is repeated. The process continues until a valid hash is found. The print statements provide feedback on the progress of the mining process.

Sample Output

```
1 version = 1
2 previous_block_hash = "00000000000000000007d28e1a9ac
3 3b37760e3b3fbbd3df2b8f7670a434f18a6"
4 merkle_root = "9d7d1c2fa42e7f520d33de8e7bb28132586d3
5 0ef7c6d9b9e446e6c12d1f7cf25"
6 timestamp = 1616966744
7 difficulty = 4  # number of leading zeros required in the hash
8 nonce = 0
```

Sample Output:

```
1 Block mined successfully!
2 Nonce: 1555
3 Hash: 000098c38b9241cbf10de81db3d3c4f2a4cf4d43a4b79d0
4 3a81c2b2e0d0e9a92
5
6 Note: The actual nonce and hash values will vary each
7 time the code is executed due to the random nature of
8 the proof-of-work algorithm.
```

2.7.8   Program to Create a Merkle Tree in Blockchain

```
 1  import hashlib
 2
 3  def build_merkle_tree(leaves):
 4      num_leaves = len(leaves)
 5
 6      # If there is only one leaf, return it as the Merkle root
 7      if num_leaves == 1:
 8          return leaves[0]
 9
10      # If the number of leaves is odd, duplicate the last leaf
11      if num_leaves % 2 == 1:
12          leaves.append(leaves[-1])
13          num_leaves += 1
14
15      # Compute the hash of each pair of leaves
16      pairs = [leaves[i] + leaves[i+1] for i in
17      range(0, num_leaves, 2)]
18      hashes = [hashlib.sha256(pair.encode()).hexdigest()
19      for pair in pairs]
20
21      # Recursively build the Merkle tree from the hashes
22      return build_merkle_tree(hashes)
23
24  # Example usage
25  leaves = ["apple", "banana", "cherry", "date"]
26  merkle_root = build_merkle_tree(leaves)
27  print("Merkle root:", merkle_root)
28
29  # Print all nodes
30  def print_merkle_tree(node, depth=0):
31      indent = " " * depth * 4
32      print(indent + node)
33      if len(node) == 64: # Check if the node is
34      a hash value
35          print_merkle_tree(node[:32], depth+1)
36          print_merkle_tree(node[32:], depth+1)
37
38  print_merkle_tree(merkle_root)
```

Explanation of Code

The provided code performs operations related to Merkle trees. It begins by importing the hashlib library, which allows for the computation of SHA-256 hashes. The build_merkle_tree function is then defined, which takes a list of leaves as input and recursively constructs a Merkle tree from them. The number of leaves is determined by obtaining the length of the input list.

If there is only one leaf, it is returned as the Merkle root since there are no hashes to compute. However, if the number of leaves is odd, the last leaf is duplicated to ensure an even number of leaves. This duplication prevents missing or extra nodes during the tree construction process.

The algorithm proceeds by combining pairs of leaves and hashing them using SHA-256. This step involves creating a list comprehension that concatenates pairs of leaves and applies the hashlib.sha256 function to compute their hash values. The resulting list of hashes is then passed recursively back into the build_merkle_tree function to construct the next level of the tree.

Once the entire Merkle tree has been built, the Merkle root is returned as the final result. To facilitate visualization and analysis, the print_merkle_tree function is defined. It takes a node in the Merkle tree as input and recursively prints all nodes in the tree. Each node's indentation level corresponds to its depth within the tree.

Within the print_merkle_tree function, an indentation string is created based on the current node's depth. The function then prints the current node and proceeds with a recursive call to print its left and right children (if any). This decision is made by checking the length of the node. If the length is 64, it signifies that the node represents a hash value rather than a leaf node.

To display the entire Merkle tree, the print_merkle_tree function is invoked with the Merkle root as its input parameter. This will print the complete tree structure, with nodes indented according to their depth in the tree.

2.7.9 Program to Prove Membership and Nonmembership in a Merkle Tree Blockchain

```
import hashlib

# Define the Merkle Tree
merkle_tree = {
    'root': 'e12f41f456d48c058ea1e1f2d8b4bb3c3b4f4d9b',
    'levels': [
        ['2d0d2e33e58209a957e83c5e5e5d5a36a7c1b130',
         'd64ee0abce60be7e75a97c1f56bbd57bc9ac2c0c',
         '17600fcdefe24fcf129a7728ca84f0c70de7321a',
         '7f8a3a75369f3b529d3fb3277a8f01b969b7d1d1'],
        ['054a1ea24f240d7eafee90a01b7f75b77a21c7a6',
         '6a644c6e5b631d2c6a5d6b55833c8e8285c13fa5'],
        ['67b7e8a847f858cde48b659cea6991a2c6c17b3b']
    ]
}

# Define the element to be proved
element = 'hello'

# Compute the hash of the element
element_hash = hashlib.sha256(element.encode()).hexdigest()

# Define a function to generate the Merkle proof for a
given element
def generate_merkle_proof(element_hash, merkle_tree):
    proof = []
    current_hash = element_hash

    for level in merkle_tree['levels']:
        if len(level) == 1:
            break

        if current_hash in level:
            sibling_index = level.index(current_hash) - 1

            if sibling_index < 0:
                sibling_index = 1
```

```
38
39                sibling_hash = level[sibling_index]
40                proof.append(sibling_hash)
41
42                current_hash = hashlib.sha256((current_hash +
43                sibling_hash).
44                encode()).hexdigest()
45
46       return proof
47
48  # Generate the Merkle proof for the element
49  proof = generate_merkle_proof(element_hash, merkle_tree)
50
51  # Verify the proof of membership
52  current_hash = element_hash
53
54  for sibling in proof:
55        current_hash = hashlib.sha256((current_hash + sibling).
56        encode()).
57        hexdigest()
58
59  if current_hash == merkle_tree['root']:
60        print(f"{element} is a member of the blockchain")
61  else:
62        print(f"{element} is not a member of the blockchain")
63
64  # Define an element that is not in the blockchain
65  non_member_element = 'world'
66
67  # Compute the hash of the non-member element
68  non_member_element_hash = hashlib.sha256(non_member_element.
69  encode()).
70  hexdigest()
71
72  # Generate the Merkle proof for the non-member element
73  non_member_proof = generate_merkle_proof(non_member_element_hash,
74  merkle_tree)
75
76  # Verify the proof of non-membership
77  current_hash = non_member_element_hash
78
79  for sibling in non_member_proof:
80        current_hash = hashlib.sha256((current_hash +
81        sibling).encode()).
82        hexdigest()
83
84  if current_hash == merkle_tree['root']:
85        print(f"{non_member_element} is a member of
86        the blockchain")
87  else:
88        print(f"{non_member_element} is not a member of
89        the blockchain")
```

2.7.10 Explanation of Code

The code begins by importing the hashlib module, which enables the computation of SHA-256 hashes. A Merkle tree is then defined using a dictionary structure, consisting of a "root" key representing the root hash and a "levels" key containing a list of lists representing each level of the tree. The element to be proved is specified as the string "hello," and its SHA-256 hash is computed using the hashlib.sha256() function, storing the resulting hash in the variable element_hash.

To generate the Merkle proof for a given element hash and Merkle tree, the code defines the generate_merkle_proof() function. This function iterates through the levels of the Merkle tree and checks whether the current hash exists within a level. If the current hash is found, the function determines the index of the sibling hash and appends it to the proof list. The current hash is then updated by concatenating it with the sibling hash and hashing the result using hashlib.sha256(). This process continues until a level with only one hash remains or the current hash is not found in any level. The function returns the proof list.

The code generates the Merkle proof for the element by calling the generate_merkle_proof() function and stores it in the proof variable. To verify the proof of membership, the code reconstructs the Merkle root hash based on the element hash and sibling hashes in the proof. It iterates through each sibling hash, concatenates it with the current hash, computes the resulting hash, and updates the current hash accordingly. Finally, it compares the final current hash with the root hash of the Merkle tree. If they match, it indicates that the element is a member of the blockchain.

The code also demonstrates the process of verifying the proof of nonmembership. It defines a nonmember element as the string "world," computes its hash using hashlib.sha256(), and generates the Merkle proof for the nonmember element using the generate_merkle_proof() function. Similar to the proof of membership verification, it reconstructs the Merkle root hash based on the nonmember element hash and sibling hashes in the non_member_proof. The final current hash is then compared with the root hash of the Merkle tree.

2.7.11 Program to Demonstrate How to Prove the Membership and Nonmembership of an Element in a Merkle Tree Blockchain

```
 1  import hashlib
 2
 3  # Define the Merkle Tree
 4  merkle_tree = {
 5      'root': 'e12f41f456d48c058ea1e1f2d8b4bb3c3b4f4d9b',
 6      'levels': [
 7          ['2d0d2e33e58209a957e83c5e5e5d5a36a7c1b130',
 8           'd64ee0abce60be7e75a97c1f56bbd57bc9ac2c0c',
 9           '17600fcdefe24fcf129a7728ca84f0c70de7321a',
10           '7f8a3a75369f3b529d3fb3277a8f01b969b7d1d1'],
11          ['054a1ea24f240d7eafee90a01b7f75b77a21c7a6',
12           '6a644c6e5b631d2c6a5d6b55833c8e8285c13fa5'],
13          ['67b7e8a847f858cde48b659cea6991a2c6c17b3b']
14      ]
15  }
16
17  # Define the element to be proved
18  element = 'hello'
19
20  # Define an element that is not in the blockchain
21  non_member_element = 'world'
```

Explanation of Code

This code implements a Merkle tree and provides functions to generate and verify proofs for membership and nonmembership in a blockchain. It defines a Merkle tree structure and elements to be verified. The generate_merkle_proof function generates proofs by traversing the tree and appending sibling hashes, and verify_merkle_proof and verify_non_membership_proof check the validity of proofs. The code demonstrates proof generation and verification for specific elements in a blockchain.

Sample Output

```
hello is a member of the blockchain
world is not a member of the blockchain
```

2.7.12 Program in Python that Demonstrates RSA Digital Signature Scheme

```
import hashlib
import rsa

# Generate RSA key pair
private_key, public_key = rsa.newkeys(2048)

# Function to create a digital signature
def create_signature(message, private_key):
    hashed_message = hashlib.sha256(message.encode()).
    digest()
    signature = rsa.sign(hashed_message, private_key,
    'SHA-256')
    return signature

# Function to verify the digital signature
def verify_signature(message, signature, public_key):
    hashed_message = hashlib.sha256(message.encode()).
    digest()
    try:
        rsa.verify(hashed_message, signature, public_key)
        print("Signature is valid.")
    except rsa.VerificationError:
        print("Signature is invalid.")

# Message to be signed
message = "Hello, World!"

# Create digital signature
signature = create_signature(message, private_key)
print("Digital Signature:", signature)

# Verify the digital signature
verify_signature(message, signature, public_key)
```

Explanation of Code

This code demonstrates the RSA digital signature scheme in Python. First, the necessary libraries are imported, including `hashlib` for hashing and `rsa` for RSA operations.

A key pair is generated using rsa.newkeys(2048), which produces a 2048-bit RSA private key and its corresponding public key.

The create_signature function takes a message and a private key as input. It hashes the message using the SHA-256 algorithm and then signs the hashed message with the private key using RSA. The resulting digital signature is returned.

The verify_signature function takes a message, a signature, and a public key as input. It hashes the message using SHA-256 and then verifies the signature using the public key. If the verification is successful, it prints "Signature is valid." Otherwise, it prints "Signature is invalid."

In the code, a sample message, "Hello, World!," is used to demonstrate the digital signing process. The create_signature function is called with the message and the private key to generate the digital signature. The resulting signature is printed.

Finally, the verify_signature function is called with the message, signature, and public key to verify the digital signature. Based on the verification result, either "Signature is valid" or "Signature is invalid" is printed.

It is important to note that SHA-256 is used for hashing, and the `rsa` library provides the necessary functions for RSA key generation, signing, and verification. To run the code, the `rsa` library needs to be installed in the Python environment using "pip install rsa."

Sample Output

```
 1 Message: Hello, World!
 2
 3 Private Key:
 4 n: 10420999931509909067660158975836516859389706670366
 5 87746986206206550802414234991112633329019663600003823
 6 18995608831999989656063898971961469825817788534 7619
 7 e: 65537
 8 d: 35570052323466067026895703515031521379368486 2127
 9 39310332254192836808546035963812214021984730540526
10 14246852613047824575332999577126885152981401605812597
11
12 Public Key:
13 n: 10420999931509909067660158975836516859389706703668
14 77469862062065508024142349911126333290196636000382318
15 99560883199998965606389897196146982581777885347619
16 e: 65537
17
18 Digital Signature: 6be95364118a615684827bca6b3e02a70
19 e45296a6e2d08bea1c06
20 433f4652e7e5585aa1e838b255399d6ccf3eaebca4195d6b3cb7a
21 ee7d1fb3ad3b50f87931ee6e8b149c1df3c2a43b0bfa2e159a8ae
22 9d74328cb5fb60f64964873f8f7d4ce9f9f768b3e7f90a4dcecf
23 22b0dbbc4c5f550bea32b39f5b76ae4ef3a46a3d3277dabdd
24
25 Signature is valid.
```

2.8   Summary

This chapter provided an overview of hash functions, secure hash algorithms, Merkle trees, and public key cryptography, focusing on their applications in blockchain technology. The chapter began by discussing the properties of hash functions, their role in data structures, and their resistance to tampering. It emphasized the computational challenge involved in tampering with hash functions, which makes them suitable for maintaining data integrity. The chapter also explored the role of hash functions in blockchain technology and the importance of ensuring data immutability. It introduced the Secure Hash Algorithm (SHA) and discussed different hashing patterns to enhance security. Public key cryptography was introduced, explaining the use of public and private keys for encryption and digital signatures. The SHA was highlighted as a widely used cryptographic hash function. The chapter also delved into Merkle trees, explaining their creation process, structure, and role in ensuring data integrity in blockchains. It covered proof of membership and nonmembership in a Merkle tree, highlighting the advantages and various applications of Merkle trees beyond blockchain technology. The use of Merkle trees for proof of reserves was discussed, which helped prove the existence of funds in a blockchain system. Public key cryptography was revisited, with a specific focus on digital signing in the context of blockchain technology. The chapter concludes with laboratory work exercises using Python to practically implement the discussed concepts, including generating hash codes, solving puzzles, implementing a blockchain, verifying hash properties, mining processes, creating Merkle trees, and proving membership/nonmembership in a Merkle tree blockchain. The provided code explanations and a demonstration of the RSA digital signature scheme using Python rounded out the chapter.

2.9   Exercise

This section gives exercises based on topics covered in this chapter.

2.9.1   Multiple Choice Questions

1. Which of the following is a characteristic of hash functions?
   a. Deterministic
   b. Reversible
   c. Unique output
   d. All of the above
   Answer: d. All of the above
2. What is the purpose of mining in a blockchain?
   a. To validate transactions
   b. To generate new coins
   c. To create new blocks
   d. All of the above
   Answer: d. All of the above
3. Which algorithm is commonly used in blockchain for creating hash codes?
   a. SHA-512
   b. SHA-256

    c. SHA-1

    d. MD5

    Answer: b. SHA-256

4. What is a Merkle tree?

    a. A data structure used to store blockchain transactions

    b. A type of consensus algorithm

    c. A cryptographic hash function

    d. A tree structure used to efficiently verify data integrity

    Answer: d. A tree structure used to efficiently verify data integrity

5. What is the role of a Merkle tree in a blockchain?

    a. To create new blocks

    b. To verify the integrity of transactions

    c. To store data in a secure manner

    d. To generate new coins

    Answer: b. To verify the integrity of transactions

6. Which property of a hash function ensures that no two different inputs will result in the same output?

    a. Collision resistance

    b. Pre-image resistance

    c. Second pre-image resistance

    d. None of the above

    Answer: a. Collision resistance

7. What is the advantage of using a Merkle tree in a blockchain?

    a. Faster transaction processing

    b. Reduced storage requirements

    c. Improved data integrity verification

    d. All of the above

    Answer: c. Improved data integrity verification

8. Which proof algorithm is used to verify membership in a Merkle tree?

    a. Proof of work

    b. Proof of stake

    c. Proof of membership

    d. None of the above

    Answer: c. Proof of membership

9. Which algorithm is used to create a SHA-3 hash in Python?

    a. sha3_256

    b. sha_256

    c. sha1

    d. md5

    Answer: a. sha3_256

10. What is the purpose of a hash pointer in a data structure?

    a. To store a unique identifier for the data structure

    b. To enable efficient data retrieval

    c. To ensure the integrity of the data structure

    d. All of the above

    Answer: d. All of the above

2.9.2   Short Answer Questions

1. How does a hash function work?
2. What is a Merkle tree and what is its role in blockchain?
3. What is proof of membership and how is it used in a Merkle tree?
4. What are some advantages of using Merkle trees in blockchain?
5. What is the purpose of using hash pointers in data structures?
6. What is SHA-256 and how is it used in blockchain?
7. What is the difference between SHA and Keccak hash algorithms?
8. Can you give an example of a real-world application that uses blockchain technology?

2.9.3   Long Answer Questions

1. Explain the role of hash functions in blockchain technology.
2. Describe the mining process in blockchain, including how new blocks are added to a chain.
3. What is a Merkle tree and how is it used in blockchain? Explain its advantages and how it helps to ensure the security of a blockchain.
4. Explain the difference between proof of membership and proof of nonmembership in a Merkle tree.
5. What are some real-world applications of blockchain technology? Discuss the potential benefits and drawbacks of implementing blockchain in these applications.
6. How does SHA-256 work and how is it used in blockchain? Compare and contrast it with other hash algorithms like SHA and Keccak.
7. Describe a real-world example of how hash pointers and data structures are used in blockchain.
8. What are some potential challenges and limitations of blockchain technology? How might these challenges be addressed?

2.9.4   Practical Questions

1. Write a Python program to verify hash properties, including collision resistance and pre-image resistance.
2. Write a program to demonstrate the mining process in blockchain, including how new blocks are added to a chain.

2.9.5   Programming Questions

1. Write a program in Python to generate a Bitcoin address from a given public key.
2. Implement a function in JavaScript to calculate the transaction fee for a Bitcoin transaction based on the transaction size and current fee rates.
3. Create a Java program to interact with the Bitcoin blockchain using a popular Bitcoin library. Perform actions such as retrieving transaction details, querying block information, and verifying transaction signatures.
4. Develop a smart contract in Solidity for a simple escrow system on the Ethereum blockchain, where funds are released based on predefined conditions.

5. Write a Python script to retrieve the current price of Bitcoin from a cryptocurrency exchange's API and display it to the user.

6. Implement a function in C++ to calculate the hash of a Bitcoin block header using the SHA-256 hashing algorithm.

7. Create a web application using HTML, CSS, and JavaScript that allows users to generate and manage Bitcoin wallets, including features such as address generation, balance checking, and transaction history.

8. Develop a Python program to monitor the mempool of the Bitcoin network and display the transactions with the highest fees in real time.

9. Write a script in Ruby to connect to a Bitcoin full node using the JSON-RPC interface and retrieve information about the latest blocks mined.

10. Implement a function in Solidity to create a time-locked smart contract that holds Ether until a specific block number is reached, at which point the funds can be released.

Bitcoin

3

3.1   What Is Bitcoin

Bitcoin is a digital currency or cryptocurrency that was created in *2009* by an unknown person or group of people using the name Satoshi Nakamoto. Bitcoin operates on a decentralized system, which means it is not controlled by any central authority or financial institution.

The cryptocurrency uses a technology called blockchain, which is a decentralized ledger that records all transactions made using Bitcoin. Bitcoin transactions are verified by network nodes through cryptography and are recorded on the blockchain. This makes it very difficult for anyone to manipulate or counterfeit Bitcoin transactions.

Bitcoin can be used to buy goods and services online and in some physical stores that accept it as a form of payment. It can also be traded on various cryptocurrency exchanges for other currencies or assets.

3.2   History

Bitcoin has had a number of historical milestones throughout its relatively short history. Here are a few of the most notable ones:

- First Bitcoin transaction: On *January 12, 2009*, the first Bitcoin transaction took place when Satoshi Nakamoto sent *10* Bitcoins to Hal Finney, a programmer and early Bitcoin enthusiast.
- First Bitcoin exchange: The first Bitcoin exchange, called BitcoinMarket.com, was launched in *March 2010*. At the time, the exchange rate was around *$0.003* per Bitcoin.
- Bitcoin Pizza Day: On *May 22, 2010*, Laszlo Hanyecz, a programmer, paid 10,000 Bitcoins (worth around *$41* at the time) for two pizzas. This event is now known as Bitcoin Pizza Day and is celebrated annually by the Bitcoin community.
- Mt. Gox hack: In *February 2014*, Mt. Gox, one of the largest Bitcoin exchanges at the time, filed for bankruptcy after losing around *850,000* Bitcoins (worth around *$450* million at the time) in a hack.
- Bitcoin halving: Bitcoin undergoes a halving event every four years, in which the rewards for mining new blocks are cut in half. The first Bitcoin halving occurred in *November 2012*, the second in *July 2016*, and the third in *May 2020*.

© The Author(s), under exclusive license to APress Media, LLC, part of Springer Nature 2024
R. S. Mangrulkar, P. Vijay Chavan, *Blockchain Essentials*,
https://doi.org/10.1007/978-1-4842-9975-3_3

– All-time high: Bitcoin's all-time high was reached in *December 2021*, when it peaked at just under *$20,000* per Bitcoin.
– Institutional adoption: In recent years, a number of large corporations and financial institutions, such as Tesla and MicroStrategy, have invested in Bitcoin as a hedge against inflation and currency devaluation.

3.3   Predicted Market

The predicted market for Bitcoin is a subject of much debate and speculation. While some experts believe that Bitcoin has a bright future and will continue to grow in value, others are more skeptical and believe that it may not be a sustainable investment in the long run.

One potential factor that could affect the market for Bitcoin is increased regulation. As governments and financial institutions become more involved in the cryptocurrency space, they may seek to impose regulations or restrictions that could limit the growth and adoption of Bitcoin.

Another potential factor is competition from other cryptocurrencies. While Bitcoin was the first and remains the most well-known cryptocurrency, there are now thousands of other cryptocurrencies available, and some of them may offer better features or more attractive investment opportunities than Bitcoin.

Despite these potential challenges, many experts remain bullish on Bitcoin's long-term prospects. They argue that its limited supply, decentralized nature, and increasing adoption by institutions and individuals make it an attractive investment and store of value. Some even predict that Bitcoin's price could reach hundreds of thousands or even millions of dollars per coin in the coming years.

3.4   Wallet

A Bitcoin wallet is a software application or hardware device that is used to store, send, and receive Bitcoin. It is essentially a digital wallet that holds a user's private keys, which are used to access their Bitcoin holdings on the blockchain.

There are several types of Bitcoin wallets, including:

– Software wallets: These are digital wallets that can be downloaded and installed on a computer or mobile device. They can be further categorized into desktop wallets, mobile wallets, and web wallets.
– Hardware wallets: These are physical devices that store a user's private keys offline. They are considered to be the most secure type of Bitcoin wallet.
– Paper wallets: These are physical copies of a user's private keys that are printed out on paper. They are also considered to be a relatively secure option, but they can be vulnerable to physical damage or theft.

Bitcoin wallets have a public address and a private key. The public address is used to receive Bitcoin, and the private key is used to access and send Bitcoin from a wallet. It is important to keep the private key secure and not share it with anyone, as anyone who has access to it can access and control the user's Bitcoin holdings.

When sending Bitcoin from a wallet, the user will typically enter the recipient's public address and the amount they wish to send. The transaction is then verified and recorded on the blockchain, and the recipient will receive the Bitcoin in their own wallet.

Public Keys as Identities

Public keys in Bitcoin are used as identities in the sense that they uniquely identify a user's Bitcoin address on the blockchain. Each Bitcoin address is associated with a public key, which is generated from the user's private key using mathematical cryptography.

When a user wants to receive Bitcoin, they will share their public key or Bitcoin address with the sender. The sender can then use the public key to create a transaction on the blockchain, which will transfer the specified amount of Bitcoin to the user's address.

While public keys are not typically used as personal identities like names or social security numbers, they do serve as unique identifiers within the Bitcoin network. This is important for maintaining security and preventing fraud, as each transaction on the blockchain is verified by other nodes in the network using public key cryptography.

It is worth noting that while public keys are necessary for using Bitcoin, they do not reveal any personal information about the user. In fact, one of the key benefits of using Bitcoin is that it allows for pseudonymous transactions, in which users can send and receive Bitcoin without revealing their true identities.

3.4.1 Bitcoin Wallets

A Bitcoin wallet, along with other cryptocurrency wallets like Ethereum or XRP, is a digital wallet for securely storing and managing digital assets. It acts as a protected vault for the encryption material that grants access to a specific cryptocurrency's public address, enabling transactions on its network. Alexandre Kech, CEO of Onchain Custodian, explains that a crypto wallet not only holds digital coins but also safeguards them using a unique private key, akin to a password for an online bank account. This private key ensures that only authorized individuals, including the wallet owner, can access the funds stored within.

Crypto wallets provide various functionalities, including storing, sending, and receiving different cryptocurrencies and tokens. While some wallets support basic transactions, others offer additional features like integrated access to DApps built on blockchain technology. These dapps can facilitate activities such as lending cryptocurrency to earn interest on holdings, expanding the wallet's utility beyond simple fund storage and transfers.

3.4.2 Custodial Wallet

A custodial wallet is a type of digital wallet where a third-party service provider manages and secures the private keys of the wallet on behalf of the user. Private keys are a crucial component of a cryptocurrency wallet as they enable users to access and manage their cryptocurrency funds.

With a custodial wallet, the service provider takes on the responsibility of securing the private keys and ensuring the safekeeping of user funds. This can be advantageous for users who are new to the world of cryptocurrency and may not be familiar with the technical aspects of managing their own private keys.

However, custodial wallets also have some drawbacks. First, users must trust the service provider to keep their funds safe, which can be a risk if the provider is hacked or goes out of business. Second, users do not have full control over their funds as they must rely on the service provider to manage their private keys.

3.4.3   Noncustodial Wallet

A noncustodial wallet, also known as a self-custody wallet, is a type of digital wallet that allows users to have full control over their private keys and manage their cryptocurrency funds directly without the involvement of a third-party service provider.

Unlike custodial wallets, where a service provider manages the private keys and stores users' funds on their behalf, noncustodial wallets store private keys locally on users' devices, such as a computer or smartphone. This means that the user is responsible for safeguarding their private keys and ensuring the security of their funds.

Noncustodial wallets are preferred by many cryptocurrency enthusiasts because they offer greater security and privacy. With a noncustodial wallet, users exercise full control over their funds and can manage their cryptocurrency assets without relying on a third-party service provider. This reduces the risk of hacks, fraud, or theft that may occur when a third party is involved.

However, noncustodial wallets require users to have a basic understanding of how private keys work and how to store them securely. Users must also ensure that they have a backup of their private keys in case they lose access to their device or their private keys are accidentally deleted.

3.4.4   Software Wallet

A software wallet is a type of digital wallet that is installed on a computer or mobile device and is used to store, manage, and transact with cryptocurrencies. It is a software application that interacts with a blockchain network to enable users to send and receive cryptocurrency payments.

Software wallets come in two main types: desktop wallets and mobile wallets. Desktop wallets are software applications that are installed on a personal computer, while mobile wallets are applications that are installed on a smartphone or tablet.

Software wallets offer users the flexibility to manage their cryptocurrency assets from their own devices, without the need for a third-party service provider. They also offer a high degree of security, provided that users take appropriate measures to protect their private keys and secure their device.

However, software wallets also have some risks. If a device is compromised by malware or a virus, the private keys can be stolen and user funds lost. Additionally, if users lose their device or forget their private keys, they may lose access to their funds permanently.

3.4.5   Hardware Wallet

Hardware wallets are crucial components in the blockchain ecosystem, offering both security and utility. They allow users to interact with multiple blockchains simultaneously, including Ethereum, Alt. Coins, Bitcoin, Lumens, and more, all from a single device. These wallets can be easily backed up using a single recovery phrase, ensuring the safety of one's assets.

Functioning as portable devices, hardware wallets serve as secure keys to access cryptocurrency assets from anywhere. They also enable easy login to decentralized applications (dApps) without the need to create new accounts. Additionally, they can be used to log in to regular applications such as Google and Facebook.

The primary advantage of hardware wallets is the protection they provide of private keys. By keeping the keys isolated from the Internet, they serve as a form of cold storage, minimizing the risk of online attacks that would compromise assets. Furthermore, hardware wallets allow users to sign and confirm transactions on the blockchain. The unique signature generated using a private key ensures that only the user can authorize transactions, preventing unauthorized access to one's funds.

3.4.6 Features of Digital Wallet

Digital wallets offer a range of features that make them popular among consumers. These features typically include easy registration processes, the ability to execute transactions and transfer funds, access to payment history, and additional features like online and in-store payments. For example, the Paytm digital wallet provides a straightforward registration process, Quick Response (QR)-enabled technology for convenient transactions, and simplified payment processes for bills and services. Digital wallets are designed to be user-friendly, with intuitive interfaces that allow users to manage transactions, check balances, and perform various functions with ease.

3.4.7 Difference Between Digital Wallet and Bank Accounts

There is a major difference between a digital wallet and bank accounts as given in Table 3-1.

3.4.8 Top Digital Wallet

Let us dive into the world of digital wallets and explore the features and benefits of the most popular options available, which empower users with secure and convenient ways to manage their finances in the digital age.

- **Apple Pay**
  - All operations are performed using device.
  - Ability to track all costs for optimization.
  - High-level security with minimal risk of unauthorized intervention.
  - Service data inaccessible to intruders if phone lost.
- **Cash App**
  - Customers can buy and sell Bitcoins directly from their Cash App balance.
  - High level of data protection, encryption, and offline storage of Bitcoins.

Table 3-1 Difference between Digital Wallet and Bank Accounts

Digital Wallets	Bank Accounts
Safer for online payments as scammers cannot access all funds	Prone to scams and potential loss of all funds
Easier and free to open without interaction with a bank	Requires bank interaction and may involve fees
Convenient to use with simple password and mobile phone authentication	Lengthy card details input required
Instantaneous transactions regardless of time or holidays	Transaction speed may vary and may be affected by bank processing times
Allows global payments and transfers regardless of location	Tied to a specific country or region
Can offer offline payment options with issued cards	Primarily used for online and in-person transactions

- Limited transparency for other transactions using the app.
- *1.5%* commission for instant transfers; international digital payments not supported.
- **Dwolla**
  - Advanced features for developers and first-class technical support.
  - Fast payment processing and a "virtual wallet" for sending, storing, and receiving funds.
  - High transaction fees for certain tariff plans and limited features for ordinary users.
- **Google Pay**
  - Security and protection of personal data, with support for multiple cards.
  - Fast transactions and support for any gadget with the Android system.
  - Limited availability of contactless payment terminals and ATMs not supporting the system.
  - Complete dependence on the smartphone for functionality.
- **PayPal**
  - Quick registration and high degree of protection for online payments.
  - Cooperation with well-known trading platforms and support for multiple currencies.
  - Relatively low transaction speed and limited availability for some regions.
- **Samsung Wallet**
  - Immediate activation and fast, secure online payments.
  - Rewarding application with defense-grade security through Samsung Knox.
  - Limited to Samsung devices and certain restrictions for charging and usage.
- **Venmo**
  - Easy transfer and receipt of money, along with online shopping.
  - Rarely charges commissions and interactive social features.
  - Available only in USA, fee for instant transfers, and limited privacy settings.
- **Zelle**
  - Free application with easy and fast usage for sending and receiving money.
  - Funds are protected up to *$250,000* per account.
  - Does not protect approved payments from fraud and requires waiting for incorrect transfers.
- **Walmart Pay**
  - Works on both iOS and Android devices with several layers of security.
  - Stores receipts electronically and supports various payment methods.
  - Limited to the USA and specific to Walmart stores.
- **Amazon Pay**
  - Low transaction fees and a high level of security.
  - Simple registration procedure and no monthly service fee.
  - Integration with stores may take time; limited customer support response time.

3.5 Digital Keys and Addresses

Fundamentally, digital credentials and addresses serve as the basis for trust and security in cryptocurrency ecosystems. The private key, which is a closely guarded secret, enables proprietors to assert control over their digital assets, while the public key and associated cryptocurrency address facilitate transparent and secure transactions, allowing users to receive funds with confidence.

3.5.1   Private Keys

To understand the concept of private keys in the context of cryptocurrencies like Bitcoin, let us break down the information provided and illustrate it with examples.

Private keys are essential for controlling and securing funds associated with a Bitcoin address. They are randomly generated numbers and must be kept secret at all times. Revealing a private key to others would give them control over the Bitcoins associated with that key. Losing a private key results in permanent loss of the funds secured by it. What follows is a step-by-step explanation of generating a private key.

Entropy generation: The first step in generating a private key is to obtain a secure source of entropy or randomness. This can be achieved through various methods such as using the random number generator provided by the operating system. For example, Bitcoin software utilizes the OS's random number generator, which may be initialized by human-generated randomness (e.g., mouse movements).

Random number selection: A private key can be any number between *1* and a constant value *(n − 1)*, where *n* represents the order of the elliptic curve used in Bitcoin. Typically, a *256*-bit number is randomly chosen. The selection process involves picking a *256*-bit number and checking if it is less than $n - 1$. This can be accomplished by feeding a larger string of random bits into the *SHA256* hash algorithm, which produces a *256*-bit number. If the result is within the desired range, it is considered a suitable private key. Otherwise, the process is repeated with a new random number.

Cryptographically secure pseudorandom number generation: It is crucial to use a cryptographically secure pseudorandom number generator (CSPRNG) to create a private key. It should have a seed from a source with sufficient entropy. Using a reliable and secure random number generator library is recommended to ensure the correct implementation of the CSPRNG.

3.5.2   Public Keys

To understand the concept of public keys in elliptic curve cryptography (ECC), let us break down the information provided and illustrate it with examples, a program, and a diagram.

ECC is a type of asymmetric or public key cryptography based on the discrete logarithm problem. In ECC, a public key is derived from a private key using elliptic curve multiplication. Let us go through the steps, which follow.

Elliptic curve definition: Bitcoin uses a specific elliptic curve called *secp256k1*, defined by a mathematical function. This curve is defined over a finite field of prime order. Although it is difficult to visualize due to the nature of a finite field, we can use a simplified example to understand the concept.

Generator point: A predetermined point on an elliptic curve called the generator point (G) is used for key generation. The generator point is the same for all Bitcoin users and is defined as part of the *secp256k1* standard.

Private key to public key calculation: To generate a public key (K), the private key (k) is multiplied by the generator point (G) using elliptic curve multiplication. The resulting point K is the public key.

3.6   Addresses in Bitcoin

Bitcoin addresses are virtual identifiers used to send and receive Bitcoins. They are comparable to email addresses for sending and receiving emails. Bitcoin addresses are usually alphanumeric and range from *26* to *35* characters in length. They have private keys that enable transactions between addresses. Bitcoin addresses come in different types, including Segregated Witness (SegWit) or Bech32 addresses, Legacy or P2PKH addresses, Compatibility or P2SH addresses, and Taproot or BC1P addresses. Each type has its own features and benefits. It is possible to send bitcoins across different address types as Bitcoin addresses are cross-compatible. However, it is important to double-check the receiving address to avoid sending Bitcoins to the wrong address. Testing the address with a small amount of bitcoins can help gain confidence before making larger transactions. Recovering Bitcoins sent to the wrong address is challenging, but reaching out to the address owner or using the OP_RETURN feature may help in some cases. It is crucial to verify the address before sending bitcoins to ensure accuracy.

P2PKH or Legacy Address Format
If your Bitcoin address starts with a *1*, you're using a P2PKH or legacy address, for example, `1BvBMSEYstWetqTFn5Au4m4GFg7xJaNVN2`. P2PKH stands for Pay-to-Pubkey Hash, which means paying to a hash of the recipient's public key. Legacy addresses are not SegWit compatible, but you can still send Bitcoin from a P2PKH address to a SegWit address without any problems. However, transactions from a P2PKH address typically have higher fees due to their larger size.

P2SH Address Format
P2SH addresses have a structure similar to P2PKH addresses but start with a *3*, for example `3J98t1WpEZ73CNmQviecrnyiWrnqRhWNLy`. P2SH stands for Pay-to-Script Hash and enables more complex functionality than legacy addresses. It is commonly used for multisig addresses, where multiple digital signatures are required to authorize a transaction. P2SH addresses are also used for nonnative SegWit transactions through P2WPKH-in-P2SH. For most users, the important thing is that this address type is widely supported and can be used to send funds to both P2PKH and bech32 addresses.

Bech32 Address Format
Bech32 addresses have a distinct appearance, starting with "bc1," and are longer than legacy or P2SH addresses due to the prefix. Bech32 is the native SegWit address format, supported by most software and hardware wallets, but not fully embraced by all exchanges. While less than one percent of Bitcoin is currently stored in bech32 addresses, this number is gradually increasing.

Bitcoin Cash Address Formats
Bitcoin Cash (BCH) addresses can follow either the legacy format (starting with a 1) or the Cash Address (Cash Addr) format. The Cash Addr format is based on bech32 and starts with "q" or "bitcoincash:q." BCH wallets can support both formats, allowing users to switch between them. The primary reason for using the Cash Addr format is to distinguish BCH from BTC (Bitcoin) and prevent funds from being sent to the wrong address.

3.7 Transaction

Bitcoin's primary function is to facilitate transactions. Bitcoin's other features are all built around making it possible to produce, broadcast, validate, and, finally, add transactions to the global database of transactions (the blockchain). In the Bitcoin network, monetary transfers are encoded in data structures called transactions. Bitcoin's blockchain, a decentralized global database that acts as a global double-entry accounting system, records all transactions publicly.

3.7.1 Transaction Lifecycle

There are multiple steps involved in the creation of, validation of, and addition to the blockchain that constitute the lifespan of a Bitcoin transaction.

3.7.1.1 Creation and Broadcasting

The process of transferring money begins when an authorized document is created and signed by one or more parties. Once the transaction has been validated, it is broadcast on the Bitcoin network, where each node is responsible for validating and spreading the news of the transaction to other nodes.

3.7.1.2 Verification and Inclusion

A mining node checks the transaction and verifies its legitimacy. When a transaction has been validated, it is added to the blockchain by being included in a block of previous transactions. To be permanently recorded and recognized as legitimate by all participants, subsequent blocks (confirmations) must be used. A new transaction life cycle can begin when the money are spent by the new owner.

3.7.2 Creating Transactions

The process of creating a Bitcoin transaction is analogous to that of writing a paper check. Until it is actually carried out, the transaction functions as an instrument conveying the intent to transfer funds and is not visible to the financial system. It is not necessary for the person who initiates a transaction to be the person who signs it, as is the case with a check.

Anyone, whether online or offline, can establish a transaction, even an unauthorized signer. An accounts payable clerk, for instance, may draft Bitcoin transactions that the CEO would then have to approve. Bitcoin transactions, unlike checks, do not specify a specific account as the funding source.

The transaction must be signed by the owner(s) of the original money in order to begin the creation process. The transaction is valid and contains all the information required to execute the funds transfer once it has been properly prepared and signed. The final step is for the valid transaction to be broadcast to the Bitcoin network and added to the public ledger.

3.7.3 Broadcasting Transactions to the Bitcoin Network

Delivering a Bitcoin transaction to the network guarantees that it will be seen by many nodes and added to the blockchain. Thousands of Bitcoin nodes need to receive a small data structure of about 300–400 bytes, which represents a transaction.

As long as many nodes are employed to guarantee propagation, senders are not required to trust the nodes used for broadcasting. Since the transaction is signed and does not include any private information, nodes do not need to trust the identity of the sender. Unlike credit card transactions, which require encrypted networks, Bitcoin transactions can be broadcast publicly via any suitable network transport technology.

WiFi, Bluetooth, near-field communication, barcodes, web forms, and even less conventional means like packet radio and satellite relay can all be used to broadcast Bitcoin transactions. Due to Bitcoin's decentralized structure, transactions can be completed through a number of different channels, making it extremely difficult to stop them from being created and completed.

3.7.4   Propagating Transactions on the Bitcoin Network

When a Bitcoin transaction is delivered to a node on the Bitcoin network, that node is responsible for verifying the legitimacy of the transaction. If the transaction is genuine, the node will forward it to other nodes in the network and signal back to the sender that the transaction was successful. In the event of an invalid transaction, the node will send a rejection message back to the sender.

Each node in the Bitcoin network establishes connections with multiple other nodes when the network first boots up. All of the nodes in the network are treated as equals since the network takes the shape of a decentralized, topology-free mesh. Through a technique known as flooding, transactions are broadcast from a central node to all of the peer nodes with which it communicates. Once a transaction is processed and accepted by the network, it spreads out to every node in an exponential fashion.

The Bitcoin network is made to spread transactions and blocks quickly and reliably, protecting against spam, denial-of-service attacks, and other possible problems. Each node checks transactions on its own, which stops bad transactions from growing past a single node.

3.7.5   Data Structures for Transaction

A transaction is a data structure that encodes a transfer of value from a source of funds, called an input, to a destination, called an output. Transaction inputs and outputs are not related to accounts or identities. Instead, you should think of them as Bitcoin amounts – chunks of Bitcoin – being locked with a specific secret that only the owner, or person who knows the secret, can unlock.

The structure of a transaction is composed of several fields, as illustrated in Table 3-2.

The *Version* field specifies the rules that this transaction follows. The *Input Counter* field indicates the number of inputs included in the transaction, while the *Input* fields contain one or more transaction inputs.

Similarly, the *Output Counter* field denotes the number of outputs included, and the *Output* fields contain one or more transaction outputs.

Finally, the *Lock Time* field represents a Unix timestamp or block number, which serves as a condition that must be met before the transaction can be added to the blockchain.

Table 3-2 Bitcoin
Transaction Structure

Field	Description
Version	Transaction version number
Input Counter	Number of inputs in transaction
Input 1	Input details for first input
Input 2	Input details for second input
…	…
Output Counter	Number of outputs in transaction
Output 1	Output details for first output
Output 2	Output details for second output
…	…
Lock Time	Transaction lock time

3.7.6 Types of Transactions

Different types of transactions in the Bitcoin system have different functions and characteristics. Some typical business deals are as follows:

3.7.6.1 Standard Transaction

A standard transaction entails an uncomplicated exchange of value between two parties. It consists of inputs that refer to prior transaction outputs as the source of funds and outputs that assign the transferred value to new recipients.

3.7.6.2 Multisignature Transaction

A multisignature transaction necessitates the approval of multiple parties prior to the expenditure of funds. Multiple public keys, often pertaining to distinct individuals or entities, are utilized as inputs for the transaction. Typically, the outputs of the transaction are then locked with a script that specifies the required number of signatures to expend the funds.

3.7.6.3 Segregated Witness (SegWit) Transaction

Segregated Witness is an upgrade to the Bitcoin protocol that isolates the transaction signature data (witness) from the actual transaction data. SegWit transactions have a unique structure and use a unique transaction format, allowing for an increase in transaction capacity and enhanced scalability.

3.7.6.4 Coinbase Transaction

The SegWit protocol enhancement separates transaction signature data (witness) from the transaction data themselves. SegWit transactions have a distinct structure and use a different transaction format, enabling increased transaction capacity and enhanced scalability.

3.7.6.5 Lock Time–Enabled Transaction

Lock time enables the sender of a transaction to specify a future time or block height at which the transaction will become valid. Lock time–enabled transactions are useful for a variety of use cases, including the creation of time-locked transactions, the implementation of conditional spending, and the creation of payment channels similar to the Lightning Network.

3.7.7 Transaction Input and Output

Unspent transaction outputs (UTXOs) are the foundational building block of a bitcoin transaction. UTXOs are immutable units of bitcoin currency that are locked to a specific proprietor, recorded on the blockchain, and recognized by the entire network as currency units. The bitcoin network keeps track of the millions of available (unspent) UTXOs. Every time a user receives bitcoin, the quantity is recorded as a UTXO in the blockchain. Consequently, a user's bitcoins could be dispersed as UTXO across hundreds of transactions and hundreds of blocks. In practice, there is no such thing as a Bitcoin address or account balance; only scattered UTXOs are locked to specific proprietors. The wallet application generates the notion of a user's Bitcoin balance. The wallet computes the user's balance by searching the blockchain and summing all of the user's UTXOs.

Bitcoins can be divided into multiples of satoshis to make bitcoin transactions easier to conduct while making them readable by people. Once created, UTXOs must be consumed in their entirety and generate change. For example, a transaction with a *20*-Bitcoin UTXO would consume the entire *20*-Bitcoin UTXO and produce two outputs: paying *1* Bitcoin to the recipient and returning *19* Bitcoins in change back to the wallet. Most bitcoin transactions generate change. A user's wallet application automatically selects various units from their available UTXOs to compose an amount greater than or equal to the desired transaction amount.

The wallet application can use strategies like combining smaller units, finding exact change, or using a single unit larger than the transaction value and making change. This complex assembly of spendable UTXOs is done by the user's wallet and is invisible to users. Transaction inputs are the UTXOs consumed by a transaction, while outputs are the UTXOs created by a transaction. This chain of transactions consuming and creating UTXOs moves chunks of Bitcoin value from owner to owner, generating change and ensuring the stability of the digital currency.

3.8 Digital Signature

The Elliptic Curve Digital Signature Algorithm (ECDSA) is used to implement digital signatures in Bitcoin. ECDSA is an elliptical curve-based cryptographic algorithm that provides secure digital signatures. Senders use their private key to generate a digital signature for transaction data when creating a Bitcoin transaction. This signature serves as evidence that the proprietor of the private key authorized the transaction. ECDSA guarantees a transaction's integrity and authenticity by employing the mathematical properties of elliptical curves. In addition to ECDSA, Bitcoin employs the SIGHASH (signature hash) function. SIGHASH is utilized to specify which aspects of a transaction are encompassed by the digital signature. It permits the signer to select which aspects of the transaction they are authorizing and which portions can be altered without invalidating the signature. By specifying a specific SIGHASH type, the signer can determine whether the signature includes the entire transaction, specific inputs, or specific outputs. This flexibility enables more complex transaction schemes, such as transactions requiring multiple signatures or transactions with affixed conditions. Bitcoin's combination of ECDSA and SIGHASH ensures the security, authenticity, and adaptability of digital signatures across the network. It enables participants to securely authorize transactions with their private keys while retaining control over transactions' individual components.

3.9   Mining and Consensus in Bitcoin

Mining and consensus are fundamental components of the Bitcoin network, playing a vital role in preserving the system's security, integrity, and decentralized nature. What follows is an overview of Bitcoin mining and consensus.

3.9.1   Mining

Mining is the process of adding new transactions to a blockchain and securing the network through the resolution of complex mathematical riddles. Network participants, known as miners, compete to solve a cryptographic conundrum known as proof of work (PoW).

Miners collect valid transactions into blocks and then apply a mathematical function (hashing) to the block's data, which includes a reference to the previous block. They modify a small piece of data known as a nonce until they discover a hash that meets certain criteria, such as having a specific number of leading zeros. This requires a significant amount of computational capacity and energy.

The newly mined block is broadcast to the network by the first miner to discover a valid hash satisfying the criteria. Other miners then verify the block's transactions for validity. If consensus is achieved that the block is valid, it is added to the blockchain and the miner is compensated with newly minted Bitcoins and transaction fees from the included transactions.

Bitcoin mining serves the two following primary purposes:

Transaction validation: Miners ensure the integrity and accuracy of the Bitcoin ledger by validating and including valid transactions in new blocks.

Blockchain security: As a security mechanism, the computational effort required for mining (PoW) serves as a security measure. Bitcoin consensus is the agreement among network participants regarding the status of the blockchain and the legitimacy of transactions. Nakamoto consensus, named after Bitcoin's pseudonymous inventor, Satoshi Nakamoto, is the consensus mechanism utilized by Bitcoin. Nakamoto consensus is attained through the consensus of the majority of miners. Miners determine collectively which chain is deemed "longest" and, therefore, legitimate. This is determined by the chain with the most accumulated PoW, indicating the greatest investment of computational effort in its creation.

This makes it extraordinarily challenging and resource intensive for malicious actors to manipulate the blockchain.

3.9.2   Consensus

All participants concur to follow the longest valid chain with the most accumulated PoW according to the Nakamoto consensus. This consensus mechanism guarantees that the network agrees on the order and validity of transactions without relying on a centralized authority. If multiple miners simultaneously discover valid blocks, transient forks may occur. Nevertheless, as more blocks are added to one of the competing forks, it grows longer and eventually surpasses the other forks, resulting in a single, accepted blockchain.

Consensus in Bitcoin is essential for maintaining the network's security, immutability, and trustworthiness. It enables participants to reach a consensus on the blockchain's current state and ensures that transactions are accepted or rejected based on predetermined rules.

3.9.3   Decentralized Consensus in Bitcoin

Fundamental to the Bitcoin network is decentralized consensus, which enables agreement among participants without the need for a central authority. Combining cryptographic techniques and incentive mechanisms, Bitcoin reaches decentralized consensus. Here is an overview of Bitcoin's decentralized consensus:

3.9.3.1 Peer-to-Peer Network
Bitcoin operates as a peer-to-peer (P2P) network in which all participants, known as nodes, interact and communicate directly with one another. Each node keeps a copy of the entire blockchain, ensuring both transparency and redundancy.

3.9.3.2 Consensus Mechanism: PoW
PoW, Bitcoin's consensus mechanism, requires miners to solve computational challenges in order to add new blocks to the blockchain. This requires a significant amount of computational power, making it difficult and resource-intensive to modify the blockchain's history.

The PoW consensus mechanism guarantees that the majority of mining power is held by trustworthy participants. To attempt to manipulate the blockchain, an attacker would need to control more than fifty percent of the network's mining power, which is extremely impractical and economically prohibitive.

3.9.3.3 Blockchain Validation
The blockchain is independently validated by every node in the Bitcoin network. By verifying the rules defined by the Bitcoin protocol, including transaction validity, block structure, and consensus rules, nodes ensure the veracity and integrity of the blockchain.

3.9.3.4 Incentive Mechanisms
Bitcoin uses incentive mechanisms to encourage participants to act in the best interest of the network. Bitcoins and transaction fees are awarded to miners for successfully mining and adding nodes to the blockchain. This encourages miners to compete fairly, invest resources, and adhere to consensus rules in order to preserve the security and stability of the network.

3.9.3.5 Fork Resolution
If multiple valid blocks are created at the same moment, a temporary fork may occur, and the longest chain with the most PoW will be adopted. The network will eventually reach consensus on a single chain thanks to this approach to handling forks.

3.9.3.6 Decentralization Benefits
Bitcoin's decentralized consensus offers several advantages.

Decentralization disperses power among participants, making it difficult for a single entity to manipulate transactions or control the network. In addition, Bitcoin transactions are resistant to censorship because there is no central authority, allowing for the freedom of financial transactions. Moreover, as consensus is reached through the network's rules and cryptographic mechanisms, participants can interact and transact with one another without needing to trust one another. Bitcoin is based on decentralized consensus, which enables a decentralized and trustless financial system. It assures that participants can agree on the state of the blockchain and the validity of transactions without relying on centralized control.

3.9.4 Mining and Racing in Bitcoin

In Bitcoin mining, miners compete to solve a mathematical puzzle and be the first to add a new block to the blockchain in a procedure known as mining and racing. Table 3-3 is titled "Mining and Racing in Bitcoin" and it is used to organize and present information related to various aspects of Bitcoin mining and the potential risks associated with it, such as the 51% attack.

Table 3-3 Mining and Racing in Bitcoin

Aspect	Description
Mining	Mining algorithm:
	Proof of work (PoW)
	Miners' reward:
	Newly minted bitcoins and transaction fees
Mining Pools	Purpose:
	Combining computational power
Mining Hardware	CPU Mining
	GPU Mining
	ASIC Mining
Mining Difficulty	Adjustment period:
	Approximately every 2 weeks
	Purpose:
	Maintain block time (10 minutes)
Mining Software	Popular software:
	CGMiner, BFGMiner, BitMinter
Mining Farms	Purpose:
	Large-scale mining operations
	Location:
	Often in regions with cheap electricity
Mining Pools	Popular pools:
	Slush Pool, F2Pool, Antpool
Racing	Purpose
51% Attack	Definition:
	Control of over 50% of network's mining power
	Consequences:
	Double-spending, network manipulation
	Prevention:
	Network security and decentralization

What follows is an overview of Bitcoin mining and racing.

3.9.4.1 Mining Process

Miners collect all legitimate network transactions and combine them into a block. The block also includes a reference to the hash of the preceding block, creating a succession of blocks (the blockchain). The miners then endeavor to solve a cryptographic puzzle referred to as PoW for the new block.

3.9.4.2 Race to Solve the Puzzle

Mining is a contest between miners to solve the PoW puzzle and locate a valid hash for a new block. Miners use their computational power to compute the hash of a block's data, repeatedly modifying a small piece of data known as a nonce until a hash satisfying certain criteria is found (e.g., containing a specific number of leading zeros). This procedure requires a significant amount of computational effort and energy.

3.9.4.3 First Miner's Advantage

The network is notified of a newly mined block by the first miner to discover a valid hash that meets the puzzle's requirements. Other miners then validate the block's legitimacy by ensuring it adheres to consensus rules and contains valid transactions. Upon reaching consensus that the block is legitimate, it is added to the blockchain.

3.9.4.4 Block Reward

The Bitcoins awarded to the miner who successfully mines a new block are known as a block reward. This encourages miners to employ computational resources and take part in the mining process. Miners may receive transaction fees in addition to the block reward.

3.9.4.5 Mining Difficulty Adjustment

The Bitcoin network dynamically adjusts the mining difficulty to maintain a constant rate of block creation. This modification is made approximately every 2016 blocks (approximately every two weeks) to ensure that new blocks are added to the blockchain on average every ten minutes.

3.9.4.6 Continuous Racing

The mining and racing procedure continues so long as there are valid transactions to be included in blocks. Miners compete to find the next valid Bitcoin block in order to receive rewards and contribute to the network's security and stability.

In Bitcoin, mining and racing constitute a competitive process that guarantees the creation of new blocks and the inclusion of valid transactions in the blockchain. The competition to solve the PoW puzzle encourages miners to invest in computational power, secure the network, and preserve the decentralized nature of the Bitcoin system.

3.9.5   Cost of Mining in Bitcoin

Bitcoin mining incurs substantial costs due to the required resources and associated expenses. What follows is a summary of the costs associated with Bitcoin mining.

3.9.5.1 Hardware Costs

Bitcoin mining necessitates mining rigs or Application-Specific Integrated Circuits (ASICs). These machines are designed specifically to execute the computational tasks required for mining. The initial investment required to acquire mining equipment can be substantial, spanning from hundreds to thousands of dollars per rig.

3.9.5.2 Electricity Costs

The mining industry consumes a considerable quantity of electricity. Mining necessitates a significant amount of computational capacity, resulting in substantial electricity costs. Miners must consider the local electricity rates and calculate the energy consumption of their mining apparatus in order to estimate their ongoing costs.

3.9.5.3 Cooling and Maintenance Costs

The intense computational activities of mining equipment generate heat. Effective cooling systems are required to prevent combustion and prolong the life of mining machinery. These cooling solutions, such as fans and specialized cooling systems, require additional expenditures. Maintenance and monitoring of the mining hardware must be performed routinely to ensure peak performance and minimize disruption.

3.9.5.4 Operating Costs

In addition to hardware and electricity costs, mining incurs additional operating expenses. Expenses associated with Internet connectivity, facility rental (if mining operations are conducted in a dedicated space), mining software licenses, and other miscellaneous expenses may be included.

3.9.5.5 Competition and Return on Investment

The level of competition influences the expense of Bitcoin mining. As more miners join the network, the mining difficulty rises, necessitating more computational power and, as a result, increased electricity consumption. Individual miners' return on investment (ROI) is diminished as a result of escalating competition.

3.9.5.6 Market Volatility

Bitcoin's price volatility is an additional factor that impacts mining costs. The fluctuating price of Bitcoin has a direct impact on the profitability of Bitcoin mining. A higher Bitcoin price can make mining more profitable, whereas a significant decline in price can make mining less lucrative or even unprofitable for some miners.

Costs associated with Bitcoin mining include hardware expenses, utility costs, cooling and maintenance expenses, operating expenses, competition, and market volatility. To determine the viability and profitability of a mining operation, miners must meticulously evaluate these costs and conduct exhaustive calculations.

3.9.6 Consensus Attacks in Bitcoin

Consensus attacks, also known as *51%* attacks, pose potential security and integrity hazards to the Bitcoin network. These assaults take advantage of the majority control of mining power to manipulate the blockchain and possibly double-spending transactions. What follows is an overview of Bitcoin consensus attacks.

Table 3-4 51% Attacks in
Cryptocurrencies - Details
and Past Incidents

Aspect	Description
Definition	Control threshold:
	Over 50% of network's mining power
Consequences	Double-spending
	Network manipulation
	Erosion of trust
Prevention	Network security
	Decentralization
	Vigilance
Past incidents	Mt. Gox (2014) - Bitcoin
	Ethereum Classic (2020) - Ethereum Classic
	Verge (2018) - Verge
	Feathercoin (2013) - Feathercoin

3.9.6.1 The Importance of Consensus

Bitcoin requires consensus to ensure that all participants concur on the state of the blockchain and the legitimacy of transactions. Consensus prevents malevolent actors from altering transaction history or counterfeiting Bitcoins. It is attained through the consensus of the majority of trustworthy network participants.

3.9.6.2 51% Attack

A *51%* attack occurs when a single entity or group of cooperating entities controls more than fifty percent of the network's total mining capacity. This majority control enables the attacker to potentially control the blockchain and dictate the norms of consensus. Table 3-4 delineates the definition of a 51% attack within the realm of cryptocurrency. The provided explanation elucidates that a 51% attack transpires when an entity acquires dominion over more than 50% of the mining power within a network. This term elucidates the requisite threshold for the occurrence of such an attack, thereby enhancing readers' comprehension.

3.9.6.3 Potential Attack Scenarios

If an adversary controls the preponderance of mining power, the following attacks are possible:

Double-spending: With majority control, an adversary can create two conflicting transactions and attempt to spend the same Bitcoins twice. Initially, one transaction can be disseminated to the network and then a competing block privately mined. Once the secret chain becomes lengthier than the publicly known chain, it can be released, effectively replacing the original transaction and spending the same amount of Bitcoins twice.

Block reorganization: By mining a lengthier private chain that conflicts with the public chain, an adversary can reorganize the blockchain. This can be done to invalidate previously confirmed transactions, reverse payments, or interfere with the network's normal operation.

Denial of service: An attacker who controls the majority of mining power can prevent other miners from effectively adding blocks to the blockchain. This can disrupt transaction confirmations and reduce network performance overall.

3.9.6.4 Mitigating Consensus Attacks

Although a *51%* attack is theoretically possible, several factors mitigate the risks:

Incentives for honesty: There are economic incentives for honest behavior and adherence to consensus norms among miners. Any attempt to manipulate the network could erode trust, decrease Bitcoin's value, and harm the attacker's own investments.

Decentralization: The decentralized nature of cryptocurrency mining guarantees that no single entity will be able to control the entire network. This decentralization makes acquiring majority control of mining power difficult and expensive.

Community vigilance: The Bitcoin community monitors the network for suspicious activity. Rapid detection and disclosure of potential attacks deter criminals.

Network upgrades: Periodic Bitcoin protocol updates and enhancements resolve known vulnerabilities and strengthen the network's resistance to attack.

3.9.6.5 Security Measures

Bitcoin developers and miners investigate alternative consensus mechanisms, such as proof of stake (PoS), which rely on participants holding coins rather than computational power, in order to increase security. These mechanisms seek to mitigate the risk of *51%* attacks by reducing the amount of network control a single entity can exert.

While consensus assaults remain a concern, the Bitcoin network is robust and secure thanks to its decentralized nature, economic incentives, vigilant community, and ongoing development efforts.

3.10   Forking

Forking in the context of Bitcoin refers to the division of the blockchain into two distinct branches, resulting in two distinct versions of the protocol and network. Forks can arise for a variety of reasons and be divided into *two* primary types: hard and soft.

3.10.1 Hard Fork

The new version of the protocol is incompatible with the preceding version. It entails a significant modification to the network's rules or consensus mechanism, resulting in the permanent separation of the blockchain.

In a hard fork, network nodes and miners must switch to the new software version in order to continue participating in the forked blockchain. If some nodes and miners choose not to upgrade, a schism will occur, resulting in two distinct chains, each with its own set of rules and network participants.

Hard forks can introduce substantial changes to the network, such as altering the block size limit, introducing new features, or modifying the consensus algorithm. Examples of hard forks in Bitcoin's history include the Bitcoin Cash (BCH) fork and the Bitcoin SV (BSV) fork.

3.10.2 Soft Fork

Soft forks are upgrades to the Bitcoin protocol that are compatible with the preceding version. This entails implementing modifications or introducing new rules that adhere to the consensus rules of the existing blockchain.

Soft forks allow nodes and miners who have not converted to the new software to continue participating in the network without interruption. Upgraded nodes enforce the new rules, whereas nonupgraded nodes continue to recognize as valid the blocks generated by the upgraded nodes.

Soft forks typically introduce conservative changes, such as tightening rules, introducing restrictions, or enabling new features within the existing framework. SegWit implementation is an example of a soft fork in Bitcoin, as it introduced a new transaction format without splitting the blockchain.

Soft forks are designed to be backward-compatible to preserve the network's continuity and prevent the blockchain from splitting into two distinct chains.

Both hard and soft divisions play crucial roles in the evolution and development of blockchain networks such as Bitcoin. They permit modifications, enhancements, and experimentation, but their impact on network compatibility and potential for chain splits varies.

3.11   Laboratory Work

This section presents the implementation of Bitcoin-related concepts using Python.

3.11.1 Program to Generate Private Keys Securely on a Hardware Wallet

```
from Crypto.Random import get_random_bytes
from Crypto.Cipher import AES
from Crypto.Protocol.KDF import scrypt
from Crypto.Util.Padding import pad
import hashlib

# Set up the parameters for key generation
password = b'password'  # Set a password for added security
salt = get_random_bytes(16)
N = 2 ** 14
r = 8
p = 1
key_len = 32  # 256-bit key

# Generate a derived key from the password and salt
dk = scrypt(password, salt, key_len, N, r, p)

# Use the derived key to encrypt a private key on the hardware wallet
private_key = get_random_bytes(32)  # Generate a random private key
iv = get_random_bytes(16)  # Generate a random initialization vector
cipher = AES.new(dk, AES.MODE_CBC, iv)
ciphertext = cipher.encrypt(pad(private_key, AES.block_size))

# Save the encrypted private key and salt to the hardware wallet
with open('private_key.enc', 'wb') as f:
    f.write(ciphertext)

with open('salt.bin', 'wb') as f:
    f.write(salt)
```

This program generates a private key and encrypts it using Advanced Encryption Standard (AES) encryption with a derived key generated from a user-provided password and a random salt. The encrypted private key and salt are then saved to the hardware wallet.

To sign transactions securely on a hardware wallet, you can use the following Python code using the `pycryptodomex` library:

```
from Crypto.Cipher import AES
from Crypto.Protocol.KDF import scrypt
from Crypto.Util.Padding import pad, unpad
import hashlib

# Load the encrypted private key and salt from the hardware wallet
with open('private_key.enc', 'rb') as f:
    ciphertext = f.read()

with open('salt.bin', 'rb') as f:
    salt = f.read()

# Derive the key from the password and salt
password = b'password'  # Enter the password used to generate the
derived key
N = 2 ** 14
r = 8
p = 1
key_len = 32
dk = scrypt(password, salt, key_len, N, r, p)

# Decrypt the private key
iv = ciphertext[:16]
cipher = AES.new(dk, AES.MODE_CBC, iv)
private_key = unpad(cipher.decrypt(ciphertext[16:]), AES.block_size)

# Sign the transaction using the decrypted private key
tx_data = b'transaction_data'
hash_data = hashlib.sha256(tx_data).digest()
signature = sign(hash_data, private_key)

# Verify the signature (optional)
public_key = get_public_key(private_key)
verify(hash_data, signature, public_key)
```

3.11.2 Program to Generate Public-Private Key Pairs, Encrypting and Storing Private Keys Securely and Signing Transactions Using the Private Key

```
import os
import json
import base64
from Crypto.PublicKey import RSA
from Crypto.Cipher import PKCS1_OAEP
from Crypto.Signature import pkcs1_15
from Crypto.Hash import SHA256

# Generate public-private key pairs
key = RSA.generate(2048)
private_key = key.export_key()
public_key = key.publickey().export_key()

# Encrypt and store private key securely
password = input("Enter password: ")
```

```
16  cipher_rsa = PKCS1_OAEP.new(key)
17  encrypted_private_key = cipher_rsa.encrypt(password.encode() +
18  private_key)
19  with open('private_key.txt', 'wb') as f:
20      f.write(encrypted_private_key)
21
22  # Load encrypted private key and decrypt
23  with open('private_key.txt', 'rb') as f:
24      encrypted_private_key = f.read()
25  cipher_rsa = PKCS1_OAEP.new(key)
26  decrypted_private_key = cipher_rsa.decrypt(encrypted_private_key)
27
28  [len(password):]
29
30  # Sign transactions using the private key
31  message = 'Hello, world!'
32  hash_message = SHA256.new(message.encode())
33  signature = pkcs1_15.new(key).sign(hash_message)
34
35  # Verify the signature
36  try:
37      pkcs1_15.new(key.publickey()).verify(hash_message, signature)
38      print("Signature is valid")
39  except (ValueError, TypeError):
40      print("Signature is invalid")
```

This program uses the Crypto library to generate public–private key pairs, encrypt and store private keys securely, and sign transactions using the private key. The private key is encrypted using a password supplied by the user and then stored in a file. When users want to sign a transaction, they enter the password to decrypt the private key and use it to sign the transaction. The signature can then be verified using the public key.

3.11.3 Program to Demonstrate Some of the Features of a Digital Wallet

```
1   import requests
2
3   # Function to check balance of a wallet
4   def check_balance(address):
5       url = f"https://api.blockcypher.com/v1/btc/main/addrs/{address}
6       /balance"
7       response = requests.get(url)
8       if response.status_code == 200:
9           balance = response.json()['balance']
10          print(f"Balance of {address}: {balance} satoshis")
11      else:
12          print("Error checking balance")
13
14  # Function to view transaction history of a wallet
15  def view_history(address):
16      url = f"https://api.blockcypher.com/v1/btc/main/addrs/
17      {address}/full"
18      response = requests.get(url)
19      if response.status_code == 200:
20          history = response.json()['txs']
21          for tx in history:
22              print(f"Transaction hash: {tx['hash']}")
```

```
23          print(f"Amount: {tx['total']} satoshis")
24          print(f"Confirmations: {tx['confirmations']}\n")
25    else:
26        print("Error viewing transaction history")
27
28 # Function to create multiple addresses within a wallet
29 def create_address():
30     url = "https://api.blockcypher.com/v1/btc/main/addrs"
31     response = requests.post(url)
32     if response.status_code == 201:
33         address = response.json()['address']
34         print(f"New address created: {address}")
35     else:
36         print("Error creating new address")
37
38 # Function to set transaction fees
39 def set_fees(fees):
40     # Your code to set transaction fees goes here
41     print(f"Transaction fees set to {fees} satoshis")
42
43 # Sample usage of the functions
44 address = "1BvBMSEYstWetqTFn5Au4m4GFg7xJaNVN2"
45 check_balance(address)
46 view_history(address)
47 create_address()
48 set_fees(100)
```

This program uses the `requests` library to interact with the Bitcoin blockchain application programming interface (API) provided by BlockCypher. The check_balance() function takes a Bitcoin address as input and retrieves the balance of that address. The view_history() function retrieves the transaction history of the address. The create_address() function creates a new Bitcoin address within the wallet. The set_fees() function sets the transaction fees for the wallet.

Note that this program is just an example; in a real-world implementation, you would need to handle errors and edge cases appropriately, as well as implement additional features and security measures.

3.11.4 Program to Compare the Features of Popular Digital Wallets, Rank Them Based on User Reviews and Ratings, and Recommend a Digital Wallet Based on User Preferences

```
1 import requests
2
3 # List of popular digital wallets
4 wallets = ["Coinbase", "Binance", "Trezor", "Ledger",
5 "Exodus"]
6
7 # Function to compare features of digital wallets
8 def compare_features(wallets):
9     for wallet in wallets:
10        url = f"https://api.coingecko.com/api/v3/coins/
11        {wallet.lower()}?localization=en"
12        response = requests.get(url)
13        if response.status_code == 200:
14            features = response.json()['description']['en']
15            print(f"{wallet} features: {features}\n")
```

```
16        else:
17            print(f"Error retrieving {wallet} features")
18
19 # Function to rank digital wallets based on user reviews
20 and ratings
21 def rank_wallets(wallets):
22     url = "https://api.coingecko.com/api/v3/coins/markets?
23     vs_currency=usd&order=market_cap_desc&per_page=10&page=1&
24     sparkline=false"
25     response = requests.get(url)
26     if response.status_code == 200:
27         data = response.json()
28         rankings = {}
29         for wallet in wallets:
30             for item in data:
31                 if wallet.lower() in item['name'].lower():
32                     rankings[wallet] = item['market_cap_rank']
33         sorted_rankings = sorted(rankings.items(), key=lambda x: x[1])
34         print("Digital wallet rankings based on market cap:")
35         for rank, wallet in enumerate(sorted_rankings, start=1):
36             print(f"{rank}. {wallet[0]}")
37     else:
38         print("Error retrieving digital wallet rankings")
39
40 # Function to recommend a digital wallet based on
41 user preferences
42 def recommend_wallet(preferences):
43     recommended_wallet = ""
44     # Your code to recommend a wallet based on user
45
46     preferences goes here
47     print(f"We recommend {recommended_wallet}
48     based on your preferences")
49
50 # Sample usage of the functions
51 compare_features(wallets)
52 rank_wallets(wallets)
53 recommend_wallet(["low fees", "mobile app"])
```

This program uses the CoinGecko API to retrieve information about digital wallets. The compare_features() function takes a list of digital wallets as input and retrieves the features of each wallet. The rank_wallets() function retrieves the market cap rankings of the wallets and ranks them accordingly. The recommend_wallet() function takes a list of user preferences as input and recommends a wallet based on those preferences.

Note that this program is just an example, and in a real-world implementation, you would need to handle errors and edge cases appropriately, as well as implement additional features and security measures.

3.11.5 Program to Deploy a Smart Contract to Blockchain Using a Tool Like Remix IDE

```
 1  # Deploying a simple smart contract to the blockchain
 2  using Remix IDE
 3  # Assumes you have installed the Metamask browser
 4  extension and connected to the desired network
 5
 6  from web3 import Web3
 7  import json
 8
 9  # connect to the local blockchain
10  web3 = Web3(Web3.HTTPProvider('http://localhost:8545'))
11
12  # load the compiled smart contract
13  with open('MyContract.json') as f:
14      contract_data = json.load(f)
15  abi = contract_data['abi']
16  bytecode = contract_data['bytecode']
17
18  # get the account to deploy the contract from
19  web3.eth.defaultAccount = web3.eth.accounts[0]
20
21  # create the contract object
22  my_contract = web3.eth.contract(abi=abi, bytecode=bytecode)
23
24  # deploy the contract to the blockchain
25  tx_hash = my_contract.constructor().transact()
26  tx_receipt = web3.eth.waitForTransactionReceipt(tx_hash)
27
28  # get the contract address
29  contract_address = tx_receipt.contractAddress
30
31  # interact with the contract
32  contract_instance = web3.eth.contract(address=contract_address,
33  abi=abi)
34
35  # call a function on the contract
36  result = contract_instance.functions.my_function().call()
37
38  # send a transaction to the contract
39  tx_hash = contract_instance.functions.my_function(my_arg).
40  transact()
41  tx_receipt = web3.eth.waitForTransactionReceipt(tx_hash)
42
43  # get the state of the contract
44  state = contract_instance.functions.get_state().call()
```

This program assumes that you have compiled your smart contract and saved the resulting ABI and bytecode in a JSON file called MyContract.json. It connects to a local blockchain running on http://localhost:8545, gets the first account on the blockchain to deploy the contract from, and deploys the contract using the constructor function. It then interacts with the contract by calling a function and sending a transaction and obtains the state of the contract by calling a function that returns the state.

3.11.6 Program that Measures the Transaction Throughput of EOA–EOA Transactions and CA–CA Transactions Using Various Gas Limits on the Ethereum Network

```
1  from web3 import Web3
2
3  # Connect to an Ethereum node using Web3
4  web3 = Web3(Web3.HTTPProvider('http://localhost:8545'))
5
6  # Define gas limits to test
7  gas_limits = [100000, 200000, 300000, 400000, 500000]
8
9  # Measure transaction throughput for EOA-EOA transactions
10 for gas_limit in gas_limits:
11     # Create two new externally owned accounts
12     sender = web3.eth.account.create()
13     receiver = web3.eth.account.create()
14
15     # Send transactions from sender to receiver
16     num_transactions = 100
17     start_time = web3.eth.getBlock('latest')['timestamp']
18     for i in range(num_transactions):
19         tx = {
20             'from': sender.address,
21             'to': receiver.address,
22             'value': 1,
23             'gas': gas_limit,
24             'gasPrice': web3.toWei('1', 'gwei'),
25             'nonce': web3.eth.getTransactionCount(sender.address)
26         }
27         signed_tx = sender.signTransaction(tx)
28         tx_hash = web3.eth.sendRawTransaction(signed_tx.rawTransaction)
29         web3.eth.waitForTransactionReceipt(tx_hash)
30
31     end_time = web3.eth.getBlock('latest')['timestamp']
32     throughput = num_transactions / (end_time - start_time)
33     print(f'EOA-EOA transaction throughput with
34     gas limit {gas_limit}: {throughput:.2f} tx/sec')
35
36 # Measure transaction throughput for CA-CA transactions
37 for gas_limit in gas_limits:
38     # Compile and deploy a simple contract
39     contract_source_code = """
40     pragma solidity ^0.8.0;
41
42     contract TestContract {
43         uint public value;
44
45         function setValue(uint _value) public {
46             value = _value;
47         }
48     }
49     """
50     compiled_contract = web3.eth.contract(abi=contract_interface['abi'],
51     bytecode=contract_interface['bin'])
52     deploy_txn = compiled_contract.constructor().buildTransaction({
53         'from': web3.eth.accounts[0],
54         'gas': 1000000,
```

```
55      'gasPrice': web3.toWei('1', 'gwei')
56    })
57    signed_txn = web3.eth.account.signTransaction(deploy_txn,
58    private_key=web3.eth.accounts[0])
59    txn_hash = web3.eth.sendRawTransaction(signed_txn.rawTransaction)
60    txn_receipt = web3.eth.waitForTransactionReceipt(txn_hash)
61    contract_address = txn_receipt.contractAddress
62
63    # Send transactions to the contract
64    num_transactions = 100
65    start_time = web3.eth.getBlock('latest')['timestamp']
66    for i in range(num_transactions):
67        tx = {
68            'from': web3.eth.accounts[0],
69            'to': contract_address,
70            'gas': gas_limit,
71            'gasPrice': web3.toWei('1', 'gwei'),
72            'data': compiled_contract.functions.setValue(i).
73            buildTransaction()['data'],
74            'nonce': web3.eth.getTransactionCount
75            (web3.eth.accounts[0])
76        }
77        signed_tx = web3.eth.account.signTransaction
78        (tx, private_key=web3.eth.accounts[0])
79        tx_hash = web3.eth.sendRawTransaction(signed_tx.
80        rawTransaction)
81        web3.eth.waitForTransactionReceipt(tx_hash)
82
83    end_time = web3.eth.getBlock('latest')['timestamp']
84    throughput = num_transactions / (end_time - start_time)
85    print(f'CA-CA transaction throughput with gas limit
86
87    {gas_limit}: {throughput:.2f} tx/sec')
```

First, the Web3 module to interact with the Ethereum network is imported.

Next, a connection is established to an Ethereum node using Web3. In this example, a connection is made with a node running locally on port 8545.

Gas limits testing represent the maximum amount of gas that can be used in a transaction.

We measure the transaction throughput for Externally Owned Account (EOA)–EOA transactions for each gas limit by doing the following steps:

First, we create two new Ethereum accounts (EOAs) using the web3.eth.account. create() method. These accounts will be used to send and receive transactions. Next, we fund the accounts with some Ether using the web3.eth.sendTransaction() method. This is necessary to have enough Ether to pay for transaction fees. Then we measure the time it takes to send a certain number of transactions (in this case, 100) from one account to the other using the web3.eth.sendTransaction() method. We use the specified gas limit for each transaction. Finally, we calculate the transaction throughput (transactions per second) for each gas limit by dividing the number of transactions sent by the time it took to send them. After measuring the transaction throughput for EOA–EOA transactions, we measure the transaction throughput for CA–CA transactions by doing the following steps: First, we deploy a new smart contract to the Ethereum network using the web3.eth.contract() method. This smart contract will be used to send and receive transactions. Next, we measure the time it takes to send a certain number of transactions (in this case, 100) between the smart contract and itself using the contract.functions.transfer() method. We use the specified gas limit for each transaction. Finally, we calculate the transaction throughput (transactions per second) for each gas limit by dividing the number of transactions sent by the time it took to send them. We print out the results of the experiments, showing the transaction throughput for each gas limit and transaction type.

3.11.7 Program that Uses Web3 to Categorize Ethereum Addresses as EOA or Contract Addresses and Evaluates Its Accuracy and Performance on a Large Dataset of Addresses

```python
from web3 import Web3

# Connect to a local Ethereum node
web3 = Web3(Web3.HTTPProvider('http://localhost:8545'))

# Load a large dataset of Ethereum addresses
with open('addresses.txt', 'r') as f:
    addresses = f.read().splitlines()

# Define a function to categorize an address as EOA or
#contract
def categorize_address(address):
    # Check if the address is a valid Ethereum address
    if not web3.isChecksumAddress(address):
        return 'Invalid'

    # Check if the address has a code field (i.e.,
    it's a contract address)
    code = web3.eth.getCode(address)
    if code:
        return 'Contract'

    # If the address doesn't have a code field, it's an EOA
    return 'EOA'

# Test the categorize_address() function on a few example addresses
print(categorize_address('0x627306090abaB3A6e1400e9345bC60c78a8BEf57'))  #
    EOA
print(categorize_address('0x4e83362442b8d1bec281594cea3050c8eb01311c'))  #
    Contract
print(categorize_address('0x0000000000000000000000000000000000000000'))  #
    Invalid

# Categorize all the addresses in the dataset
results = {}
for address in addresses:
    category = categorize_address(address)
    if category in results:
        results[category] += 1
    else:
        results[category] = 1

# Print the results
print(results)
```

We import the Web3 module and connect to a local Ethereum node using Web3(HTTPProvider('http://localhost:8545')). We load a large dataset of Ethereum addresses from a text file using open('addresses.txt', 'r'). We define a function called categorize_address() that takes an Ethereum address as input and returns a string indicating whether the address is an EOA or a contract address. We use web3.isChecksumAddress() to check whether the address is a valid Ethereum address and web3.eth.getCode() to check whether the address has a code field (indicating that it's a contract address).

We test the categorize_address() function on a few example addresses to make sure it is working correctly.

We iterate over all the addresses in the dataset and use the categorize_address() function to categorize each address. We keep track of the number of addresses in each category using a dictionary called results.

We print out the results of the categorization, which shows the number of addresses in each category (EOA, Contract, and Invalid).

3.11.8 Program that Simulates the Life Cycle of a Transaction on the Ethereum Network and Measures the Time and Resources Required

```
import time

# Step 1: Transaction Creation
start_time = time.time()
# code to create the transaction goes here
transaction_creation_time = time.time() - start_time
print("Time taken to create transaction:",
transaction_creation_time)

# Step 2: Transaction Validation
start_time = time.time()
# code to validate the transaction goes here
transaction_validation_time = time.time() - start_time
print("Time taken to validate transaction:",
transaction_validation_time)

# Step 3: Inclusion in a Block
start_time = time.time()
# code to include transaction in a block goes here
transaction_inclusion_time = time.time() - start_time
print("Time taken to include transaction in block:",
transaction_inclusion_time)

# Step 4: Confirmation
start_time = time.time()
# code to confirm the transaction goes here
transaction_confirmation_time = time.time() - start_time
print("Time taken to confirm transaction:",
transaction_confirmation_time)

# Resource Usage
# code to measure resource usage goes here
```

3.11.9 Program for Implementing ECDSA

```
from ecdsa import SigningKey, SECP256k1
import hashlib

# Generate a private key
private_key = SigningKey.generate(curve=SECP256k1)

# Get the public key from the private key
public_key = private_key.get_verifying_key()

# Sign a message with the private key
message = b"Hello, world!"
signature = private_key.sign(message)

# Verify the signature with the public key
assert public_key.verify(signature, message)

# Hash the message with SHA-256
hashed_message = hashlib.sha256(message).digest()

# Generate a Bitcoin-style signature from the ECDSA
signature
r, s = private_key.sign_digest(hashed_message, sigencode=ecdsa.util.
sigencode_der_canonize)

# Print the signature in hex format
print("Signature:", r.hex(), s.hex())
```

This code generates a random ECDSA private key, derives the public key from it, signs a message with the private key, and verifies the signature with the public key. It then hashes the message with SHA-256 and generates a Bitcoin-style signature from the ECDSA signature, which is printed in hex format.

3.11.10 Program to Create a Bitcoin Transaction and Sign It with a SIGHASH Flag Using the bitcoinlib Library

```
from bitcoinlib.transactions import Transaction, Input, Output
from bitcoinlib.keys import Key
from bitcoinlib.encoding import to_hex

# Create a new transaction
tx = Transaction()

# Add an input to the transaction
txin = Input('prev_txid', 0)
tx.add_input(txin)

# Add an output to the transaction
txout = Output('address', 100000)
tx.add_output(txout)

# Set the SIGHASH flag to sign only the current input
txin.script_sig.sighash_flag = 1
```

```
19 # Sign the transaction with the private key
20 private_key = Key('private_key')
21 sig = private_key.sign_input(tx, 0)
22
23 # Set the signature in the transaction input
24 txin.script_sig.signature = sig + bytes([txin.script_sig.sighash_flag])
25
26 # Print the signed transaction in hex format
27 print(to_hex(tx.serialize()))
```

This code creates a new Bitcoin transaction with one input and one output, sets the SIGHASH flag to sign only the current input, signs the transaction with a private key, and sets the signature in the transaction input. Finally, it prints the signed transaction in hex format. Note that this is a very basic example, and there are many more details to consider when creating and signing Bitcoin transactions in practice.

3.11.11 Program for Bitcoin Mining

```
1 import hashlib
2 import time
3
4 class Block:
5     def __init__(self, transactions, previous_block_hash):
6         self.timestamp = time.time()
7         self.transactions = transactions
8         self.previous_block_hash = previous_block_hash
9         self.nonce = 0
10        self.hash = self.calculate_hash()
11
12    def calculate_hash(self):
13        block_header = str(self.timestamp) + str(self.transactions) + \
14                       str(self.previous_block_hash) + str(self.nonce)
15        return hashlib.sha256(block_header.encode()).hexdigest()
16
17    def mine_block(self, difficulty):
18        print('Mining block...')
19        start_time = time.time()
20
21        while self.hash[:difficulty] != '0' * difficulty:
22            self.nonce += 1
23            self.hash = self.calculate_hash()
24
25        end_time = time.time()
26        time_elapsed = end_time - start_time
27
28        print('Block mined:', self.hash)
29        print('Time elapsed:', time_elapsed)
30
31 difficulty = 2
32
33 print('Mining genesis block...')
34 transactions = ['transaction1', 'transaction2', 'transaction3']
35 previous_block_hash = '00000000000000000000000000000000
36 00000000000000000000000000000000'
37
38 block = Block(transactions, previous_block_hash)
```

```
39  block.mine_block(difficulty)
40
41  print('Mining block 1...')
42  transactions = ['transaction4', 'transaction5', 'transaction6']
43  previous_block_hash = block.hash
44
45  block = Block(transactions, previous_block_hash)
46  block.mine_block(difficulty)
47
48  print('Mining block 2...')
49  transactions = ['transaction7', 'transaction8', 'transaction9']
50  previous_block_hash = block.hash
51
52  block = Block(transactions, previous_block_hash)
53  block.mine_block(difficulty)
```

3.11.11.1 Sample Input

```
1  difficulty = 3
2
3  print('Mining genesis block...')
4  transactions = ['transaction1', 'transaction2', 'transaction3']
5  previous_block_hash = '0000000000000000000000000000000
6  0000000000000000000000000000000000000'
7
8  block = Block(transactions, previous_block_hash)
9  block.mine_block(difficulty)
10
11  print('Mining block 1...')
12  transactions = ['transaction4', 'transaction5', 'transaction6']
13  previous_block_hash = block.hash
14
15  block = Block(transactions, previous_block_hash)
16  block.mine_block(difficulty)
17
18  print('Mining block 2...')
19  transactions = ['transaction7', 'transaction8', 'transaction9']
20  previous_block_hash = block.hash
21
22  block = Block(transactions, previous_block_hash)
23  block.mine_block(difficulty)
```

3.11.11.2 Sample Output

```
1   Mining genesis block...
2   Mining block...
3   Block mined: 0003a3cc9df93547ef75f22ec54c8358f72b44a757
4   bdd43a5402da2b59c55b6f
5   Time elapsed: 0.016009807586669922
6   Mining block 1...
7   Mining block...
8   Block mined: 0000c04aafff7a00d0e124de7a92a23531fb2e06c1
9   c6e51a2f9c2325e5f5e55e
10  Time elapsed: 0.14003205299377441
11  Mining block 2...
12  Mining block...
13  Block mined: 00002a1e310ef75a0a94bb44b484b2da2b883a919
```

```
14  b6f9a59ce1a2a4707b8310e
15  Time elapsed: 1.1625428199768066
```

In this example, the difficulty level is set to 3, which means that the block hash must have three leading zeros to be considered valid. The program creates three blocks, with each block referring to the previous block's hash. The program then mines each block using the PoW algorithm, which involves incrementing the nonce value until a valid block hash is found. The program prints out the block hash and the time elapsed to mine the block for each block.

3.11.12 Program that Demonstrates How to Identify 51% Attacks on a Blockchain

```python
1   import hashlib
2
3   class Block:
4       def __init__(self, data, previous_hash):
5           self.data = data
6           self.previous_hash = previous_hash
7           self.hash = self.calculate_hash()
8
9       def calculate_hash(self):
10          sha = hashlib.sha256()
11          sha.update(self.data.encode('utf-8') +self.previous_hash.encode('
    utf-8'))
12          return sha.hexdigest()
13
14  class Blockchain:
15      def __init__(self):
16          self.chain = [self.create_genesis_block()]
17
18      def create_genesis_block(self):
19          return Block("Genesis Block", "0")
20
21      def add_block(self, new_block):
22          new_block.previous_hash = self.chain[-1].hash
23          new_block.hash = new_block.calculate_hash()
24          self.chain.append(new_block)
25
26      def validate_chain(self):
27          for i in range(1, len(self.chain)):
28              current_block = self.chain[i]
29              previous_block = self.chain[i-1]
30
31              if current_block.hash != current_block.calculate_hash():
32                  print('Invalid hash for block', i)
33                  return False
34
35              if current_block.previous_hash != previous_block.hash:
36                  print('Invalid previous hash for block', i)
37                  return False
38
39          print('Blockchain is valid')
40          return True
41
42      def get_chain_length(self):
43          return len(self.chain)
```

```
44
45   def get_chain_hashrate(self):
46       total_hashrate = 0
47       for block in self.chain:
48           total_hashrate += int(block.hash, 16)
49       return total_hashrate
50
51   def check_for_51_percent_attack(self):
52       chain_length = self.get_chain_length()
53       total_hashrate = self.get_chain_hashrate()
54       for i in range(0, chain_length):
55           block_hash = int(self.chain[i].hash, 16)
56           if block_hash / total_hashrate > 0.51:
57               print('51% attack detected at block', i)
58               return True
59
60       print('No 51% attack detected')
61       return False
```

In this program, we define a `Block` class that contains data, a hash of the previous block, and a hash of itself. We then define a `Blockchain` class that keeps track of a list of blocks and contains functions for adding blocks, validating the chain, and checking for a 51% attack.

The validate_chain() function iterates over each block in the chain and checks whether the hash and previous hash are valid. The get_chain_length() function returns the length of the chain, and the get_chain_hashrate() function calculates the total hash rate of the chain.

The check_for_51_percent_attack() function checks whether any block in a chain has a hash greater than 51% of the total hash rate of the chain. If a block has a hash greater than 51%, then the function prints out the block number and returns True. If no block has a hash greater than 51%, the function prints out a message indicating that no 51% attack was detected and returns False.

By calling the check_for_51_percent_attack() function on a valid blockchain, we can identify whether a 51% attack has occurred on the blockchain or not.

3.11.13 Program to Demonstrate the Concept of Forking

```
1   import threading
2   import time
3   import hashlib
4
5   class Block:
6       def __init__(self, index, data, previous_hash):
7           self.index = index
8           self.timestamp = time.time()
9           self.data = data
10          self.previous_hash = previous_hash
11          self.hash = self.calculate_hash()
12
13      def calculate_hash(self):
14          sha = hashlib.sha256()
15          sha.update(str(self.index).encode('utf-8') + str(self.timestamp)
16          .encode('utf-8') + str(self.data).encode('utf-8') +
17          str(self.previous_hash).encode('utf-8'))
18          return sha.hexdigest()
19
20  class Blockchain:
```

```
21      def __init__(self):
22          self.chain = [self.create_genesis_block()]
23
24      def create_genesis_block(self):
25          return Block(0, "Genesis Block", "0")
26
27      def add_block(self, data):
28          previous_block = self.chain[-1]
29          index = previous_block.index + 1
30          previous_hash = previous_block.hash
31          new_block = Block(index, data, previous_hash)
32          self.chain.append(new_block)
33
34      def print_chain(self):
35          for block in self.chain:
36              print("Block #" + str(block.index) +
37                  " with hash: " + block.hash)
38
39  def thread_1(blockchain):
40      blockchain.add_block("Transaction 1 from thread 1")
41      blockchain.add_block("Transaction 2 from thread 1")
42
43  def thread_2(blockchain):
44      blockchain.add_block("Transaction 1 from thread 2")
45      blockchain.add_block("Transaction 2 from thread 2")
46
47  if __name__ == '__main__':
48      blockchain = Blockchain()
49
50      t1 = threading.Thread(target=thread_1, args=(blockchain,))
51      t2 = threading.Thread(target=thread_2, args=(blockchain,))
52
53      t1.start()
54      t2.start()
55
56      t1.join()
57      t2.join()
58
59      blockchain.print_chain()
```

In this program, we define a Block class that represents a block in a blockchain, and we define a Blockchain class that represents the blockchain itself. We also define two functions, thread_1 and thread_2, that add blocks to the blockchain. We create two threads, one for each function, and start them. Finally, we wait for both threads to complete and print out the blockchain.

When the threads add blocks to the blockchain, they both use the same blockchain instance, which means they are both modifying the same data structure. This is similar to a fork in a blockchain, where two groups of nodes are modifying the same blockchain data structure, potentially creating two different chains.

When we run this program, we can see that the two threads add blocks to the blockchain, but they do not produce two different chains. Instead, the blocks are added in a deterministic order, and the final blockchain contains all the blocks from both threads in the same order. This is because Python's Global Interpreter Lock (GIL) prevents true parallelism, meaning only one thread can execute at a time. In a real blockchain, with true parallelism, forking can occur and nodes may create different chains.

3.11.14 Program to Detect and Deal with 51% Attacks in the Bitcoin Blockchain

```python
import requests
import time

# Define the URL of a Bitcoin block explorer API
api_url = "https://blockchain.info/q"

# Function to check the current hash rate
def get_hash_rate():
    try:
        response = requests.get(f"{api_url}/getdifficulty")
        if response.status_code == 200:
            return float(response.text)
    except requests.RequestException as e:
        print("Error:", str(e))
    return None

# Function to check the number of blocks mined in the last hour
def blocks_mined_last_hour():
    try:
        response = requests.get(f"{api_url}/getnethashps/3600")
        if response.status_code == 200:
            return int(response.text)
    except requests.RequestException as e:
        print("Error:", str(e))
    return None

# Main loop for monitoring
while True:
    current_hash_rate = get_hash_rate()
    blocks_last_hour = blocks_mined_last_hour()

    if current_hash_rate is not None and blocks_last_hour is not None:
        # Adjust these thresholds as needed
        if current_hash_rate < 0.5 and blocks_last_hour < 5:
            print("Potential 51% attack detected!")
            # You could implement an alert or response mechanism here
        else:
            print("Bitcoin network is operating normally.")

    # Wait for some time before checking again (e.g., every ten minutes)
    time.sleep(600)
```

Explanation of Code

This program examines the network's present hash rate and the number of blocks mined within the last hour. If both values fell below certain (adjustable) thresholds, a message indicating a potential 51% attack is displayed. In a real-world scenario, you would need a more advanced system and presumably the cooperation of other Bitcoin network participants and miners to counteract such an attack.

Please be aware that addressing a 51% attack in Bitcoin requires a coordinated effort from miners, developers, and the larger Bitcoin community. Individual users cannot prevent or mitigate these assaults effectively on their own.

3.12 Summary

This chapter provided a comprehensive introduction to Bitcoin, covering various aspects of its technology and ecosystem. The chapter began with an explanation of what Bitcoin is and its historical background. It then delved into the predicted market trends and the concept of a digital wallet. The chapter also explored digital keys and addresses, transactions, digital signatures, and mining and consensus in Bitcoin.

Additionally, the chapter discussed forking, including hard forks and soft forks, which result in the creation of two separate chains. The chapter concludes, in the next section, with laboratory work examples, including programs related to generating private keys, creating digital wallets, deploying smart contracts, and implementing ECDSA.

Throughout the chapter, readers gain an understanding of Bitcoin's fundamental concepts, its market potential, the role of wallets and addresses, transaction processes, the importance of digital signatures, the mining and consensus mechanism, and the implications of forking in the Bitcoin network.

The laboratory work examples provide hands-on experience in working with Bitcoin-related tools and concepts, allowing readers to gain practical skills in key areas of Bitcoin technology.

3.13 Exercise

This section gives exercises based on topics covered in this chapter.

3.13.1 Multiple Choice Questions

1. What is Bitcoin?
    a. A centralized digital currency
    b. A decentralized digital currency
    c. A physical form of currency
    d. A government-regulated currency
2. What is the purpose of a digital wallet in Bitcoin?
    a. To securely store and manage Bitcoin
    b. To mine new Bitcoins
    c. To regulate Bitcoin transactions
    d. To create new Bitcoins
3. What is the difference between a custodial and noncustodial wallet?
    a. Custodial wallets require a fee for each transaction, while noncustodial wallets are free.
    b. Custodial wallets are managed by a third party, while noncustodial wallets give users full control over their funds.
    c. Custodial wallets can only be accessed online, while noncustodial wallets are offline.
    d. Custodial wallets offer higher security features than noncustodial wallets.
4. Which type of wallet is a Ledger Nano S?
    a. Custodial wallet
    b. Noncustodial wallet
    c. Software wallet
    d. Hardware wallet

5. What are private keys in Bitcoin?
   a. Keys used to access public Wi-Fi networks
   b. Keys that unlock Bitcoin transactions
   c. Keys used to encrypt Bitcoin transactions
   d. Keys that control the Bitcoin mining process
6. What is the purpose of a transaction in Bitcoin?
   a. To transfer Bitcoin from one address to another
   b. To create new Bitcoin
   c. To regulate the Bitcoin market
   d. To mine new Bitcoin blocks
7. What is the consensus mechanism in Bitcoin mining?
   a. Proof of stake (PoS)
   b. Proof of work (PoW)
   c. Delegated proof of stake (DPoS)
   d. Byzantine fault tolerance (BFT)
8. What is the cost associated with Bitcoin mining?
   a. The cost of purchasing Bitcoin hardware
   b. The cost of electricity consumed during mining
   c. The cost of Bitcoin transaction fees
   d. The cost of Bitcoin storage in digital wallets
9. What is a hard fork in Bitcoin?
   a. A temporary split in the blockchain
   b. A permanent split in the blockchain
   c. An upgrade to the Bitcoin protocol
   d. A change in Bitcoin mining difficulty
10. What is the main purpose of laboratory work in "Bitcoin 1"?
    a. To simulate real-world Bitcoin transactions
    b. To explore the features of different digital wallets
    c. To provide practical experience with Bitcoin-related concepts and tools
    d. To analyze the market trends of Bitcoin

3.13.2 Short Answer Questions

1. Define Bitcoin:
2. What is the significance of a digital wallet in Bitcoin?
3. Differentiate between a custodial and noncustodial wallet.
4. Name two types of digital wallets used for storing Bitcoin.
5. Explain the concept of private keys in Bitcoin.
6. What is the purpose of a transaction in the Bitcoin network?
7. Briefly describe the consensus mechanism in Bitcoin mining.
8. What factors contribute to the cost of Bitcoin mining?
9. Define a hard fork in the context of Bitcoin.
10. What is the main purpose of laboratory work in "Bitcoin 1"?

3.13.3 Long Answer Questions

1. Explain the process of creating a Bitcoin transaction, including the key components involved and the steps taken to ensure its validity and security.
2. Discuss the role of miners in the Bitcoin network and how they contribute to the consensus mechanism. Explain the mining process and the incentives for miners to participate in securing the network.
3. Describe the concept of the blockchain in Bitcoin and its role in maintaining a transparent and decentralized ledger. Discuss the process of adding transactions to the blockchain and the benefits it provides in terms of security and trust.
4. Compare and contrast the different types of digital wallets used for storing Bitcoin, including software wallets, hardware wallets, and paper wallets. Discuss their respective advantages, disadvantages, and security considerations.
5. Analyze the impact of transaction fees on the Bitcoin network. Discuss the factors that influence transaction fees, the role of miners in fee selection, and the challenges associated with scaling the network to accommodate increased transaction volume.
6. Explain the concept of a hard fork in Bitcoin and discuss the potential consequences and challenges associated with a fork. Provide examples of notable hard forks in Bitcoin's history and their implications for the network and its users.
7. Discuss the potential risks and security considerations involved in using Bitcoin, including the vulnerabilities of digital wallets, the risks of centralized exchanges, and the importance of secure practices such as private key management and transaction verification.
8. Explore the current and future challenges facing the Bitcoin network, including scalability issues, regulatory concerns, and the potential impact of emerging technologies such as quantum computing. Discuss potential solutions and advancements that could address these challenges and ensure the long-term viability of Bitcoin.

Ethereum Blockchain

4

The Ethereum blockchain is a decentralized, open source platform that enables the creation and execution of smart contracts. It was introduced in 2015 by Vitalik Buterin and has since become one of the most popular blockchain networks. Ethereum allows developers to build decentralized applications (DApps) on top of its blockchain, providing them with a robust infrastructure and a wide range of functionalities. Its native cryptocurrency, Ether (ETH), is used for various purposes within the network, such as paying transaction fees and incentivizing.

4.1   Overview of Ethereum Blockchain

Ethereum is a revolutionary technology that facilitates the seamless, low-cost transfer of the cryptocurrency Ether (ETH) to anyone in the world. However, its functionality extends far beyond that of a digital currency. Ethereum is a robust platform that enables developers to create and deploy decentralized applications (DApps) that are irrepressible and resistant to censorship.

Some of its key features are as follows:

Send Cryptocurrency to Anyone for a Small Fee: ETH, the native cryptocurrency of Ethereum, enables users to transmit and receive digital currency. Using Ethereum's network, users can transfer ETH from one account to another in a secure manner and for relatively low fees compared to conventional financial systems. A distributed network of nodes processes and verifies these transactions, ensuring a trustworthy and untraceable transmission of value.

Powering DApps: Ethereum offers a robust infrastructure for the development of DApps in addition to basic cryptocurrency transfers. DApps are software applications that utilize the smart contract functionality of the Ethereum blockchain to operate. These applications may include financial tools such as decentralized exchanges and lending platforms, as well as social networks, amusement applications, and supply chain solutions.

Unstoppable and Censorship-Resistant: Its permissionless and censorship-resistant nature is one of Ethereum's most significant strengths. DApps deployed on Ethereum operate on a decentralized network, as opposed to traditional applications and platforms that can be controlled or shut down by central authorities. Once a smart contract has been deployed, it becomes part of the blockchain and is accessible to all parties. This ensures that DApps cannot be readily shut down or censored, providing a level of freedom and resilience that is exclusive to decentralized systems.

© The Author(s), under exclusive license to APress Media, LLC, part of Springer Nature 2024
R. S. Mangrulkar, P. Vijay Chavan, *Blockchain Essentials*,
https://doi.org/10.1007/978-1-4842-9975-3_4

Permissionless Blockchain and Smart Contracts: Anyone can participate in the Ethereum network as a user or node without requiring permission from a central authority. As developers can freely construct on the platform, this accessibility promotes inclusivity and encourages innovation. In addition, Ethereum's blockchain is capable of executing smart contracts, which are agreements written in code that execute themselves. Smart contracts facilitate the automation of a variety of processes and agreements without the need for intermediaries, thereby reducing costs and increasing productivity.

Ethereum is an innovative technology that transcends merely being a cryptocurrency. It is a flexible platform that enables the transmission of value (cryptocurrency) and empowers developers to build a vast array of DApps. Ethereum enables trustless interactions, censorship resistance, and the development of an open, decentralized ecosystem for the benefit of everyone by leveraging the power of smart contracts and operating on a permissionless blockchain.

4.1.1 Key Features

As one of the most influential blockchain platforms, Ethereum possesses a number of distinguishing features and qualities that set it apart from conventional systems. Let's examine the most important ones:

Smart Contracts: One of Ethereum's defining features is its ability to execute smart contracts. Smart contracts are self-executing agreements with terms and conditions directly written into code. They enable automation and self-enforcement of contractual obligations without the need for intermediaries, reducing reliance on traditional legal systems and enhancing trust in digital interactions.

Decentralization: Ethereum operates as a decentralized network, meaning there is no central authority or single point of control. The platform is supported by a distributed network of nodes globally, each participating in transaction validation and smart contract execution. This decentralization provides greater security, resilience, and censorship resistance compared to centralized systems.

Ethereum Virtual Machine (EVM): The EVM is a crucial component of the Ethereum platform. It is a runtime environment that executes smart contracts written in various programming languages, with Solidity being the most common. The EVM ensures that the same code is executed consistently across all nodes, achieving consensus on the output of smart contracts.

Ether (ETH) cryptocurrency: Ethereum has its native cryptocurrency, ETH, which serves multiple purposes within the network, including paying transaction fees and for computational services. It is also used as a medium of exchange and a digital asset.

Interoperability and Standards: Ethereum follows standards that define how tokens and smart contracts should be created and function on the network. The most well-known standard is ERC-20, which governs the creation and implementation of fungible tokens. ERC-721 is another notable standard for nonfungible tokens (NFTs), which represent unique assets.

DApps: Ethereum facilitates the development and deployment of DApps. DApps are software applications that run on the Ethereum blockchain and interact with smart contracts. DApps span various industries, including finance, gaming, supply chain, governance, and more.

Upgradeable Protocols: Ethereum's upgradeable protocol enables the implementation of Ethereum Improvement Proposals (EIPs) to improve the platform's functionality and address issues. However, upgrades require community consensus and careful consideration due to potential network disruptions and compatibility concerns.

Community and Development: Ethereum has a large and vibrant community of developers, enthusiasts, and contributors. The open source nature of the platform encourages continuous development, fostering innovation and collaboration among participants.

Ethereum 2.0: Ethereum is transitioning from a proof-of-work (PoW) to a proof-of-stake (PoS) consensus mechanism through Ethereum 2.0 upgrade. PoS is expected to improve the scalability, security, and energy efficiency of the network.

Immutable Blockchain: Once data are recorded on the Ethereum blockchain, they become immutable, meaning they cannot be altered or deleted. This characteristic ensures the permanence and transparency of transactions and smart contract interactions.

4.1.2 EVM

While the EVM's physical instantiation cannot be likened to a cloud or an ocean wave, it is nonetheless managed as a single entity by thousands of interconnected computers, each running the Ethereum client.

The Ethereum protocol was designed specifically to ensure that this unique state machine runs without interruption or change. All the accounts and the smart contracts built on Ethereum exist in this ecosystem. Ethereum only ever exists in one so-called canonical state per chain block, and the EVM specifies the criteria for arriving at a new valid state at each chain block.

4.2 History of Ethereum

Vitalik Buterin came up with the idea for Ethereum in 2013. In 2015, DApps were made available. It acquired many new features and changed from PoW to PoS in 2022, as a result of which it used less energy. Today, Ethereum is a leading blockchain tool that pushes for new ideas in a decentralized world. Various milestones in Ethereum's history are summarized in Table 4-1.

4.2.1 Ledger to State Machine

Blockchain and distributed ledger technology (DLT) platforms have experienced rapid growth in recent years, offering public, permissioned, and private networks, each with its own smart contract capabilities. However, the fundamental concept of a distributed ledger and its transaction processing is at the heart of each of these platforms. In this article, we will examine this similarity from a computer science perspective. Table 4-2 provides a structured and organized comparison of blockchain and DLT platforms.

The ledger maintains two essential properties: immutability and append-only. Requests or commands involving validation and consensus mechanisms are used to add transactions to a distributed ledger. Once a transaction is recorded, a state transition is triggered. For instance, if Alice sends ten coins to Bob, Alice's wallet balance will diminish by ten, while Bob's wallet balance will increase by ten.

The current state of the ledger is a direct result of all previous transactions. In a distributed environment, this integrity is essential for achieving consensus among multiple nodes. Thus, the

Table 4-1 History of Ethereum

Year	Key Milestone
2013	Ethereum concept proposed by Vitalik Buterin in a whitepaper
2014	Ethereum project announced and development begins
2015	Ethereum's public testnet, Olympic, is launched for developers
2015	Ethereum's Frontier, the first live release, goes live
2016	The DAO, a decentralized autonomous organization, is launched and subsequently hacked, leading to a contentious hard fork
2017	Ethereum's market capitalization surpasses $100 billion, making it one of the largest cryptocurrencies
2017	The Ethereum Enterprise Alliance (EEA) is formed to promote Ethereum's adoption in the business world
2018	Ethereum's network upgrade, Constantinople, is initiated to improve scalability and reduce transaction costs
2020	Ethereum 2.0 begins its phased launch, transitioning from a PoW to PoS consensus mechanism
2021	Ethereum's network upgrade, London, introduces EIP-1559, changing the fee structure and burning transaction fees
2021	Ethereum's price reaches an all-time high, surpassing $4,000 per ETH
2022	Development and upgrades continue in the Ethereum ecosystem, with a focus on scalability and sustainability

Table 4-2 Comparison: Ledger to State Machine

Concept	Description
Blockchain and DLT Platforms	These technologies have seen rapid growth, offering various types of networks: public, permissioned, and private. Each of these networks incorporates smart contract capabilities tailored to its specific use case
Fundamental Concept	The core concept shared by all blockchain and DLT platforms is the idea of a distributed ledger. This ledger serves as a decentralized and tamper-proof record of transactions
Transaction Processing	At the heart of these platforms lies the transaction processing mechanism. This mechanism is fundamental to the operation of distributed ledgers, ensuring the secure and reliable recording of transactions

ledger functions as a form of state machine. It can be defined as a "ledger state machine" with the following characteristics:

– Transactions cause a state transition.
– The machine state is a pure function of all preceding transactions.

Despite lacking the simplicity of a finite state machine (FSM) and the complete computational capacity of a Turing machine, this model offers a number of useful characteristics as a result of the following properties:

– It is infinite, not constrained by the limitations of a FSM.
– It is not necessarily a model of computation and lacks the full power of a Turing machine.

Despite not offering the simplicity of a FSM or the complete computational capability of a Turing machine, this model possesses several useful features due to its key properties:

- The state does not need to be explicitly stored as it can always be recomputed.
- Consequently, the state can be regenerated at any point in history.
- Records and the state are easy to replicate due to their immutability.
- Computation on records and the state is easily scalable due to the ease of replication.

It is crucial to define the concept in this manner in order to facilitate the subsequent steps:

- Comparing this model with how relational database technology systems typically operate.
- Comparing various blockchain platforms and frameworks regarding how their state machines function, based on the assertion that all blockchain frameworks share this common concept.
- Defining low-level constructs in code that serve as the basis for designing blockchains from first principles.

Notably, these ideas and concepts are not entirely novel; similar discussions can be found by searching for terms such as "blockchain state machine" or by realizing that the state of an AggregateRoot in the Command Query Responsibility Segregation/Event Sourcing (CQRS/ES) paradigm is a pure function of all the events that impacted it.

4.2.2   Ethereum Network

Transactions and smart contracts on the Ethereum network are validated and processed by a distributed network of computers called nodes. Each participant in the network has its own copy of the full blockchain, including all of the data on past transactions and the code for any smart contracts.

A machine becomes a node in the Ethereum network when it runs an application that allows it to participate in the network, such as an Ethereum client. This node is accountable for confirming the correctness of smart contracts and transactions and keeping the blockchain in sync with other nodes.

Together, the network's nodes reach consensus on its current state, guaranteeing the integrity and uniformity of the blockchain and the legality of all transactions. Ethereum's network is resilient and resistant to single points of failure because of its decentralized structure and the consensus process (usually PoW or migrating to PoS).

The simplest form of Ethereum network is given in Figure 4-1. It has a consensus mechanism as PoW that interacts with other nodes in the Ethereum network. It also has Ethereum state, which maintains the state of Ethereum, an EVM that executes smart contracts and a pool of transactions. These transactions are supposed to be present in the memory of Ethereum clients, which can be further validated and mined in blockchain. Apart from the aforementioned components, a peer-to-peer (P2P) module is responsible for communicationg with other Ethereum client nodes present in the Ethereum network.

There is no central host or authority in the Ethereum network, where independent nodes are connected.

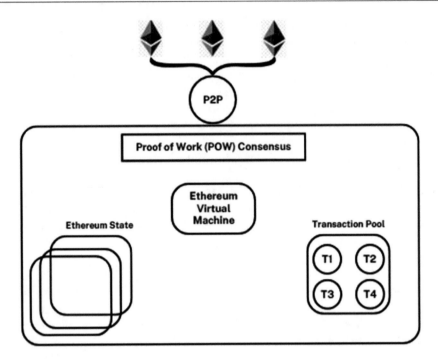

Figure 4-1 Ethereum network

4.3   Smart Contracts

Smart contracts are computer programs that are stored on a blockchain-based platform and auto-matically implement portions of a contract. They can function independently or in conjunction with traditional text-based contracts, executing duties such as the transfer of funds between parties. On the blockchain, the code is replicated across multiple nodes, providing security and permanence. Smart contracts are written in programming languages such as Solidity and require execution parameters that are both specific and objective. Currently, they can only perform elementary duties, such as cryptocurrency transfers. As blockchain adoption increases, more complex smart contracts will be developed. However, many years will pass before code will be able to accommodate subjective legal criteria. Before they can be executed on certain blockchains, smart contracts must pay a transaction fee known as "gas."

Currently, smart contracts are best adopted for automatically executing payment of funds upon the occurrence of a predetermined event or imposing monetary penalties based on objective conditions. They reduce the need for human intervention, escrow agents, and judicial systems, thereby reducing the cost of execution and enforcement. For example, they could automate payment transfers upon product delivery and streamline procure-to-pay processes. On the enforcement side, if payment is not received, they could disable access to Internet-connected assets.

Smart contracts are essential components of numerous blockchain applications; however, their enforceability as legal agreements under contract law in the United States highlights a number of legal and practical considerations that must be addressed prior to their widespread commercial application.

4.4 Challenges in Implementing Smart Contracts

The challenges in implementing smart contracts are as follows:

- Nontechnical Parties: Nontechnical parties may find it difficult to negotiate, draft, and comprehend smart contracts, necessitating the use of technical experts to precisely encode the agreement in code.
- Off-Chain Resources: Smart contracts are frequently required to interact with off-chain resources, which can contribute to potential data accuracy issues and reliance on trusted third-party oracles.
- Final Agreement Uncertainty: Determining the final agreement in smart contracts can be difficult when the text and code contradict one another, necessitating clarification as to which takes precedence.
- The automated nature of smart contracts may not align with actual business practices, as parties are unable to readily excuse breaches or tolerate partial performance.
- Modifying and Terminating: Due to the immutability of blockchains, amending smart contracts can be difficult and expensive, and parties may encounter difficulties in terminating contracts without self-help remedies.
- Objectivity and Ambiguity: During negotiations, the objectivity required by smart contracts may conflict with the flexibility and ambiguity prevalent in traditional text-based contracts.
- Payment Guarantees: Although smart contracts can orchestrate payment, practical complications can arise when the necessary funds are not readily available in wallets associated with the contracts.
- Allocation of Risk: Smart contracts introduce new risks, such as coding errors and cyberattacks, which may necessitate a clear allocation of risk between parties and third-party developers.
- Governing Law and Venue: Parties may be required to specify governing law and venue clauses for global adoption of smart contracts in order to guarantee predictable dispute resolution.
- Best Practices: As the adoption of smart contracts continues to evolve, best practices include the use of hybrid approaches that combine text and code, address risk allocation, and specify the applicable law and venue.

4.4.1 Smart Contract Life Cycle

The smart contract life cycle refers to the phases a smart contract undergoes, beginning with its initial publication on the blockchain and ending with its possible destruction. What follows is a concise description of each phase.

- **Published to the zero address**
  (0x000000000000 000000000000000000000000000000000000000): When a smart contract is created, it is deployed to the blockchain network and given a unique address. The zero address, typically represented as 0x0000000000000
  000000000000000000000000000000000000000, is a special address used to indicate that a contract has been published but has not yet been allocated a unique address on the blockchain. At this point, the contract is not active and cannot be carried out.
- **Invoked by transaction**
  Once the smart contract is published and designated a unique address on the blockchain, it can be invoked or interacted with via transactions. Users or other contracts can initiate interactions with

the functions and state of a smart contract. When triggered by a valid transaction, the contract's code will be executed on the blockchain, and it may perform actions or modify its internal state accordingly.

– **May be destroyed**
  It is possible to design a smart contract so that it can be terminated or destroyed. This is typically implemented as a special function that allows the contract creator or designated users to terminate the contract, releasing any resources it was utilizing and removing it permanently from the blockchain. It is essential to observe, however, that not all smart contracts have this "self-destruct" feature. Whether a contract can be terminated depends on how its originator programmed it.

EVM Language Set LLL (Lisp-like, earliest but seldom used), Serpent (Python-like), Solidity (JavaScript-like), Vyper (Python-like), and Bamboo (Erlang-like) are the high-level programming languages for the EVM. These languages are employed for writing smart contracts and interacting with the Ethereum blockchain.

4.4.2   Introducing Solidity

Solidity is a high-level programming language designed specifically for writing Ethereum smart contracts.

– Solidity is one of the primary languages for constructing smart contracts on the Ethereum blockchain. Solidity was developed by Gavin Wood, one of Ethereum's cofounders.
– Solidity remains the most widely used high-level language for creating Ethereum smart contracts. Its early acceptance, comprehensive documentation, sizable development community, and advanced feature set all contribute to its widespread appeal.
– It has many useful features and functions that are required for creating sophisticated and safe smart contracts. It enables programmers to design and implement their own data structures, deal with inheritance, control access, and carry out business logic.
– Despite its widespread adoption, Solidity is not problem-free. Reentrancy attacks, integer overflow, and other traps in blockchain development should be carefully considered while writing safe smart contracts in Solidity.
– Solidity, the most popular language for Ethereum smart contracts, is constantly improving and developing best practices for constructing secure and efficient contracts thanks to the hard work of the community. Newer languages, such as Vyper, have evolved as an alternative to Solidity in an effort to remedy some of its shortcomings, most notably in the areas of security and readability.

4.4.2.1 Solidity Data Types
Among the most important data types in the Solidity programming language used by Ethereum are the following:

bool: The `bool` data type is used to represent boolean values, which can be either `true` or `false`. It is fundamental for conditional statements and logical operations in smart contracts.

int, uint: These are data types used to represent signed (with `int`) and unsigned (with `uint`) integers, respectively. They come in different variants, like `int8`, `int16`, `uint8`, `uint16`, and so on, up to `int256` and `uint256`. The default is `uint256`, which means an unsigned integer with 256 bits.

fixed, ufixed: These are fixed-point number types. They are similar to floating-point numbers, but the decimal point is fixed, making them suitable for financial calculations with high precision.

address: The `address` data type is used to store Ethereum addresses. Addresses are used to represent user accounts or smart contracts on the Ethereum network. The size of an address is 20 bytes.

Arrays: Solidity allows you to create arrays, which are collections of elements of the same type. They can be either dynamic (length can change during execution) or static (fixed length).

Time units: Solidity provides time units to work with time-related values. For example, you can use `seconds`, `minutes`, `hours`, `days`, and `weeks` as units to express time durations in smart contracts.

Ether units: Ethereum has a native cryptocurrency, ETH. Different units are used to express ETH, depending on its denomination:

`wei`: The smallest unit of ETH (1 wei = 1 ETH/10^18).

`finney`: 1 ETH = 1,000 finney.

`szabo`: 1 ETH = 1,000,000 szabo.

`ether`: The base unit, 1 ETH = 1 ether.

4.4.3 Global Variables

Global variables in Solidity are preset variables that can be accessed anywhere in a smart contract. These variables are crucial for understanding the current transaction, its context, and where the blockchain currently stands. Developers of smart contracts can then access and make use of this vital information while the contract is executed.

– **msg** – the transaction call.

- **msg.sender**: Ethereum address of sender who initiated current transaction. It indicates the account or smart contract that triggered the execution of the current function.
- **msg.value**: Amount of Ether (in wei) sent along with the transaction call. It represents the value or payment attached to the transaction.
- **msg.gas**: Amount of gas remaining for the current transaction. It indicates the available gas for executing the current function, and any unused gas is refunded to the sender.
- **msg.data**: Data payload of the transaction. It includes the function selector and any additional parameters provided when calling a smart contract function.
- **msg.sig**: First four bytes of **msg.data**, representing the function selector. It is used to determine which function in the smart contract is being called.

– **tx** – the transaction.

- **tx.gasprice**: Gas price (in wei) set by transaction sender. The gas price determines the amount of ETH the sender is willing to pay for each unit of gas used in the transaction.

– **block** – the block the transaction is in.

- **block.coinbase**: Address of the miner who mined the block. It represents the Ethereum account that receives the block reward for successfully mining the block.
- **block.difficulty**: Difficulty level of block. The difficulty value is a measure of how hard it was to mine the block and is adjusted dynamically to maintain a consistent block production rate.
- **block.gaslimit**: Maximum amount of gas allowed in block. It limits the total gas consumption of all transactions within the block.

- **block.number**: Block number of current block. It is a sequential number assigned to each new block in the blockchain.
- **block.timestamp**: Timestamp of current block, measured in seconds since the epoch (January 1, 1970). It represents the time when the block was mined.

4.4.3.1 Constructing and Destroying Contracts

Constructing and destroying contracts are important aspects of the life cycle of smart contracts in Solidity. What follows is an explanation of how contracts are constructed and destroyed.

Constructing Contracts

Contracts in Solidity are created using a constructor function, which is a special function with the same name as the contract itself. The constructor is executed only once, at the time of contract deployment. It is used to initialize the contract's state and perform any setup required for the contract to function correctly.

In older versions of Solidity, the constructor function had the same name as the contract, but since the release of Solidity version 0.5.0, it has been explicitly defined using the `constructor` keyword.

During deployment, the constructor is called with the initial parameters provided, and it sets the initial values for state variables and other contract settings.

Destroying Contracts

A contract in Solidity can be destroyed using the `selfdestruct` function. This function allows the contract to be terminated, and its remaining ETH balance (if any) is sent to a designated address.

The `selfdestruct` function takes a single parameter, which is the address where the contract's remaining ETH balance will be sent.

The person who triggers the `selfdestruct` function (i.e., the sender of the transaction that calls `selfdestruct`) claims the contract's ETH balance. It is essential to handle contract destruction with caution, as once a contract is destroyed, its code and state can no longer be accessed.

It is important to note that the ability to destroy a contract and claim its ETH balance is only possible if the contract author has explicitly enabled this functionality in the contract's code. In other words, the contract creator must include a valid implementation of the `selfdestruct` function in the contract's code for this feature to be available.

Function Syntax and Function Modifiers in Solidity

Function Syntax

In Solidity, functions are defined using the following syntax:

```
function FunctionName([parameters])
{public|private|internal|external}
[pure|constant|view|payable] [modifiers]
[returns (return types)]
```

- **FunctionName**: Name of function.
- **[parameters]**: Optional list of input parameters for function, separated by commas.
- **public|private|internal|external**: Specifies visibility of function. For example, `public` makes the function accessible from outside the contract, while `private` restricts access to within the contract.

– **pure|constant|view|payable**: Optional keywords to specify the function type.

- **pure**: The function does not modify the contract's state and does not read from the contract's storage. It is often used for utility functions with no side effects.
- **constant** or **view**: The function does not modify the contract's state but can read from the contract's storage.
- **payable**: The function can receive ETH along with the function call.

Function Modifiers

Function modifiers are used to modify other functions in Solidity. They use an underscore (_) as a placeholder for the modified function. Here's an example of a function modifier:

```
modifier onlyOwner {
  require(msg.sender == owner);
  _;
}
```

In this example, the `onlyOwner` modifier checks whether the `msg.sender` is the owner of the contract. If the condition is met, the underscore (_) indicates where the modified function's code will be inserted. This allows you to add custom checks or pre- and postprocessing logic to functions by reusing the modifier.

Error Handling in Solidity

Error handling in Solidity is a crucial aspect of smart contract development to ensure the integrity of the contract's state and prevent unexpected behavior. Solidity provides different mechanisms for error handling, each serving specific purposes:

1. **Guarantee state**:
   - In Solidity, if a condition evaluates to `false` during contract execution, an exception is thrown, and the entire transaction is reverted. This helps in guaranteeing the integrity of the contract's state. If any condition that is essential for the correct execution of a function is not met, the function will throw an exception and revert any changes made to the contract's state before the exception.
2. **assert**:
   - The `assert` function is used to check for internal programming errors. It is typically used to ensure that certain conditions that are expected to be true hold true at a specific point in the contract. A failed assertion indicates a serious issue in the contract's logic, and the contract execution is halted immediately and all changes reverted.
   - It is important to note that `assert` should not be used for regular input validation or external condition checks, as it is not intended for error handling during normal contract execution.
3. **require**:
   - The `require` function is used for input validation and checking external conditions that are expected to hold true during contract execution. It is a common error-handling mechanism used to ensure the validity of function arguments and inputs.

- If a `require` statement evaluates to `false`, then the contract execution is immediately halted, and all changes are reverted. This helps prevent incorrect inputs from propagating through the contract and ensures that only valid transactions will be processed.
- The `require` function can also take a second argument, which is an error message string. This can be used to provide more descriptive error messages when a condition fails, making it easier to identify the cause of the error.

Using a Function Modifier

Solidity makes it possible to restrict access to a function using a function modifier. A function modifier is a special function that can modify the behavior of other functions. It is often used to add additional checks or conditions to function execution. Let's look at an example of how to restrict access to a function using a function modifier:

```
modifier onlyOwner {
  require(msg.sender == owner);
  _;
}

function takeFunds(uint256 amt) public onlyOwner {
  msg.sender.transfer(amt);
}
```

4.5   Ethereum Development Tools

Ethereum development tools comprise a comprehensive range of software and services that facilitate the process for developers to create, test, deploy, and engage with applications and smart contracts on the Ethereum blockchain. These tools optimize the development process, improve efficiency, and guarantee the resilience of DApps. This document presents a comprehensive overview of the essential tools utilized in Ethereum development. A few popular tools are given below:

- **Node.js and npm**: Node.js and npm are widely used tools in the field of web development. Node.js is a runtime environment for executing JavaScript code on the server side, facilitating server-side scripting. Additionally, npm (Node Package Manager) is employed to effectively manage and distribute software packages. Node.js is widely utilized by developers for executing JavaScript-based tools and scripts. Additionally, npm serves as a valuable tool for facilitating the installation and maintenance of libraries, dependencies, and frameworks.
- **Git**: Git, which tracks versions, is a distributed version control system that enables multiple users to collaborate on a project. Git is a software application that serves as a version control system, enabling collaborative project work and facilitating the monitoring and administration of source code modifications. Git is a highly prevalent tool utilized by developers to efficiently oversee diverse iterations of their code, enable collaborative efforts on distinct branches, and guarantee smooth coordination among team members.
- **Text editors and integrated development environments (IDEs)**: IDEs are also used for development. Developers employ code editors, such as Visual Studio Code, or IDEs, like Remix, to author, modify, and manage code. The aforementioned tools include features such as syntax highlighting, autocompletion, debugging functionalities, and specialized extensions designed specifically for Ethereum development.

- **Ganache**: Ganache offers a localized Ethereum blockchain environment that facilitates the testing of smart contracts and DApps. The platform provides functionalities such as real-time mining, customizable gas prices, and an intuitive interface for simulating interactions with the Ethereum network.
- **Truffle**: The term "truffle" pertains to an underground variety of delectable fungus. The Truffle framework is extensively acknowledged and implemented within the Ethereum Transactions development community. A variety of tools are provided by the platform to aid in the compilation, testing, and deployment of smart contracts. Truffle provides assistance throughout the development process by offering a project structure, deployment procedures, and testing facilities.
- **Web3.js and ethers.js**: Web3.js and ethers.js are JavaScript libraries commonly used for interacting with the Ethereum blockchain. These JavaScript libraries serve the purpose of facilitating interaction with Ethereum networks, thereby enabling DApps to establish communication with smart contracts. Web3.js and ethers.js serve as abstraction layers for Ethereum's JSON-Remote Procedure Call (RPC) interface, enabling developers to interact with the blockchain by simplifying the process of reading and writing data.
- **Remix IDE**: The Remix IDE is a software development environment that facilitates the creation, testing, and deployment of smart contracts on the Ethereum blockchain. Remix is an online IDE that has been purposefully tailored for the construction of Ethereum smart contracts. The platform provides a Solidity code editor, debugging tools, and an integrated Ethereum simulator for the purpose of testing.
- **Infura**: Infura offers application programming interface (API)-based access to Ethereum nodes, enabling DApps to engage with the Ethereum network without the need for operating their own node. The ability to access the blockchain is of utmost importance for apps deployed on diverse platforms.
- **Hardhat**: Hardhat is a viable alternative development environment and task runner that can be utilized for Ethereum projects. The software provides sophisticated testing, debugging, and deployment functionalities, rendering it a widely favored option among developers.
- **Solc**: The Solc algorithm is an extensively implemented compiler designed for the Solidity programming language. It is renowned for its productivity and efficacy in generating Solc is a compiler that has been developed with the Solidity programming language in mind. The process in question entails the conversion of Solidity smart contracts to bytecode, which serves as the rudimentary syntax for the contract's directives. Subsequently, the EVM, the runtime environment utilized to conduct smart contracts on the Ethereum blockchain, may execute this bytecode.
- **Metamask**: Metamask is a browser extension that functions as an Ethereum wallet and facilitates smooth engagement with DApps directly through web browsers.

4.6   Ethereum Transactions

Ethereum transactions play a fundamental role in the Ethereum blockchain, enabling the transfer of value, execution of smart contracts, and various interactions within the network. A transaction is a signed message that includes information such as a recipient's address, the amount of ETH being transferred, and optional data for smart contract execution.

4.6.1   Transaction Life Cycle

The Ethereum transaction undergoes multiple stages throughout its existence. These are as follows:

1. **Creation**: The initiation of a transaction occurs when users generate and authenticate a transaction message using their private key. The content of this communication encompasses specific information such as the address of the recipient, the designated amount, and the predetermined gas limit.
2. **Submission**: The signed transaction is broadcast to the Ethereum network via a node. Miners and nodes validate and propagate the transaction across the network.
3. **Inclusion in Mempool**: The process of inclusion in the mempool refers to the acceptance of valid transactions into a designated memory pool. These transactions remain in the mempool until they are selected for inclusion in a block. In the context of transaction inclusion, there is a competitive process wherein transactions vie for inclusion based on the gas price proposed by the sender.
4. **Mining**: The process of mining involves the selection of transactions from the mempool, followed by the creation of a new block through the resolution of a cryptographic problem. The selected transactions are encompassed inside the content of the block.
5. **Execution and Confirmation**: If a smart contract call is made, the transaction's code is performed by every full node in the network. Upon successful completion, the transaction is verified, and subsequently, the Ethereum network undergoes a change in its overall state.
6. **Finality**: Finality is achieved when a transaction is incorporated into a block and subsequently confirmed by the addition of several following blocks, thereby establishing its validity. As the number of confirmations increases, the level of security and irreversibility of the transaction also increases. The user's text contains no information to rewrite.

4.7   Gas and Transaction Fees

Ethereum has garnered substantial acclaim for its comprehensive smart contract capabilities, concurrently drawing much scrutiny for its transaction fees, generally referred to as gas pricing. The expenses linked to Ethereum are widely regarded as an essential component of its ecosystem, and they carry substantial implications for the expansion of the network, its capacity to handle increased workload, and the extent of user engagement.

Gas fees encompass the costs incurred when doing transactions or engaging with smart contracts on the Ethereum network. The process of transmitting ETH or interacting with smart contracts, such as the generation of NFTs or participation in crowdsales, requires the payment of gas fees. The function of gas fees in compensating miners for their contributions to network operations is noteworthy, as they do not provide any advantages to a centralized organization.

4.7.1   Addressing Gas Fees

The core developers of Ethereum are now engaged in resolving the issue of excessive gas prices through a series of continuous improvements, including The Merge (formerly known as Ethereum 2.0 or Eth2.0). These upgrades are designed to improve the efficiency and affordability of transactions on the Ethereum network. The achievement of implementing the PoS algorithm on the Ethereum testnet demonstrates a significant advance in pursuit of these objectives.

4.7.2   Factors Affecting Gas Price

The price of gas in the Ethereum network plays a pivotal role in determining the financial implications associated with the execution of transactions and smart contracts. The phenomenon is subject to the effects of various significant elements.

- **Network Congestion:** The phenomenon of network congestion is a significant issue in the field of computer networking. Elevated levels of network activity and congestion might result in a surge in the need for block space, thereby causing a rise in gas prices. Gas prices can experience substantial increases during periods of high demand, such as when a widely used decentralized finance (DeFi) protocol is introduced or during NFT releases.
- **Gas Limit:** The gas limit is a parameter that determines the maximum amount of computational work that can be performed in a single Ethereum transaction. The cost of gasoline has a direct correlation with the transaction's gas limit. In cases where a transaction necessitates greater computing resources, it will be assigned a higher gas limit and, as a result, a higher gas price. This is done to ensure that miners give priority to including the transaction in a block.
- **Gas Auctions:** Gas auctions are a method of selling and purchasing gas resources through a competitive bidding process. Individuals have the ability to determine the amount they are willing to spend on gas fees when initiating a transaction. Miners exhibit a preference for transactions with elevated gas prices in order to optimize their financial gains. This phenomenon gives rise to a competitive atmosphere in which consumers engage in a bidding process to get expedited transaction processing.
- **Gas Tokenization:** The process of gas tokenization involves converting gas into a digital asset that may be traded or used as a form of payment. Certain applications and protocols have implemented the issuance of gas tokens, which enable users to secure prevailing gas pricing for forthcoming transactions. The process of gas tokenization has the potential to affect gas prices through its influence on the demand for gas at a specific price point.
- **Ethereum Upgrades:** The topic of discussion pertains to the upgrades being made to the Ethereum platform. Modifications to Ethereum's protocol, encompassing alterations to the gas tax framework or enhancements in network performance, have the potential to exert an influence on gas pricing. An instance of this is the implementation of EIP-1559 and the London Hard Fork, which sought to enhance the predictability of gas pricing through the introduction of a foundational cost.
- **Market Speculation:** Market speculation refers to the practice of making predictions or assumptions about future market conditions, particularly in relation to the buying and selling of financial market speculation and the occurrence of external events, which can exert an influence on gas prices as well. The presence of positive emotion and a rise in demand for apps built on the Ethereum platform can potentially lead to an escalation in gas costs. Conversely, negative news or downturns in the market may cause a decrease in gas pricing.

4.7.3   Calculating Gas Costs

The pricing of gas is expressed in gwei, which represents one billionth of the cryptocurrency ETH. The value of gwei within a gas unit experiences fluctuations as a result of changes in supply and demand, thereby influencing transaction costs. Wallet-to-wallet transfers necessitate a lower consumption of gas in comparison to intricate operations that involve smart contracts. The imposition of gas restrictions serves the purpose of guaranteeing the precision of transactions.The Gas consumptions for various ethereum operations are given in Table 4-3.

Table 4-3 Examples of Gas Consumption for Various Ethereum Operations

Operation	Gas Consumption	Description
Wallet-to-wallet transfer	21,000 gas	Basic ETH transfer
Deploying a simple contract	1,000,000 gas	Deploying a minimal smart contract
Sending an ERC-20 token	100,000 gas	Transferring an ERC-20 token
Minting NFT	150,000 gas	Creating new NFT
Interacting with DeFi protocol	2,000,000 gas	Participating in complex DeFi transaction
Playing blockchain game	500,000 gas	Interacting with blockchain-based game
Staking Ethereum	250,000 gas	Locking ETH for staking in preparation for PoS
Calling smart contract function	Variable	Gas consumption depends on function complexity

4.7.4   Gas Fee Calculation

The implementation of the London Hard Fork brought about a more sophisticated method for calculating gas fees. Individuals are required to remit a fundamental charge, which is subsequently eliminated, as well as an additional price to enhance the promptness of transaction processing. The computation of the transaction cost for Ethereum entails the multiplication of the gas units (limit) by the summation of the base and priority fees, resulting in a comprehensive estimation of the cost.

4.7.5   Implications of Base Fee

The introduction of the base fee through the London Hard Fork has significant implications for Ethereum's token economics as it facilitates deflationary dynamics by means of ETH burning. The consequences of this technique have the potential to impact the status of ETH as a store of wealth. Miners, nevertheless, encounter alterations in their revenue framework as a result of the base fee system.

4.7.6   Transaction Cost Predictability

Despite the anticipated decrease in costs following the implementation of the London Hard Fork in the Ethereum network, it is noteworthy that fees have persisted at a very elevated level. Both users and miners have the ability to modify priority fees in order to accelerate transactions, thereby preserving the dynamics of transaction costs. The priority charge structure maintains the ability of miners to exercise selection and promotes competition among users for expedited processing.

4.7.7   Future with PoS

The forthcoming implementation of The Merge, which involves the transfer of Ethereum to a PoS consensus mechanism, is expected to bring about more alterations in transaction fees. The transition of PoS from reliance on computational capacity to the utilization of locked ETH for the purpose of validating transactions is expected to have a significant impact on the dynamics of transaction fees.

4.7.8   Gas Fees and Orchid

During the interim period, several blockchains that are compatible with the EVM have emerged as viable alternatives to mitigate the issue of high gas prices associated with Ethereum. The deployment of Orchid across EVM-compatible chains facilitates the provision of decentralized virtual private network services at a lower cost, which creates opportunities for a more inclusive and competitive price framework.

4.7.9   Example 1: Wallet-to-Wallet Transfer

Assuming the intention is to ascertain the gas consumption associated with a fundamental ETH transfer from one wallet to another, let us proceed with the calculation. The gas limit allocated for this particular task is commonly set at 21,000 gas units.

Gas Consumption Formula

The formula to calculate the gas cost for a wallet-to-wallet transfer is

$$\text{Gas Cost} = \text{Gas Price} \times \text{Gas Limit},$$

where

$$\text{Gas Price} = \text{cost per gas unit in gwei},$$
$$\text{Gas Limit} = \text{number of gas units required for the operation}.$$

Let us assume the gas price is 50 gwei.

Gas Consumption Calculation

Given the gas limit for a wallet-to-wallet transfer is 21,000 and the gas price is 50 gwei, the gas cost is

$$\text{Gas Cost} = 50 \, \text{gwei} \times 21,000 \, \text{gas units} = 1,050,000 \, \text{gwei}.$$

4.7.10 Example 2: Deploying a Simple Contract

Let us calculate the gas consumption for deploying a simple smart contract. Suppose the gas limit required for this deployment is 1,000,000 gas units.

Gas Consumption Formula

The formula to calculate the gas cost for deploying a contract is the same as above:

$$\text{Gas Cost} = \text{Gas Price} \times \text{Gas Limit},$$

assuming a gas price of 80 gwei.

Gas Consumption Calculation

With a gas limit of 1,000,000 and a gas price of 80 gwei, the gas cost becomes

$$\text{Gas Cost} = 80\,\text{gwei} \times 1,000,000\,\text{gas units} = 80,000,000\,\text{gwei}.$$

4.7.11 Avoiding Ethereum Gas Fees

Outlined below are many strategies that can be employed to mitigate the impact of gas fees:

1. Optimize the transaction timing.
   The price of Ethereum's gas exhibits significant volatility over the course of a given day. It is worth noting that the price of gasoline often experiences a significant decrease within a few hours following a purchase. There is also the possibility of the opposite occurring. This phenomenon has the potential to induce cognitive dissonance among traders. In such circumstances, it is imperative to closely observe and analyze the market. Nevertheless, this process is highly labor-intensive and lacks specificity.
   There are specific periods, such as during late night hours or on weekends, during which it is possible to observe a reduced cost for gasoline. These specific instances present opportune moments for acquiring Ethereum. Furthermore, one can analyze the volatility of Ethereum by examining charts. This tool facilitates the estimation of periods characterized by significantly reduced gasoline prices.
2. Take advantage of rebate offers.
   Numerous applications and websites provide attractive discounts for the acquisition of Ethereum. One such site is Balancer, which provides a reimbursement of up to 90% for Ethereum acquisitions. Efforts are made to decrease the gas prices for traders purchasing Ethereum from their platforms.
   KeeperDao and similar applications use a mechanism wherein gas fees are levied collectively on a group of individuals. This phenomenon is beneficial as it results in a substantial reduction in the gas fees borne by individual dealers. Therefore, one can actively seek out such alternatives in order to effectively mitigate gas fees.
3. Choose transaction type carefully.
   Ethereum encompasses a variety of transactional modalities. Therefore, it can be observed that the gas fees exhibit a dynamic nature, characterized by fluctuations over time. Prior to selecting a transaction type, it is imperative to do a comparative analysis of the gas fees associated with alternative transaction types. This ensures the selection of a transaction that incurs the least amount of gas expenses.
   Nevertheless, it is imperative to take into account additional elements when analyzing the costs associated with gas expenses. When selecting cheap costs, it is advisable to prioritize transaction

security and avoid compromising on it. This is because there are situations where lower prices are correlated with increased risks.

4. Monitor network congestion to avoid delays.

Network congestion is a prevalent issue that cryptocurrency traders frequently encounter while engaging in trading activities. The significance of this matter lies in the fact that even a slight delay in trading might result in swings in prices. Consequently, this can impede the anticipated or expected profitability for a trader in relation to that particular cryptocurrency.

One can engage in constant monitoring of congestion levels and execute trades promptly upon identifying relatively low congestion. One method for accomplishing this task is examining the mempool of a given network. Typically, this space serves as the waiting room for a transaction prior to its finalization.

5. Benefit from gas tokens.

Gas tokens can be utilized by traders to achieve significant savings on miner fees and additional expenses associated with transactions. One can readily acquire gas tokens by removing all variable currency and transactions from storage. When the cost of gas is considerably reduced, the process of mining gas tokens becomes notably straightforward.

Gas tokens can be readily exchanged into ETH during the transaction processing. There exists a potential for acquiring gas tokens as incentives, which can then be utilized to cover gas fees.

6. Calculate payable gas fees beforehand

Multiple gas fee calculators are available for users to compute gas fees in advance. Two examples of platforms that provide information on gas prices are Gas Now and Etherscan's Gas Tracker. These tools are specifically designed to facilitate the prediction of gasoline prices in advance. These solutions offer real-time value, reducing the likelihood of errors. One might readily employ them to ascertain gas fees that are really time-sensitive.

7. Switch to Ethereum 2.0

Ethereum 2.0 represents a notable advancement in comparison to its predecessor, Ethereum, in all aspects. One of the most notable advancements entails the adoption of the PoS mechanism in lieu of the PoW method.

The PoS process entails the automatic selection of a validator based on their possession of a substantial quantity of a specific cryptocurrency. When participating in the competition to become a validator, there is no requirement for the utilization of complex computational or problem-solving tools. Therefore, in the context of Ethereum 2.0 trading, the gas fees imposed are either nonexistent or minimal.

4.8 Laboratory Work

This section shows the implementation of smart contracts using Python.

4.8.1 Solidity Program for Displaying Hello Message

```
pragma solidity ^0.8.17;

contract HelloWorld {
    string public greet = "Hi, Let's get introduced to Solidity";
}
```

```
pragma solidity ^0.8.17;

contract HelloWorld {
    string public greet = "Hi, Let's get introduced to Solidity";
}
```

Explanation of Code

This Solidity smart contract is a simple example of a contract that is commonly used to demonstrate the basic functionality of a programming language or platform. Let us break down the code:

SPDX License Identifier: MIT

This is a special comment that specifies the license under which the code is distributed. In this case, it uses the MIT license, which is a permissive open source license.

Compiler Version Specification

The next line of code specifies the compiler version that should be used to compile this contract. It starts with `pragma solidity`, followed by the caret (^) symbol, and then the version number `0.8.17`. This line ensures that the contract will only compile using a Solidity compiler version that is at least `0.8.17` but under `0.9.0`. This version range restriction is useful for ensuring compatibility and avoiding potential issues when using different compiler versions.

Contract Definition

The main part of the code is the contract definition. It starts with the `contract` keyword, followed by the contract's name, which in this case is "Hi, Let's get introduced to Solidity." This is a very basic contract that has no constructor, functions, or state variables defined. It only has one public state variable:

`string public greet`: This is a public string variable named "greet." The `public` modifier means that this variable can be read from other contracts or externally by anyone. The initial value of the variable is set to "Hi, Let's get introduced to Solidity." This variable will store and expose the greeting message "Hi, Let's get introduced to Solidity."

4.8.2   Program for Demonstrating Simple Increment and Decrement Functions

```
// SPDX-License-Identifier: MIT
pragma solidity ^0.8.17;

contract CounterDemo {
```

```
5    uint public counter;
6
7    // Function to get the current counter
8    function get_Counter() public view returns (uint) {
9        return counter;
10   }
11
12   // Function to increment counter by 1
13   function increment() public {
14       counter += 1;
15   }
16
17   // Function to decrement counter by 1
18   function decrement() public {
19       // This function will fail if counter = 0
20       counter -= 1;
21   }
22 }
```

Explanation of Code

The Solidity smart contract "CounterDemo" is a simple demonstration of a basic counter functionality. The contract starts with a SPDX License Identifier comment specifying the MIT license for the code. It uses Solidity compiler version 0.8.17 or higher. The contract defines a state variable "counter" of type uint (unsigned integer) to keep track of the current count. The contract provides three functions: get_Counter() is a view function that allows anyone to read the current value of the counter. increment() is a public function that increments the counter by 1. decrement() is a public function that decrements the counter by 1, but it will fail if the counter is already at 0. Overall, this contract showcases a basic example of state variables and functions in Solidity.

4.8.3 Smart Contract Development with Solidity

- Setting up a local Ethereum development environment
- Creating a basic smart contract in Solidity
- Compiling and deploying the smart contract to a local test network
- Interacting with the deployed contract using web3.js or ethers.js

Setting Up a Local Ethereum Development Environment

To set up a local Ethereum development environment, you can use tools like `ganache-cli` to create a local Ethereum test network.

```
1  npm install -g ganache-cli
2  ganache-cli
```

Creating a Basic Smart Contract in Solidity

Create a new Solidity file named Counter.sol in the contracts directory.

```solidity
// contracts/Counter.sol
// SPDX-License-Identifier: MIT
pragma solidity ^0.8.0;

contract Counter
    {
    uint256 private count;

    constructor() {
        count = 0;
    }

    function increment() public
    {
        count++;
    }

    function getCount() public view returns (uint256)
    {
        return count;
    }
}
```

Compiling and Deploying the Smart Contract

Initialize a Truffle project, create a deployment migration, and compile the contracts.

```
truffle init
```

Edit the migrations/2_deploy_contracts.js file to include the deployment code.

```javascript
// migrations/2_deploy_contracts.js
const Counter = artifacts.require("Counter");

module.exports = function (deployer) {
  deployer.deploy(Counter);
};
```

Compile the contracts.

```
truffle compile
```

Interacting with the Deployed Contract Using web3.js

Create a JavaScript file named `interact.js` in the project root directory.

```
// interact.js
const Web3 = require("web3");
const web3 = new Web3("http://localhost:8545"); // Update the URL
    ↪ if needed

const abi = require("./build/contracts/Counter.json").abi;
const address = "CONTRACT_ADDRESS"; // Replace with the actual
    ↪ contract address

const contract = new web3.eth.Contract(abi, address);

async function interactWithContract() {
  const initialCount = await contract.methods.getCount().call();
  console.log("Initial Count:", initialCount);

  await contract.methods.increment().send({ from: "
    ↪ YOUR_ACCOUNT_ADDRESS" });

  const updatedCount = await contract.methods.getCount().call();
  console.log("Updated Count:", updatedCount);
}

interactWithContract();
```

Replace `"CONTRACT_ADDRESS"` with the actual contract address and `"YOUR_ACCOUNT _ADDRESS"` with your account address.

Running the Interaction Script

In a terminal window, run the interaction script.

```
node interact.js
```

This script will interact with the deployed smart contract, incrementing the count and displaying the results.

Remember to replace placeholders such as `"CONTRACT_ADDRESS"` and `"YOUR_ACCOUNT_ ADDRESS"` with actual values from your environment.

4.8.4 Implementing Security Measures in Smart Contracts

Identifying and Analyzing Common Vulnerabilities

Start by identifying and analyzing common vulnerabilities in existing smart contracts. This step is crucial to understanding potential security risks.

Implementing Security Measures

Implement security measures to address vulnerabilities in the smart contract. For example, let us consider reentrancy protection and input validation.

Reentrancy Protection
To prevent reentrancy attacks, you can use the `nonReentrant` modifier.

```
// Reentrancy protection modifier
modifier nonReentrant() {
    require(!_reentrant, "Reentrant call detected");
    _reentrant = true;
    _;
    _reentrant = false;
}
```

Input Validation
Implement input validation to ensure that the input data meet certain criteria.

```
// Input validation example
function processPayment(uint256 amount) public {
    require(amount > 0, "Amount must be greater than zero");
    // Process the payment
}
```

Testing the Improved Smart Contract

After implementing security measures, thoroughly test the improved smart contract to demonstrate enhanced security.

Reentrancy Test
Test the reentrancy protection by creating a malicious contract that attempts reentrancy. The protected contract should reject the attack.

```
// Malicious contract for reentrancy attack
contract MaliciousContract {
    function attack(address vulnerableContract) public {
        // Attempt reentrancy attack
        vulnerableContract.call.value(1 ether)("");
    }
}
```

Input Validation Test
Test input validation by providing both valid and invalid inputs to the contract's functions.

```
// Test input validation
```

```
 2 contract TestInputValidation {
 3     function testProcessPayment() public {
 4         // Try valid payment
 5         processPayment(100);
 6
 7         // Try invalid payment
 8         try processPayment(0) {
 9             // Expecting a revert due to input validation
10             revert("Invalid input should trigger revert");
11         } catch Error(string memory) {
12             // Expecting an error
13         } catch {
14             // Catch-all for unexpected errors
15             revert("Unexpected error");
16         }
17     }
18 }
```

Remember that this is a simplified example; real-world security measures and testing would involve more complexity and thoroughness.

4.8.5 Developing an ERC-20 Token

- Designing the contract for an ERC-20 token following the standard specifications
- Implementing token functionalities such as transfer, approve, and transferFrom
- Deploying the ERC-20 token contract to the Ethereum blockchain
- Testing token transactions and interactions using a Web3 interface

Designing the ERC-20 Token Contract

Design a contract for an ERC-20 token following the standard specifications.

```
 1 // ERC-20 Token Contract
 2 pragma solidity ^0.8.0;
 3
 4 contract ERC20Token {
 5     string public name = "MyToken";
 6     string public symbol = "MTK";
 7     uint8 public decimals = 18;
 8     uint256 public totalSupply;
 9
10     mapping(address => uint256) public balanceOf;
11     mapping(address => mapping(address => uint256)) public
      ↪ allowance;
12
```

```
13  event Transfer(address indexed from, address indexed to,
    ↪ uint256 value);
14  event Approval(address indexed owner, address indexed spender
    ↪ , uint256 value);
15
16  constructor(uint256 _initialSupply) {
17      totalSupply = _initialSupply * 10 ** uint256(decimals);
18      balanceOf[msg.sender] = totalSupply;
19  }
20
21  // Implement transfer, approve, and transferFrom functions
22  // ...
23  }
```

Implementing Token Functionalities

Implement token functionalities such as transfer, approve, and transferFrom.

```
1  function transfer(address to, uint256 value) public returns (bool
    ↪ ) {
2      require(to != address(0), "Invalid address");
3      require(balanceOf[msg.sender] >= value, "Insufficient balance
    ↪ ");
4
5      balanceOf[msg.sender] -= value;
6      balanceOf[to] += value;
7
8      emit Transfer(msg.sender, to, value);
9      return true;
10  }
11
12  function approve(address spender, uint256 value) public returns (
    ↪ bool) {
13      allowance[msg.sender][spender] = value;
14      emit Approval(msg.sender, spender, value);
15      return true;
16  }
17
18  function transferFrom(address from, address to, uint256 value)
    ↪ public returns (bool) {
19      require(from != address(0), "Invalid sender address");
20      require(to != address(0), "Invalid recipient address");
21      require(balanceOf[from] >= value, "Insufficient balance");
22      require(allowance[from][msg.sender] >= value, "Allowance
    ↪ exceeded");
23
```

```
24    balanceOf[from] -= value;
25    balanceOf[to] += value;
26    allowance[from][msg.sender] -= value;
27
28    emit Transfer(from, to, value);
29    return true;
30 }
```

Deploying the ERC-20 Token Contract

Deploy the ERC-20 token contract to the Ethereum blockchain using tools like Remix or Truffle.

Testing Token Transactions and Interactions

Test token transactions and interactions using a web3 interface.

```
1  // JavaScript code for testing ERC-20 token interactions
2  const Web3 = require("web3");
3  const web3 = new Web3("http://localhost:8545"); // Update the URL
      ↪ if needed
4
5  const abi = require("./build/contracts/ERC20Token.json").abi;
6  const address = "CONTRACT_ADDRESS"; // Replace with the actual
      ↪ contract address
7
8  const tokenContract = new web3.eth.Contract(abi, address);
9
10 async function testTokenInteractions() {
11     const accounts = await web3.eth.getAccounts();
12     const sender = accounts[0];
13     const recipient = accounts[1];
14
15     const initialBalance = await tokenContract.methods.balanceOf(
      ↪ sender).call();
16     console.log("Initial Balance:", initialBalance);
17
18     // Test transfer function
19     await tokenContract.methods.transfer(recipient, 100).send({
      ↪ from: sender });
20
21     const updatedBalance = await tokenContract.methods.balanceOf(
      ↪ sender).call();
22     console.log("Updated Balance:", updatedBalance);
23
24     // Test approve and transferFrom functions
```

```
25    await tokenContract.methods.approve(recipient, 50).send({
      ↪ from: sender });
26    await tokenContract.methods.transferFrom(sender, recipient,
      ↪ 50).send({ from: recipient });
27
28    const finalBalance = await tokenContract.methods.balanceOf(
      ↪ recipient).call();
29    console.log("Final Balance of Recipient:", finalBalance);
30 }
31
32 testTokenInteractions();
```

Remember to replace `"CONTRACT_ADDRESS"` with the actual contract address in the testing JavaScript code.

4.8.6   Building a Simple DApp

Developing a Basic DApp

Start by developing a basic DApp with a front-end interface using HTML, CSS, and JavaScript.

```
1  <!DOCTYPE html>
2  <html>
3  <head>
4      <title>Simple DApp</title>
5      <!-- Add CSS styling -->
6  </head>
7  <body>
8      <h1>Simple DApp</h1>
9      <button id="incrementBtn">Increment Count</button>
10     <p id="countDisplay">Count: <span id="countValue">0</span></p
       ↪ >
11
12     <script>
13         // JavaScript code for interacting with the smart
       ↪ contract
14     </script>
15 </body>
16 </html>
```

Integrating with a Smart Contract

Integrate the DApp with a smart contract to handle user interactions.

```
1  // JavaScript code to interact with the smart contract
2  const Web3 = require("web3");
```

```
const web3 = new Web3("http://localhost:8545"); // Update the URL
    ↪ if needed

const abi = require("./build/contracts/YourSmartContract.json").
    ↪ abi;
const address = "CONTRACT_ADDRESS"; // Replace with the actual
    ↪ contract address

const contract = new web3.eth.Contract(abi, address);

document.addEventListener("DOMContentLoaded", async () => {
    const incrementBtn = document.getElementById("incrementBtn");
    const countValue = document.getElementById("countValue");

    incrementBtn.addEventListener("click", async () => {
        await contract.methods.increment().send({ from: "
    ↪ YOUR_ACCOUNT_ADDRESS" });

        const updatedCount = await contract.methods.getCount().
    ↪ call();
        countValue.textContent = updatedCount;
    });

    // Update initial count value on page load
    const initialCount = await contract.methods.getCount().call()
    ↪ ;
    countValue.textContent = initialCount;
});
```

Deploying the DApp and the Related Smart Contract

Deploy the DApp and the related smart contract to the Ethereum blockchain using tools like Remix or Truffle.

Testing the DApp's Functionality and Usability

Test the DApp's functionality and usability by interacting with it in a Web3-enabled browser.

4.8.7   Interacting with Off-Chain Data Using Oracles

Understanding Oracles and Their Role

Begin by understanding the concept of oracles and their role in obtaining external data for smart contracts.

Integrating an Oracle Service into a Smart Contract

Integrate an oracle service into a smart contract to fetch off-chain data.

```solidity
// Solidity code to interact with an oracle
pragma solidity ^0.8.0;

interface OracleInterface {
    function getData() external returns (uint256);
}

contract DataConsumer {
    OracleInterface public oracle;
    uint256 public offChainData;

    constructor(address _oracleAddress) {
        oracle = OracleInterface(_oracleAddress);
    }

    function fetchOffChainData() public {
        offChainData = oracle.getData();
    }
}
```

Retrieving Real-World Data through an Oracle

Retrieve real-world data, such as weather information or stock prices, using the implemented oracle.

Implementing a Use Case in a DApp

Implement a use case that leverages off-chain data in a DApp.

```javascript
// JavaScript code for the DApp using off-chain data
const Web3 = require("web3");
const web3 = new Web3("http://localhost:8545"); // Update the URL
    ↪ if needed

const abi = require("./build/contracts/DataConsumer.json"
        ).abi;
const address = "CONTRACT_ADDRESS"; // Replace with the actual
    ↪ contract address

const contract = new web3.eth.Contract(abi, address);

document.addEventListener("DOMContentLoaded", async () => {
    const fetchBtn = document.getElementById("fetchBtn");
```

```
13   const dataDisplay = document.getElementById("dataDisplay");

15   fetchBtn.addEventListener("click", async () => {
16       await contract.methods.fetchOffChainData().send({ from: "
     ↪ YOUR_ACCOUNT_ADDRESS" });

18       const offChainData = await contract.methods.offChainData
     ↪ ().call();
19       dataDisplay.textContent = `Off-Chain Data: ${offChainData
     ↪ }`;
20   });
21 });
```

Remember to replace "CONTRACT_ADDRESS" with the actual contract address and "YOUR_ACCOUNT_ADDRESS" with your account address.

4.8.8   Program to Demonstrate a Basic Example of Smart Contract Interaction and Ownership Management on Ethereum Blockchain

```
1  % SPDX-License-Identifier: MIT
2  pragma solidity >=0.4.22 <0.9.0;

4  contract TokenHolder {
5      % 'TokenCreator' is a contract type defined later.
6      % It's safe to reference without creating a new contract.
7      TokenCreator creatorContract;
8      address tokenHolder;
9      bytes32 tokenName;

11     % Constructor registers the creator and the assigned name.
12     constructor(bytes32 name_) {
13         % State variables are accessed directly by their name.
14         % Functions can be accessed through 'this.f' for external
        ↪ view.
15         tokenHolder = msg.sender;

17         % Explicit type conversion from 'address' to '
        ↪ TokenCreator'.
18         creatorContract = TokenCreator(msg.sender);
19         tokenName = name_;
20     }

22     function renameToken(bytes32 newName) public {
23         % Only the creator can rename the token.
24         if (msg.sender == address(creatorContract))
25             tokenName = newName;
```

```
26      }
27
28      function transferToken(address newHolder) public {
29          % Only the current tokenHolder can transfer the token.
30          if (msg.sender != tokenHolder) return;
31
32          % Call 'isTokenTransferAllowed' from 'TokenCreator'
    ↪ contract.
33          if (creatorContract.isTokenTransferAllowed(
34          tokenHolder, newHolder))
35              tokenHolder = newHolder;
36      }
37  }
38
39  contract TokenCreator {
40      function spawnToken(bytes32 name)
41          public
42          returns (TokenHolder tokenAddress)
43      {
44          % Create a new 'TokenHolder' contract and return its
    ↪ address.
45          return new TokenHolder(name);
46      }
47
48      function updateTokenName(TokenHolder tokenAddress, bytes32
    ↪ name) public {
49          % Change the name of a token held by 'tokenAddress'.
50          tokenAddress.renameToken(name);
51      }
52
53      % Check if transferring a token to 'TokenHolder' is allowed.
54      function isTokenTransferAllowed(address currentHolder,
    ↪ address newHolder)
55          public
56          pure
57          returns (bool allowed)
58      {
59          % Check a condition to determine if transfer should
    ↪ proceed.
60          return keccak256(abi.encodePacked(currentHolder,
    ↪ newHolder))[0] == 0x7f;
61      }
62  }
```

Sample Input and Output

```
 1  % Input: Deploy TokenCreator contract, create a token, rename it,
       ↪  and transfer ownership.
 2  Deploy TokenCreator contract.
 3
 4  % Create a token holder using TokenCreator contract.
 5  Create TokenHolder "Alice" using TokenCreator.
 6
 7  % Rename the token held by Alice.
 8  Rename token to "NewTokenName".
 9
10  % Transfer ownership of the token from Alice to Bob.
11  Transfer token ownership to address "0x1234567890abcdef" (Bob's
       ↪  address).
12
13  % Output: Token ownership and name changes are reflected in the
       ↪  blockchain.
14  TokenHolder "Alice" now holds token "NewTokenName".
15  Token ownership transferred to address "0x1234567890abcdef" (Bob'
       ↪  s address).
```

Explanation of Code

This code demonstrates a fundamental example of smart contract interaction and ownership administration on the Ethereum blockchain using the Solidity programming language. The code presents a straightforward token system in which tokens can be created, possessed, renamed, and transferred between holders. The TokenHolder contract denotes token ownership and management, whereas the TokenCreator contract permits the creation of new token holders and enforces rules for token transfers. The code demonstrates concepts such as contract deployment, function invocation, conditional tests, and contract interaction. It functions as an instructional example for understanding how smart contracts can implement decentralized ownership and interaction logic.

4.8.9 Program to Create a Decentralized Blind Auction Smart Contract on the Ethereum Blockchain, Enabling Participants to Place Concealed Bids, Reveal Them, and Determine the Highest Bidder While Ensuring Secure Fund Management and Transparent Auction Outcomes. This Contract Facilitates a Trustless and Tamper-Resistant Auction Mechanism, Promoting Fairness and Efficiency in Auction Processes

```
 1  % SPDX-License-Identifier: MIT
 2  pragma solidity ^0.8.4;
 3
 4  contract ConfidentialBid {
```

```
  5   struct Offer {
  6       bytes32 hiddenValue;
  7       uint depositAmount;
  8   }
  9
 10   address payable public recipient;
 11   uint public offerStart;
 12   uint public revealStart;
 13   bool public finished;
 14
 15   mapping(address => Offer[]) public offers;
 16
 17   address public winningBidder;
 18   uint public highestOffer;
 19
 20   % Permissible withdrawals of previous offers
 21   mapping(address => uint) refunds;
 22
 23   event AuctionConcluded(address victor, uint highestOffer);
 24
 25   % Failures are described as errors.
 26
 27   % The function has been called prematurely.
 28   % Please retry after 'time'.
 29   error PrematureCall(uint time);
 30   % The function has been called too late.
 31   % It's beyond 'time'.
 32   error LateCall(uint time);
 33   % The auctionEnd function has already been invoked.
 34   error AuctionEndAlreadyInvoked();
 35
 36   % Modifiers are convenient for validating inputs to
 37   % functions. 'onlyBefore' is used with 'placeOffer' below:
 38   % The modifier's body replaces '_' with the original function
 ↪    body.
 39   modifier onlyBefore(uint time) {
 40       if (block.timestamp >= time) revert LateCall(time);
 41       _;
 42   }
 43   modifier onlyAfter(uint time) {
 44       if (block.timestamp <= time) revert PrematureCall(time);
 45       _;
 46   }
 47
 48   constructor(
 49       uint offeringDuration,
 50       uint revealingDuration,
```

```
51        address payable recipientAddress
52    ) {
53        recipient = recipientAddress;
54        offerStart = block.timestamp + offeringDuration;
55        revealStart = offerStart + revealingDuration;
56    }
57
58    % Place a concealed offer using `hiddenValue` =
59    % keccak256(abi.encodePacked(value, fake, secret)).
60    % The sent ether is refunded only if the offer is correctly
61    % disclosed during the revealing phase. The offer is valid if
62    % the ether sent with the offer is at least "value" and "fake
↪ "
63    % is false. Setting "fake" to true and not sending the exact
64    % amount are ways to hide the true offer while fulfilling
65    % the required deposit. Multiple offers can be placed by
66    % the same address.
67    function placeOffer(bytes32 hiddenValue)
68        external
69        payable
70        onlyBefore(offerStart)
71    {
72        offers[msg.sender].push(Offer({
73            hiddenValue: hiddenValue,
74            depositAmount: msg.value
75        }));
76    }
77
78    % Reveal concealed offers. Refunds are provided for all
79    % correctly revealed invalid offers except for the highest.
80    function disclose(
81        uint[] calldata values,
82        bool[] calldata fakes,
83        bytes32[] calldata secrets
84    )
85        external
86        onlyAfter(offerStart)
87        onlyBefore(revealStart)
88    {
89        uint numOffers = offers[msg.sender].length;
90        require(values.length == numOffers);
91        require(fakes.length == numOffers);
92        require(secrets.length == numOffers);
93
94        uint refundAmount;
95        for (uint i = 0; i < numOffers; i++) {
96            Offer storage offerToCheck = offers[msg.sender][i];
```

```
        (uint value, bool fake, bytes32 secret) =
            (values[i], fakes[i], secrets[i]);
        if (offerToCheck.hiddenValue != keccak256(abi.
↪ encodePacked(value, fake, secret))) {
            % Offer wasn't truly revealed. Deposit isn't
↪ refunded.
            continue;
        }
        refundAmount += offerToCheck.depositAmount;
        if (!fake && offerToCheck.depositAmount >= value) {
            if (submitOffer(msg.sender, value))
                refundAmount -= value;
        }
        % Prevent sender from reclaiming the same deposit.
        offerToCheck.hiddenValue = bytes32(0);
    }
    payable(msg.sender).transfer(refundAmount);
}

% Withdraw an offer that has been outbid.
function retract() external {
    uint amount = refunds[msg.sender];
    if (amount > 0) {
        % Setting to zero is crucial because the receiver
        % can invoke this function again as part of the
        % receiving call before `transfer` completes.
        refunds[msg.sender] = 0;

        payable(msg.sender).transfer(amount);
    }
}

% Conclude the auction and send the highest offer
% to the recipient.
function auctionEnd()
    external
    onlyAfter(revealStart)
{
    if (finished) revert AuctionEndAlreadyInvoked();
    emit AuctionConcluded(winningBidder, highestOffer);
    finished = true;
    recipient.transfer(highestOffer);
}

% This function is "internal," accessible only within
% the contract (or derived contracts).
function submitOffer(address bidder, uint value) internal
```

```
142    returns (bool successful)
143  {
144     if (value <= highestOffer) {
145        return false;
146     }
147     if (winningBidder != address(0)) {
148        % Refund the prior highest bidder.
149        refunds[winningBidder] += highestOffer;
150     }
151     highestOffer = value;
152     winningBidder = bidder;
153     return true;
154  }
155 }
```

Sample Input and Output

```
1  % Input: Deploy ConfidentialBid contract, place offers, reveal,
        ↪ and conclude auction.
2  Deploy ConfidentialBid contract.
3
4  % Place concealed offers by participants.
5  Place offer with concealed value "0xabcdef" and deposit 5 ether.
6  Place offer with concealed value "0x123456" and deposit 7 ether.
7
8  % Reveal concealed offers during the revealing phase.
9  Reveal offer values [5, 7], fake flags [false, false], and
        ↪ secrets ["0x7890", "0x5678"].
10
11 % Output: Auction concludes, highest offer is sent to the
        ↪ recipient.
12 Auction concluded. Winning bidder: Address of winning bidder.
        ↪ Highest offer: 7 ether.
```

Explanation of Code

On the Ethereum blockchain, the provided Solidity code implements a decentralized blind auction smart contract. The contract permits participants to submit hidden bids during an offering phase, followed by a disclosing phase in which bids are revealed. Bids are camouflaged using cryptographic hashes, and valid revealed bids are refunded. The contract ensures that only valid bids with adequate funding are considered, and it keeps track of the highest bidder and offer. After the conclusion of the revealing phase, the auction can be concluded by transferring the highest offer to a designated recipient. This code establishes a secure and transparent mechanism for conducting trustless blind auctions, thereby promoting auction process fairness and efficiency.

4.8.10 Program to Showcase the Vulnerability of Reentrancy Attacks in a Smart Contract Context and Demonstrate the Implementation of a Solution Using a Reentrancy Guard

```solidity
% SPDX-License-Identifier: GPL-3.0
pragma solidity ^0.8.0;

/**
    Exploitation of a contract function through multiple calls,
    circumventing its intended single use.
 */
contract CryptoVault {

    mapping(address => uint256) public coinBalances;

    function depositCoins() public payable {
        coinBalances[msg.sender] += msg.value;
    }

    % The withdraw function susceptible to re-entrancy attacks
    function retrieveCoins() public {
        uint256 coinsStored = coinBalances[msg.sender];
        require(coinsStored > 0, "insufficient balance");
        (bool success, ) = msg.sender.call{value: coinsStored
    ↪ }("");
        require(success, "retrieval failed");
        coinBalances[msg.sender] = 0;
    }

    function getCoinBalance() public view returns (uint256) {
        return address(this).balance;
    }
}

contract ExploitContract {

    CryptoVault public vault;

    constructor(address _vaultContract) {
        vault = CryptoVault(_vaultContract);
    }

    % The fallback function attempts re-entrancy if the vault
    ↪ holds a minimum balance
    receive() external payable {
        if (address(vault).balance >= 1 ether) {
            vault.retrieveCoins();
```

```
42            }
43        }
44
45        function initiateExploit() external payable {
46            require(msg.value >= 1 ether);
47            vault.depositCoins{value: 1 ether}();
48            vault.retrieveCoins();
49        }
50
51        function getBalance() public view returns (uint256) {
52            return address(this).balance;
53        }
54
55    }
56
57    % Solution: 1) Zeroing balance before function call 2)
        ↪ Implementation of Re-Entrancy Guard
58    % Example: https://github.com/OpenZeppelin
59    /openzeppelin-contracts/blob/v4.5.0/
60    contracts/security/ReentrancyGuard.sol
61
62    contract ReEntrancyProtection {
63
64        bool internal lock;
65
66        modifier noReEntrancy() {
67            require(!lock, "No re-entrancy");
68            lock = true;
69            _;
70            lock = false;
71        }
72    }
```

Sample Input and Output

```
1  % Input: Deploy CryptoVault and ExploitContract, initiate attack
2  Deploy CryptoVault contract.
3
4  % Deposit coins into CryptoVault.
5  Deposit 10 Ether into CryptoVault.
6
7  % Initiate the exploit by deploying ExploitContract.
8  Deploy ExploitContract and link it to CryptoVault.
9
10 % Trigger the exploit attack.
```

```
11  Send 1 Ether to ExploitContract's receive() function.
12  Call ExploitContract's initiateExploit() function.
13
14  % Output: Demonstration of re-entrancy attack and its prevention
15  Attack: ExploitContract repeatedly withdraws Ether from
        ↪ CryptoVault due to vulnerability.
16  Solution: ReEntrancyProtection prevents further attacks by
        ↪ guarding against re-entrancy.
```

Explanation of Code

This code in Solidity serves as an illustration of reentrancy attacks in smart contracts and proposes a remedy by implementing a reentrancy protection mechanism. The scenario presented involves a simulated contract called CryptoVault that allows users to deposit and withdraw coins. However, this contract exhibits a vulnerability wherein attackers can exploit malicious reentrant calls to repeatedly withdraw cash. The vulnerability is exemplified by the ExploitContract contract, which attempts to exploit the CryptoVault. In response to this issue, the code incorporates the ReEntrancyProtection contract, which employs a reentrancy guard to mitigate these attacks by imposing limitations on recursive function invocations. In general, the code underscores the significance of protecting against reentrancy vulnerabilities and demonstrates a way to mitigate them by implementing preventive measures.

4.9   Mist Browser

The Mist Browser is a web browser specifically designed for the Ethereum blockchain. It allows users to access and interact with DApps built on the Ethereum network. With Mist Browser, users can securely manage their Ethereum accounts, view smart contracts, and execute transactions directly from the browser interface. It provides a user-friendly experience by simplifying the process of navigating and interacting with the decentralized web. Additionally, Mist Browser supports various Ethereum standards like ERC-20 tokens, making it convenient for users.

The advantages of using Mist Browser include its enhanced security features, as it allows users to securely manage their Ethereum accounts and execute transactions directly from the browser interface. It also provides a user-friendly experience by simplifying the process of navigating and interacting with DApps. Additionally, Mist Browser supports various Ethereum standards like ERC-20 tokens, making it convenient for users to access and manage their digital assets.

4.9.1   Guidlines for Using Mist Browser

To use the Mist browser, you can start by downloading and installing it on your device. Once installed, open the browser to see a user-friendly interface. From there you can navigate through websites by typing the URL in the search bar or by clicking on bookmarks and links. Additionally, you can customize your browsing experience by adjusting settings such as privacy preferences and appearance.

The Mist browser was designed with the purpose of serving as an essential component within the ecosystem of DApps on the Ethereum network. The initial graphical user interface (GUI) provided users with the ability to access the blockchain, which was previously only accessible through the command line interface. The developers aimed to provide a comprehensive platform for the operation and implementation of diverse Ethereum apps and projects.

Regrettably, technological limitations at that time rendered the fulfillment of the technical prerequisites for a completely decentralized app browser system unattainable. Consequently, the Mist browser project was discontinued, leading to the removal of the software from circulation in March 2019. One possible way to rewrite the user's text to be more academic is to acquire further knowledge pertaining to the Mist browser and the objectives pursued by its developers.

4.9.2   Mist and Geth

Mist is a GUI application that provides an easy-to-use interface for interacting with the Ethereum blockchain and managing Ethereum accounts. Geth, short for "Go Ethereum," is one of the official implementations of the Ethereum client software. It is the software responsible for participating in the Ethereum network, validating transactions, and maintaining a copy of the Ethereum blockchain.

4.9.3   Geth's Role

Geth plays a crucial role in the Ethereum network. It operates as a full Ethereum node, which means it connects to other nodes on the Ethereum network to send and receive transactions and blocks. It also synchronizes with the Ethereum blockchain by downloading and processing all the data stored on the blockchain. Apart from this, it also validates transactions and smart contracts, ensuring the integrity of the network. It also provides an interface for developers and users to interact with the Ethereum network using command-line instructions and JSON-RPC API.

4.10   Summary

This chapter presented a comprehensive examination of the Ethereum blockchain, emphasizing its fundamental characteristics and the Ethereum Virtual Machine (EVM). The chapter delved into the historical progression of Ethereum's development, tracing its evolution from a ledger-based system to a state machine. Additionally, it examined the underlying structure of the Ethereum network. The chapter also gave an introduction to the notion of smart contracts, highlighting the challenges associated with their implementation. Additionally, it provided an overview of the Solidity programming language. The chapter also explored Ethereum transactions, encompassing the life cycle of transactions and the computation of gas fees. The chapter further examined the various factors that influence the fluctuation of gas prices in the market. Additionally, it explored the potential consequences of implementing base fees and analyzed the anticipated shift toward Ethereum 2.0's PoS mechanism in the future. In the final section, the chapter will conclude by presenting a series of practical laboratory experiments that encompass several subjects, including the establishment of smart contracts, implementation of security measures, utilization of ERC-20 tokens, creation of DApps, and the interaction with off-chain data through the utilization of oracles.

The chapter delved into many facets of Ethereum's architecture, transactions, and development tools, offering readers a thorough comprehension of the Ethereum ecosystem and its underlying mechanisms. In addition, the usefulness of Mist Browser was described. Moreover, the incorporation of practical, experiential experiments serves to augment the educational process by facilitating the application of academic principles to tangible, real-life situations.

4.11   Exercise

This section gives exercises based on topics covered in the chapter.

4.11.1 Multiple Choice Questions

1. What is the primary purpose of gas fees in the Ethereum network?
   a. To generate profits for Ethereum Inc.
   b. To fund development of Ethereum software
   c. To compensate miners for network resources
   d. To cover transaction validation costs
2. Which Ethereum development tool provides a local blockchain environment for testing smart contracts and DApps?
   a. Ganache
   b. Truffle
   c. Remix IDE
   d. Metamask
3. In Ethereum, what is the main benefit of using gas tokens?
   a. They provide a discount on Ethereum purchases.
   b. They are used to increase transaction security.
   c. They reduce the amount of gas needed for transactions.
   d. They are a form of cryptocurrency for gas payments.
4. What type of mechanism does Ethereum 2.0 use for transaction validation?
   a. Proof of work (PoW)
   b. Proof of stake (PoS)
   c. Proof of concept (PoC)
   d. Proof of authority (PoA)
5. Which Ethereum transaction type is associated with minting NFTs?
   a. Wallet-to-wallet transfer
   b. Deploying a simple contract
   c. Sending an ERC-20 token
   d. Minting NFTs
6. What is the primary function of the base fee introduced in Ethereum's London Hard Fork?
   a. It provides rewards to miners for transaction processing.
   b. It ensures that transactions are processed quickly.
   c. It helps stabilize gas prices during network congestion.
   d. It limits the total supply of ETH in circulation.
7. Which Ethereum development tool is specifically designed for smart contract development and provides a Solidity code editor?
   a. Ganache
   b. Truffle

    c. Remix IDE

    d. Metamask

8. What is the smallest unit of measurement in the Ethereum ecosystem?

    a. Wei

    b. Gwei

    c. Ether

    d. Nano

9. How are gas prices quoted in Ethereum?

    a. In Ethereum units (ETH)

    b. In Gwei

    c. In Bitcoin (BTC)

    d. In USD

10. When is the use of priority fees advantageous in Ethereum transactions?

    a. When gas prices are at their lowest

    b. When network congestion is high

    c. When sending a large amount of ETH

    d. When using a gas token

4.11.2 Long Answer Questions

1. Explain the concept of gas fees in the Ethereum network. How are gas fees calculated, and what is their significance in the context of Ethereum transactions? Discuss the role of miners and the purpose of gas fees in maintaining the network's functionality. Provide examples of different types of transactions and how their gas costs are determined.

2. Describe the transition from Ethereum 1.0 to Ethereum 2.0. What are the key differences between the proof-of-work (PoW) mechanism used in Ethereum 1.0 and the proof-of-stake (PoS) mechanism in Ethereum 2.0? How does this transition impact gas fees, transaction validation, and overall network efficiency?

3. Explain the factors that affect gas prices in the Ethereum network. Discuss how supply and demand, network congestion, and transaction type influence gas prices. Provide insights into how users can optimize their gas fees by choosing the right transaction timing and type.

4. Discuss the challenges and implications of high gas fees in the Ethereum ecosystem. How do high gas fees impact user experience, hinder adoption, and limit scalability? Explore the approaches and solutions that developers and users can implement to mitigate the effects of gas fees and enhance the overall usability of Ethereum-based applications.

5. Provide a comprehensive overview of Ethereum development tools. Explain the role of tools like Truffle, Remix IDE, Ganache, and Infura in the development life cycle of Ethereum applications. Discuss how these tools aid in smart contract creation, testing, deployment, and interaction with the Ethereum blockchain. Highlight the benefits and use cases of each tool.

6. Examine the concept of gas tokens and their significance in reducing gas fees for Ethereum transactions. How do gas tokens work, and how can users benefit from using them? Discuss the process of earning and redeeming gas tokens, and provide examples of scenarios where gas tokens can be particularly advantageous for users.

7. Dive into the Ethereum transaction life cycle, from initiation to confirmation. Explain each step involved in a typical Ethereum transaction, including nonce generation, gas price estimation, and contract execution. Discuss how miners select transactions to include in a block and how the transaction confirmation process ensures the integrity of the Ethereum blockchain.

8. Explore the historical development of Ethereum, from its early stages to its current state. Highlight key milestones, such as the transition from a ledger-based system to a state machine and the introduction of major upgrades like the London Hard Fork. Discuss the challenges and breakthroughs that have shaped Ethereum's evolution and contributed to its position as a leading blockchain platform.

9. Describe the role and importance of smart contracts in the Ethereum ecosystem. Explain how smart contracts are created, deployed, and executed on the Ethereum blockchain. Provide examples of real-world use cases for smart contracts, such as decentralized finance (DeFi) applications, nonfungible tokens (NFTs), and decentralized applications (DApps). Discuss the benefits and challenges of using smart contracts.

10. Discuss the implications of Ethereum's gas fee structure on the user experience and adoption of blockchain technology. Analyze the factors that contribute to the volatility of gas prices and their impact on users' willingness to participate in Ethereum-based activities. Explore potential strategies and innovations that could address the challenges posed by gas fees and create a more user-friendly environment for blockchain users.

Hyperledger

5

Hyperledger is an open-source community focused on developing enterprise-grade blockchain frameworks and tools. It aims to enable organizations to build and deploy robust, scalable, and secure blockchain solutions for various industries. With a strong emphasis on privacy, performance, and interoperability, Hyperledger offers a range of modular platforms that can be customized to meet specific business needs. By providing a collaborative environment for developers, Hyperledger fosters innovation and accelerates the adoption of blockchain technology in the corporate world.

5.1   Introduction to Hyperledger

Hyperledger is an open-source initiative that operates within the auspices of the Linux Foundation, offering a robust framework for the development of various use cases pertaining to blockchain technology. According to Brian Behlendorf, the executive director of Hyperledger, the organization can be characterized as a collective of communities with a shared goal on exploring and implementing blockchain applications within many industrial domains. This section provides an overview of the objectives and benefits associated with the utilization of Hyperledger.

5.1.1   The Purpose of Hyperledger

Hyperledger provides a robust and tailored blockchain infrastructure that facilitates the creation and maintenance of decentralized ledgers, ensuring enhanced security and individualized functionality. The provision of secrecy in transactions is very important, particularly in situations involving sensitive information, such as medical data. In contrast to public blockchains, Hyperledger facilitates the establishment of direct connections among transaction participants, thereby guaranteeing anonymity and confidentiality. The significant achievement in the progression of Hyperledger is presented in Table 5-1.

© The Author(s), under exclusive license to APress Media, LLC, part of Springer Nature 2024   167
R. S. Mangrulkar, P. Vijay Chavan, *Blockchain Essentials*,
https://doi.org/10.1007/978-1-4842-9975-3_5

Table 5-1 Milestones in the History of Hyperledger Development

Sr. No.	Milestone	Important Development
1	Inception of Hyperledger	Creation of Hyperledger project under Linux Foundation, fostering collaboration and innovation in blockchain technology
2	Introduction of Hyperledger Fabric	Launch of Hyperledger Fabric, a modular framework for enterprise-grade blockchain applications with smart contracts and privacy channels
3	Hyperledger Sawtooth Release	Release of Hyperledger Sawtooth, introducing a unique consensus algorithm framework focused on simplicity and modularity
4	Hyperledger Composer Contribution	Contribution of Hyperledger Composer, providing an intuitive way to define and deploy blockchain business networks
5	Hyperledger Indy for Decentralized Identity	Introduction of Hyperledger Indy, addressing decentralized identity solutions with tools and libraries for self-sovereign digital identities
6	Hyperledger Burrow and Smart Contracts	Inclusion of Hyperledger Burrow, adding support for Ethereum smart contracts and compatibility with existing Ethereum tools
7	Hyperledger Caliper for Benchmarking	Introduction of Hyperledger Caliper, a benchmarking tool to measure and analyze blockchain performance
8	Hyperledger Avalon and TEEs	Development of Hyperledger Avalon with Trusted Execution Environments (TEEs) for enhanced privacy and security in off-chain processing
9	Expansion of Hyperledger Ecosystem	Continuous expansion of the Hyperledger ecosystem with various projects and tools catering to diverse use cases and industry requirements
10	Continued Collaboration and Innovation	A history marked by ongoing collaboration, innovation, and active involvement of developers, researchers, and industry leaders in the Hyperledger community

5.2   Hyperledger Architecture

The architecture of Hyperledger is organized into three distinct layers: the infrastructure layer, framework layer, and tool layer. This tiered structure establishes a resilient ecosystem that supports the development of blockchain solutions. The architectural design includes a range of services that are implemented to enhance the security and efficiency of transaction processing, consensus processes, and data management. The services in the Hyperledger architecture is given in Figure 5-1.

5.2.1   Infrastructure Layer

The infrastructure layer is a crucial component of the overall system architecture.

The foundational layer encompasses the fundamental components of the Hyperledger ecosystem. The aforementioned technology serves as the foundational framework for the creation, administration, and implementation of blockchain systems. The infrastructure layer encompasses the various components that form the foundation of a system or network.

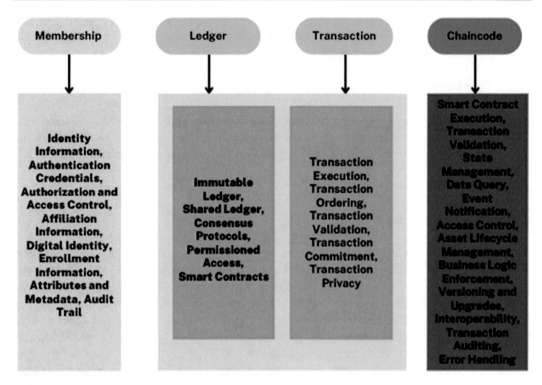

Figure 5-1 Various services in Hyperledger architecture

- **Consensus Layer:** This layer functions as the central component of the platform, carrying out the necessary business logic for the handling of transactions. The implementation of this mechanism guarantees the precision and appropriate management of both transactions and blocks.
- **Smart Contract Layer (Chaincode):** The smart contract layer, often known as chaincode, is a fundamental component of blockchain technology. The validation of transaction requests in the smart contract layer is accomplished by the execution of business logic that is defined within the Chaincode functions. Transaction states are processed and managed in a manner that is of utmost importance.
- **Communications/Protocol Layer:** In networking systems, the communications/protocol layer is an essential component. Its primary function is to oversee the transmission of data between various devices or This layer facilitates the transmission of data between network elements via a peer-to-peer communication protocol. The system is responsible for supervising the transmission of messages necessary for transaction execution and maintaining the shared ledger.

5.2.2   Framework Layer

The framework layer pertains to the conceptual structure that serves as the foundation for a specific application or system. It includes the foundational elements.

The framework layer comprises blockchain frameworks tailored to the needs of specific businesses, which aid in the development of customized blockchain applications. The platform provides an extensive selection of libraries and tools for the development of blockchain solutions that are tailored to a variety of use cases. This stratum is composed of Hyperledger Fabric, Hyperledger Indy, Hyperledger Iroha, and Hyperledger Sawtooth, among other frameworks.

5.2.3   Tool Layer

The tool layer encompasses a range of accelerators and utilities that serve to augment the development and administration of blockchain applications constructed utilizing the framework layer. The platform offers supplementary features and resources to enhance the efficiency of integrating blockchain technology.

Additional Components

- **Data Layer:** The data layer is tasked with managing many data-related functions, including but not limited to enhancing transactions, preserving audit trails, and securely storing data through the utilization of cryptographic techniques. The root of trust in the blockchain instance is established.
- **Identity Services Layer:** The identity services layer is a crucial component in the overall system architecture. An individual oversees the administration of membership registration services, with the primary objective of guaranteeing the implementation of robust protocols for authorizing and authenticating member access across various network nodes.
- **API Layer:** As a component of a software system, the application programming interface (API) layer offers a collection of protocols and interfaces that facilitate communication with other software services or components. This system improves the efficacy of service interfaces for external frameworks and tools by serving as an intermediary between them. On the blockchain network, the system oversees synchronous communication for both transmitting and receiving requests and responses.
- **Policy Services Layer:** The policy services layer is a crucial component inside the system architecture. The blockchain platform ensures the implementation of governance rules and corporate policies.

5.3   Hyperledger Community and Development

The open-source Hyperledger development community is governed by the Hyperledger Architecture Working Group. This group fosters collaboration among community members and architects to develop the ecosystem and implement underlying frameworks. Consensus mechanisms, crucial for blockchain operation, are determined based on use case requirements and can vary among Hyperledger projects like Fabric, Indy, Iroha, and Sawtooth.

5.4   Hyperledger Smart Contracts (Chaincode)

Chaincode, also known as smart contracts, forms a vital component within the Hyperledger architecture. It manages transaction states and associated business processing functions. Chaincode defines how transactions are executed, processed, and updated, playing a key role in enabling modular and scalable blockchain architecture.

With a container-based architecture, Hyperledger ensures the deployment of scalable and high-performance solutions. Chaincode serves as the central implementation of transaction handling, encompassing logic execution, processing states, and interaction with the API layer for application handling.

5.5   The Functioning of Hyperledger

Hyperledger facilitates the establishment of contract prerequisites by means of apps. The membership service is responsible for verifying contracts, while the participating peers generate identical outcomes that are transmitted to the consensus cloud. Following the process of validation, the ledgers associated with the attached peers undergo updates, ensuring the maintenance of confidentiality. This method can be effectively demonstrated by a practical example.

5.5.1   Contributor

Committees are responsible for adding verified transactions to designated ledgers, thereby guaranteeing the precision of data.

5.5.2   Endorser

The designation "endorser" pertains to a public supporter or promoter of a particular individual or organization. By simulating transactions that are unique to the network, endorsers reduce the likelihood of erroneous activities occurring. They perform an essential role in maintaining the integrity of the blockchain.

5.5.3   Consenter

The term "consenter" refers to an individual who gives their consent or approval. The process of transaction validation involves consenters confirming the outcomes of transactions by cross-referencing them with information provided by other participants, thereby establishing the ledger entries that have been officially committed. All these roles are depicted in Figure 5-2.

5.5.4   Example

Let us comprehend the concept with the aid of an illustration given in Algorithm 1 and also simplified in Figure 5-3.

5.5.5   Advantages of Hyperledger

Hyperledger provides a number of benefits that make it appropriate for enterprise applications.

- Flexibility
  Hyperledger offers a modifiable and modular platform that can be customized to the specific requirements of a business.

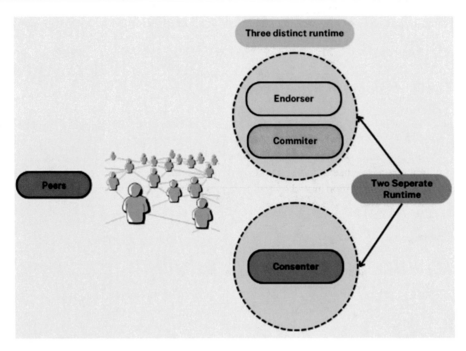

Figure 5-2 Roles and runtime

Algorithm 1 Hyperledger Transaction Process
___
1: Alice decides to send a product to Bob on a Hyperledger-based network.
2: Alice locates Bob's address on the network using her app.
3: The app queries the membership service to validate Bob's membership.
4: Hyperledger connects Alice and Bob directly for the transaction.
5: Both Alice and Bob generate transaction results.
6: The generated results from Alice and Bob must match to validate the transaction.
7: The matched result is sent to the consensus cloud for ordering and verification.
8: Once verified, the result is committed to the ledger.
9: Bob receives the product as the transaction is completed successfully.

- Security
  Hyperledger prioritizes security by integrating access control, identity management, and encryption capabilities for robust protection.
- Scalability
  Hyperledger was designed for large-scale applications and efficiently supports high transaction volumes.
- Privacy
  Hyperledger enables the development of private, permissioned blockchain networks, assuring the privacy of sensitive data.
- Interoperability
  The Hyperledger common platform simplifies system and application integration.

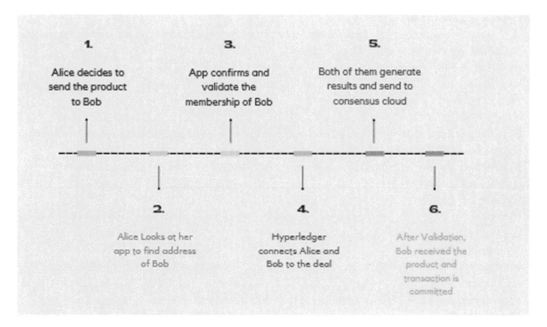

Figure 5-3 Summary of overall process

5.5.6 Limitations of Hyperledger

Hyperledger offers a number of advantages, but there are also limitations to consider.

- Complexity
  Installation and maintenance of Hyperledger can be difficult, requiring technical expertise and resources.
- Limited Decentralization
  The permissioned nature of Hyperledger restricts participation, resulting in less decentralization than public blockchains.
- Limited Community
  While Hyperledger's community is expanding, it may be smaller than that of other platforms, which could impair support availability.
- Limited Smart Contract Functionality
  The smart contract capabilities of Hyperledger are more limited than those of other blockchain platforms.

5.6   Hyperledger Projects

This section introduces various projects within the Hyperledger ecosystem.

- Hyperledger Fabric
  Hyperledger Fabric serves as a foundation for modular applications, offering benefits like permissioned networks and confidential transactions.

- Hyperledger Sawtooth
  Hyperledger Sawtooth is an open-source, enterprise-level blockchain system supporting various consensus algorithms.
- Hyperledger Indy
  Hyperledger Indy focuses on decentralized identity and provides libraries and tools for creating such identities.
- Hyperledger Iroha
  Hyperledger Iroha is designed for infrastructure projects requiring distributed ledger technology.
- Hyperledger Burrow
  Hyperledger Burrow executes smart contracts in permissioned blockchains, facilitating cross-industry applications.
- Hyperledger Caliper
  Hyperledger Caliper is a benchmark tool to measure blockchain performance using predefined use cases.
- Hyperledger Cello
  Hyperledger Cello serves as an operational dashboard for efficient blockchain management.
- Hyperledger Explorer
  Hyperledger Explorer is a user-friendly tool to view, query, and interact with blockchain data.
- Hyperledger Besu
  Hyperledger Besu is an Ethereum client suitable for both public and private blockchain networks.

5.6.1   Comparison of Hyperledger with Other Blockchain Frameworks

Table 5-2 provides an overview of the key characteristics of the three examined blockchain frameworks. These characteristics include their specific use case emphasis, the type of blockchain employed, the consensus techniques utilized, the privacy features incorporated, the level of interoperability offered, and the sectors they mostly serve.

Table 5-3 provides a comparative analysis of Hyperledger and Quorum, with a specific emphasis on their respective beginnings, community development, frameworks, privacy features, consensus algorithms, and use cases.

Hyperledger Explorer, a project under the auspices of the Linux Foundation and hosted by Hyperledger, is an open-source software tool specifically designed for the analysis and visualization of data derived from blockchain networks powered by Hyperledger Fabric. The platform offers a web-based interface that facilitates users in effectively accessing, querying, and comprehending data related to blockchain technology.

5.6.1.1 Key Features of Hyperledger Explorer
Hyperledger Explorer provides fundamental functionalities that facilitate the effective monitoring and understanding of processes within a blockchain network. These functionalities include real-time visualization of transaction data, smart contract management, and network status tracking. Additionally, Hyperledger Explorer offers a user-friendly interface that allows users to easily navigate and analyze the blockchain network's activities.

- View transaction history, smart contract details, network nodes, and user data
- Compatibility with different Hyperledger Fabric versions and connections to both single and multiple blockchain networks

Table 5-2 Comparison of Hyperledger with other blockchain frameworks

Aspect	Hyperledger	Ethereum	Corda
Use Case Focus	Enterprise use cases	Public and permissionless use	Financial services and regulated industries
Blockchain Type	Both permissioned and permissionless	Permissionless	Primarily permissioned
Frameworks	Multiple frameworks	Ethereum Virtual Machine (EVM)	Core Corda platform
Consensus Mechanism	Various (depends on framework)	Proof of work (PoW)	Pluggable consensus
Privacy Features	Fine-grained access control	Limited privacy options	Emphasis on transaction privacy
Interoperability	Supports integration with existing systems	Interoperable with other Ethereum-based projects	Emphasizes interoperability
Industries	Wide range beyond finance	Focus on financial applications	Primarily financial and regulated sectors

Table 5-3 Comparison with Quorum

Aspect	Hyperledger	Quorum
Origin	Linux Foundation	J.P. Morgan
Community	Developed under a broader community	Developed by J.P. Morgan
Frameworks	Multiple frameworks available	Private variant of Ethereum
Privacy	Supports privacy and confidentiality	Focuses heavily on transaction privacy
Consensus	Various consensus options available	Permissioned Ethereum-based consensus
Use Cases	Versatile for various industries	Primarily focused on financial applications

- REST API for seamless integration with external programs and devices
- Designed for developers, network administrators, auditors, and business analysts

5.6.1.2 Importance of Hyperledger Explorer

Hyperledger Explorer plays a crucial role in the surveillance, visualization, and analysis of blockchain networks that are built on the Hyperledger Fabric platform. The significance of this phenomenon encompasses several key aspects. First, Hyperledger Explorer provides a comprehensive view of the blockchain network, allowing users to monitor transactions, blocks, and smart contracts in real time. Additionally, it offers advanced analytics and reporting capabilities, enabling stakeholders to gain valuable insights into the network's performance and identify any potential issues or bottlenecks. Its significance includes:

- Effective monitoring and visualization of blockchain networks
- Detailed analysis of transactions, aiding in pattern recognition and fraud detection
- Comprehensive network analysis for performance enhancement
- Ensuring security, compliance, and customization

5.6.1.3 Notable Features of Hyperledger Explorer

Hyperledger Explorer provides a range of functionalities for the purpose of investigating and overseeing Hyperledger Fabric blockchain networks. These functionalities encompass:

- Dashboard providing an overview of network statistics
- Block and transaction explorers for detailed data examination
- Channel and Chaincode viewers for comprehensive network insights
- Real-time monitoring of blocks and transactions
- Customizable user interface for personalized experience
- User and network management functionalities

5.6.1.4 Architecture of Hyperledger Explorer

The architecture of Hyperledger Explorer comprises three key components:

a. User Interface: Offers a user-friendly web-based interface to display and interact with blockchain data.
b. REST API Server: Provides a REST API for communication between clients and the Hyperledger Explorer server.
c. Database: Stores blockchain-related data, supporting LevelDB and CouchDB databases.

5.6.1.5 Step-by-Step Installation of Hyperledger Explorer

To install Hyperledger Explorer, follow these steps:

```
# Step 1: Clone the Hyperledger Explorer Repository
git clone https://github.com/hyperledger/blockchain-explorer.git

# Step 2: Navigate to the Hyperledger Explorer Directory
cd blockchain-explorer

# Step 3: Checkout to the Latest Release (Replace <latest_release> with the
    actual version)
git checkout v<latest_release>

# Step 4: Create Configuration Files
cp config.json.example config.json
cp connection-profile/first-network.json connection-profile/connection-
    profile.json

# Step 5: Configure the Connection Profile
# Edit connection-profile/connection-profile.json as needed

# Step 6: Install Dependencies
npm install

# Step 7: Generate Necessary Certificates
cd app/test
./generateCertificates.sh

# Step 8: Start the Blockchain Network
# Ensure that the blockchain network is running

# Step 9: Start Hyperledger Explorer
./start.sh
```

5.6.1.6 Benefits and Uses of Hyperledger Explorer

Hyperledger Explorer is a powerful tool that offers numerous benefits and uses in the realm of blockchain technology. One of its primary advantages is its ability to provide a comprehensive view of the entire blockchain network, allowing users to easily explore and analyze the data stored on the ledger. This not only enhances transparency but also facilitates effective monitoring and auditing of transactions. Additionally, Hyperledger Explorer enables users to track the progress of smart contracts, ensuring their proper execution and identifying any potential issues or bottlenecks in real time.

Hyperledger Explorer offers numerous benefits, including:

- Enhanced network visibility and monitoring
- Detailed transaction analysis for improved performance and security
- Smart contract development and testing
- Effective network management and business intelligence

5.6.1.7 Limitations of Hyperledger Explorer

Hyperledger Explorer has certain limitations:

- Limited to Hyperledger Fabric blockchain technology
- Focused on data tracking and analysis, lacking certain advanced functions
- Complexity in setup and customization, especially for large networks
- Security considerations and lack of official documentation

5.6.2 Hyperledger Fabric in Blockchain

Hyperledger Fabric is an open-source framework that enables the development of decentralized ledger applications. The modular architecture of the system offers a significant degree of confidentiality, flexibility, robustness, and scalability, rendering it suitable for diverse businesses. Hyperledger Fabric, a blockchain architecture, is under the management of the Linux Foundation. It is designed to operate as a private and secure platform. The details are as follows.

5.6.2.1 Understanding Hyperledger Fabric

Hyperledger Fabric is specifically designed for applications at the corporate level, distinguished by its modular architecture, permissioned network, and the execution of smart contracts referred to as "chaincode." The platform places a high emphasis on the aspects of security, privacy, and scalability, thereby enabling the development of tailored blockchain solutions for various industries, including banking, supply chain, and healthcare.

Within a Hyperledger Fabric network, the various nodes engage in collaborative efforts to carry out distinct functions such as the validation of transactions, the maintenance of the ledger, and the execution of chaincode. The validation and ordering of transactions are achieved by a consensus method, which guarantees the integrity and consistency of the ledger.

5.6.2.2 Hyperledger Fabric's Operational Mechanism

Hyperledger Fabric is a blockchain technology that has been specifically developed for usage in companies and corporate contexts. It operates on a permissioned basis, meaning that access to the blockchain is restricted to authorized participants. The operational mechanism of this system encompasses various essential components and procedures that collaborate harmoniously to establish a blockchain network that is both secure and capable of scaling effectively.

Key Components:

Hyperledger Fabric functions as a permissioned blockchain network at the enterprise level, consisting of discrete entities or members. The aforementioned entities, encompassing banks, financial institutions, and supply chain networks, engage in interactions within the network by utilizing their fabric certificate authority.

Each network participant designates authorized peers who have undergone a comprehensive authorization procedure.

The establishment of network connections is facilitated through the utilization of the software development kit (SDK) of a particular programming language when developing client-side applications.

Workflow:

For every transaction within the fabric, the following steps occur:

1. **Proposal Creation:** The initiation of a transaction request is carried out by a member organization through the client application. The proposal is distributed to colleagues within each respective organization for the purpose of obtaining their endorsement.

2. **Endorsement:** The act of endorsing or expressing support for something or someone. The validation of transactions is carried out by peers through the execution of chaincode, which then provides an endorsement answer to the client application.

3. **Submission to Ordering Service:** Submission to the ordering service: Once transactions have been approved, they are transmitted to the ordering service, which organizes them into blocks and disseminates them among peer nodes within the network, spanning various network participants.

4. **Ledger Update:** The purpose of this communication is to provide an update on the ledger. The local ledgers of relevant organizations are updated by peer nodes with the new block, thereby completing the process of committing transactions.

5.6.3   Consensus in Hyperledger Fabric

Consensus in Hyperledger Fabric pertains to the procedural framework through which members within a blockchain network reach a mutual agreement over the authenticity and sequential arrangement of transactions to be incorporated into the communal ledger. Consensus is a fundamental mechanism that guarantees a uniform perspective across all participants regarding the current state of the blockchain, while also ensuring the secure and unalterable recording of transactions. Hyperledger Fabric utilizes a distinctive and adaptable consensus methodology, setting it apart from numerous other blockchain platforms.

Key aspects of consensus in Hyperledger Fabric include:

- **Pluggable Consensus:** The concept of pluggable consensus refers to the ability to easily switch between different consensus algorithms in a system. Hyperledger Fabric facilitates the integration of diverse consensus algorithms into the network, catering to various operational needs. This stands in contrast to alternative blockchain systems that employ a singular consensus process, such as proof of work (PoW) or proof of stake (PoS). The inherent flexibility of Fabric enables its adaptation to several use cases, including permissioned networks characterized by individuals who possess recognized and established trust.

- **Ordering Service:** This service is used to place orders. The concept of consensus in the context of Fabric can be delineated into two separate steps, endorsement and ordering. The endorsement phase encompasses the verification of a transaction's accuracy and its execution on a smart contract. After receiving endorsement, transactions are forwarded to the ordering service, which proceeds to generate a series of blocks that encompass the transactions in a predetermined sequence. The act of separating enables Fabric to attain enhanced levels of throughput and efficiency.

- **Kafka-Based Ordering Service:** The Kafka-based ordering service Hyperledger Fabric employs a Kafka-based ordering service as its default mechanism, which guarantees the orderly arrangement and consolidation of transactions into blocks. Kafka offers a distributed and resilient method for sequencing transactions, thereby improving the robustness of the network.
- **Channel-Level Consensus:** The concept of channel-level consensus refers to the agreement or alignment among different channels within a communication system. The concept of channels is introduced by Fabric, wherein these channels serve as private subnetworks within the overarching blockchain network. Each channel has the capability to implement its own consensus mechanism, allowing various segments of an organization to function with distinct consensus algorithms or even independent ledgers, while utilizing the same foundational infrastructure.
- **Practical Byzantine Fault Tolerance (PBFT):** PBFT is a consensus algorithm that addresses the Byzantine fault tolerance problem. Hyperledger Fabric is capable of accommodating consensus techniques such as PBFT, which offer enhanced throughput and fault tolerance capabilities. The ordering service in Fabric utilizes PBFT, which guarantees that a significant majority of nodes must reach a consensus over the sequencing of transactions.
- **Consenters and Ordering Nodes:** The individuals who provide consent and the nodes responsible for ordering. The ordering service in Fabric is composed of nodes referred to as consenters, who are responsible for packaging and disseminating transactions to peers. The responsibility for preserving consensus on the sequencing of transactions lies with these nodes.
- **Private Data and Endorsement Policies:** The topic of discussion pertains to the policies surrounding private data and endorsements. In the Fabric framework, it is possible to establish endorsement policies for certain transaction types, thereby determining the specific peers that are required to provide endorsement for a given transaction. Furthermore, the utilization of private data collecting facilitates the targeted dissemination of data exclusively to designated participants, thereby safeguarding the confidentiality of the information while simultaneously upholding agreement on the shared data. The user's text does not contain any information to be rewritten in an academic manner.

5.6.3.1 Industry Applications of Hyperledger Fabric

Hyperledger Fabric, a permissioned blockchain platform, is well suited for a wide range of industry applications that require trust, privacy, scalability, and control.

a. **Supply Chain:** The concept of supply chain refers to the interconnected network of organizations, activities, resources, and technologies involved in the production, distribution, and consumption of goods and services. Hyperledger Fabric improves the efficiency of supply chain transactions by providing heightened levels of transparency and traceability. Fabric facilitates real-time updates on the creation and distribution of products, thereby mitigating the risks associated with counterfeiting.

b. **Trading and Asset Transfer:** Trading and asset transfer are key components in the fields of finance and economics. Hyperledger Fabric enhances the efficiency of trading and asset transfer processes by reducing the need for paperwork through the implementation of a reliable and secure paperless solution. The dematerialization of assets on the blockchain enables individuals to directly access financial securities.

c. **Insurance:** The notion of insurance entails a contractual agreement among entities or individuals to transmit the potential risk. Insurance claim processing is streamlined through the automation of payment and subrogation procedures facilitated by Hyperledger Fabric. This technology ensures the implementation of secure Know Your Customer (KYC) and identity verification processes. The user's text lacks any pertinent information that necessitates rephrasing in an academic fashion.

5.6.3.2 Advantages Offered by Hyperledger Fabric

Hyperledger Fabric offers several advantages that make it a preferred choice for enterprise blockchain solutions.

a. **Open Source:** Hyperledger Fabric is open-source, allowing public accessibility, modification, and distribution of its code.
b. **Private and Confidential:** Hyperledger Fabric ensures privacy by exposing the ledger only to authenticated members, making it suitable for industries requiring data confidentiality.
c. **Access Control:** Fabric's layered access control system provides privacy and control over data exposure, even among competitors within the same network.
d. **Chaincode Functionality:** Fabric's chaincode technology facilitates the hosting of smart contracts, accommodating diverse business rules and transactions.
e. **Performance:** Hyperledger Fabric's private network architecture contributes to faster transaction speeds, enhancing performance.

5.6.3.3 Constraints of Hyperledger Fabric

Hyperledger Fabric, while robust, has certain limitations that need to be considered. One limitation is the complexity of setting up and configuring the network, which requires a deep understanding of blockchain concepts and infrastructure. Major limitations include the following:

a. **Scalability**: Fabric's permissioned network design limits scalability for large-scale public networks.
b. **Performance**: Network size, configuration, and chaincode complexity can impact Fabric's performance.
c. **Complexity**: Setting up and configuring a Fabric network requires a deep understanding of the technology.
d. **Compatibility**: Fabric's compatibility with specific programming languages may limit integration with other technologies.
e. **Cost**: Running a Fabric network incurs infrastructure costs.
f. **Interoperability**: Hyperledger Fabric's interoperability with other blockchains is restricted within a single network.

5.7   Hyperledger Consortiums and Networks

In the context of Hyperledger, consortium networks pertain to collaborative networks that are established by various organizations with the purpose of creating, managing, and sustaining a shared blockchain infrastructure. The consortium networks have numerous advantages, some of which are as follows:

- **Shared Governance:** The concept of shared governance is a fundamental principle in the field of governance and decision-making processes. The decision-making process regarding the network's rules, policies, and upgrades is undertaken collaboratively by the members of the consortium. The use of this shared governance paradigm serves to guarantee both openness and inclusivity.

- **Cost Sharing:** The concept of cost sharing refers to the practice of distributing expenses across multiple parties. Through the collaborative utilization of resources and the sharing of infrastructure, members of a consortium have the potential to mitigate the individual financial burdens involved with the establishment and upkeep of a private blockchain network.
- **Interoperability:** Interoperability refers to the ability of different systems or components to work together and exchange information. Consortium networks facilitate the smooth interchange of data and value across member organizations, promoting interoperability and enhancing the efficiency of business processes.
- **Security and Trust:** The concepts of security and trust are central to the current discussion. The consortium network comprises member organizations that are recognized entities, thereby augmenting trust and security in contrast to public blockchains.
- **Customization:** Consortium networks offer customized solutions to cater to the distinct needs and demands of member firms, thereby enhancing the efficiency and effectiveness of blockchain deployment.
- **Use Case Diversity:** Case diversity in academic research consortium networks has the capacity to facilitate a diverse array of applications, encompassing supply chain management and financial services, thereby fostering collaborative efforts across different industries. The user text contains no information to rewrite in an academic manner.

The formation of consortium networks involves defining network participants, consensus mechanisms, access controls, and smart contract rules. Hyperledger Fabric, for example, provides the tools and frameworks necessary for creating and managing consortium networks. This empowers organizations to collaborate while maintaining data privacy, security, and operational control.

5.8 Hyperledger and Blockchain as a Service (BaaS)

Hyperledger Fabric is a blockchain platform specifically developed for use in commercial environments that is designed to cater to various business use cases. The operational mechanism of this system encompasses various essential components and procedures that collaborate harmoniously to establish a blockchain network that is both secure and capable of scaling effectively.

5.8.1 Hyperledger Adoption Through BaaS

The utilization of BaaS platforms, such as IBM Blockchain Platform and Azure Blockchain, facilitates the integration and administration of Hyperledger-based blockchain networks for enterprises, thereby streamlining the process of Hyperledger adoption. BaaS platforms offer a comprehensive suite of tools, resources, and infrastructure that facilitate the development, deployment, and upkeep of blockchain applications, all while mitigating the necessity of handling intricate technical intricacies at the foundational level.

5.8.2 Advantages and Considerations

The utilization of backend as a service for the deployment of Hyperledger entails several benefits and factors that need to be taken into account.

- **Rapid Deployment:** BaaS platforms streamline the setup and configuration of Hyperledger networks, enabling quicker deployment of blockchain solutions.
- **Cost Efficiency:** Organizations can reduce costs by leveraging the infrastructure and services provided by BaaS providers, eliminating the need for extensive hardware and software investments.
- **Scalability:** BaaS platforms offer scalability features, allowing organizations to easily scale their blockchain networks as their business needs grow.
- **Expertise and Support:** BaaS providers offer technical expertise and support, assisting organizations in overcoming challenges and ensuring optimal network performance.
- **Resource Savings:** BaaS eliminates the need for in-house blockchain expertise and dedicated IT resources for network maintenance and management.
- **Data Privacy:** Considerations include data privacy and control, as organizations need to trust BaaS providers with sensitive information.
- **Vendor Lock-In:** Organizations should be aware of potential vendor lock-in when relying heavily on a specific BaaS provider.

Adopting Hyperledger through BaaS platforms provides a strategic approach for organizations to leverage blockchain technology without extensive infrastructure investments, benefiting from the convenience, support, and scalability offered by BaaS providers.

5.9 Laboratory Work

This section gives the various implementations of Hyperledger through examples.

5.9.1 Program to Demonstrate Interaction with a Hyperledger Fabric Blockchain Network Using the Hyperledger Fabric JavaScript SDK

```
// This example assumes you have the necessary Hyperledger Fabric tools and
    dependencies installed.

// Step 1: Define the required modules and dependencies
const { Gateway, Wallets } = require('fabric-network');
const fs = require('fs');
const path = require('path');

async function main() {
  try {
    // Step 2: Load the connection profile and wallet
    const ccpPath = path.resolve(__dirname, 'connection.json');
    const ccpJSON = fs.readFileSync(ccpPath, 'utf8');
    const ccp = JSON.parse(ccpJSON);

    const walletPath = path.join(process.cwd(), 'wallet');
    const wallet = await Wallets.newFileSystemWallet(walletPath);
```

```
18    // Step 3: Check if user exists in the wallet
19    const identity = await wallet.get('user1');
20    if (!identity) {
21      console.log('An identity for the user "user1" does not exist in the
      wallet')
22      return;
23    }
24
25    // Step 4: Create a gateway connection
26    const gateway = new Gateway();
27    await gateway.connect(ccp, { wallet, identity: 'user1', discovery: {
      enabled: true, asLocalhost: true } });
28
29    // Step 5: Access the network
30    const network = await gateway.getNetwork('mychannel');
31
32    // Step 6: Access the contract
33    const contract = network.getContract('mycontract');
34
35    // Step 7: Submit a transaction (e.g., create a new asset)
36    await contract.submitTransaction('CreateAsset', 'asset1', 'Description',
      'Owner', 'Status');
37
38    console.log('Transaction has been submitted');
39
40    // Step 8: Disconnect from the gateway
41    gateway.disconnect();
42  } catch (error) {
43    console.error('Error: ${error}');
44    process.exit(1);
45  }
46 }
47
48 main();
```

Sample Input and Output

```
1  // Input data for creating a new asset
2  const assetId = 'asset123';
3  const description = 'Product ABC';
4  const owner = 'Manufacturer';
5  const status = 'In Transit';
6
7  // Query input data
8  const queryAssetId = 'asset123';
```

```
1  // Output
2  Transaction has been submitted
3
4  Query result for asset asset123: In Transit
```

Explanation of Code

The provided JavaScript program demonstrates how to interact with a Hyperledger Fabric blockchain network using the Hyperledger Fabric JavaScript SDK. The program is designed to perform a simplified supply chain use case. It follows a series of steps to establish a connection to the blockchain network, access a specific smart contract, and submit a transaction.

The program starts by importing necessary modules and dependencies, including the `fabric-network` module for interacting with the Hyperledger Fabric network. It defines an `async` function named `main()` that serves as the main entry point for the program.

In the initial steps, the program loads the connection profile from a JSON file (`connection.json`) and creates a wallet to store user identities for secure interaction with the network. It then checks whether a specific user identity (`'user1'`) exists in the wallet, which is necessary for submitting transactions.

Next, the program creates a connection to the network using the `Gateway` class. It connects using the parsed connection profile and user identity, while enabling network discovery for locating network components. Once connected, it accesses a specific channel (`'mychannel'`) within the network and obtains a contract object associated with a smart contract named `'mycontract'`.

To simulate a transaction, the program submits a transaction to the network. It uses the `submitTransaction` method of the contract and provides arguments such as asset ID, description, owner, and status. In this example, these arguments are placeholders and should be replaced with actual data relevant to the use case.

After successfully submitting the transaction, the program logs a message confirming the submission. It then disconnects from the network gateway to release resources and connections.

The program includes error handling to catch and display any exceptions that may occur during execution, ensuring that errors are properly logged. Overall, this code serves as a foundational framework for initiating transactions on a Hyperledger Fabric blockchain network, offering insights into connecting, accessing contracts, and submitting data to the blockchain ledger.

5.9.2 Program to Demonstrate How Hyperledger Fabric Could Be Used in a Healthcare Context to Manage Patient Medical Records

```
const { Contract } = require('fabric-contract-api');

%\begin{lstlisting}[frame=single,caption={healthcare.js}]
%const { Contract } = require('fabric-contract-api');

class HealthcareContract extends Contract {
    async initLedger(ctx) {
        console.info('Initializing Ledger');
    }

    async createMedicalRecord(ctx, patientId, doctorId, diagnosis, treatment)
    {
        const medicalRecord = {
            patientId,
            doctorId,
            diagnosis,
            treatment,
            timestamp: new Date(),
        };
```

```
19
20      await ctx.stub.putState(patientId, Buffer.from(JSON.stringify(
    medicalRecord)));
21      console.info('Medical record created:', medicalRecord);
22  }
23
24  async queryMedicalRecord(ctx, patientId) {
25      const recordBytes = await ctx.stub.getState(patientId);
26      if (!recordBytes || recordBytes.length === 0) {
27          throw new Error('Medical record for patient ${patientId} not
    found');
28      }
29
30      const medicalRecord = JSON.parse(recordBytes.toString());
31      return medicalRecord;
32  }
33 }
34
35 module.exports = HealthcareContract;
```

Code Listing 5-1 Smart Contract – healthcare.js

```
1 const { Gateway, Wallets } = require('fabric-network');
2 const fs = require('fs');
3 const path = require('path');
4
5 async function main() {
6     try {
7         const ccpPath = path.resolve(__dirname, 'connection.json');
8         const ccpJSON = fs.readFileSync(ccpPath, 'utf8');
9         const ccp = JSON.parse(ccpJSON);
10
11        const walletPath = path.join(process.cwd(), 'wallet');
12        const wallet = await Wallets.newFileSystemWallet(walletPath);
13
14        const identity = await wallet.get('user1');
15        if (!identity) {
16            console.log('An identity for the user "user1" does not exist in
    the wallet');
17            return;
18        }
19
20        const gateway = new Gateway();
21        await gateway.connect(ccp, { wallet, identity: 'user1', discovery: {
    enabled: true, asLocalhost: true } });
22
23        const network = await gateway.getNetwork('mychannel');
24        const contract = network.getContract('healthcare');
25
26        // Create a medical record
27        await contract.submitTransaction('createMedicalRecord', 'patient1', '
    doctor1', 'Fever', 'Rest and hydration');
28
29        // Query a medical record
30        const record = await contract.evaluateTransaction('queryMedicalRecord
    ', 'patient1');
31        console.log('Medical Record:', record.toString());
32
33        gateway.disconnect();
```

```
34    } catch (error) {
35        console.error('Error: ${error}');
36        process.exit(1);
37    }
38 }
39
40 main();
```

Code Listing 5-2 interact.js

Sample Input and Output

Creating a Medical Record

```
1 createMedicalRecord('patient123', 'doctor456', 'Fever', 'Rest and hydration')
    ;
```

Code Listing 5-3 Sample Input – Creating a Medical Record

Querying a Medical Record

```
1 {
2     "patientId": "patient123",
3     "doctorId": "doctor456",
4     "diagnosis": "Fever",
5     "treatment": "Rest and hydration",
6     "timestamp": "2023-08-17T12:34:56Z"
7 }
```

Code Listing 5-4 Sample Output – Querying a Medical Record

```
1 const { Contract } = require('fabric-contract-api');
2
3 class GovernmentContract extends Contract {
4     async initLedger(ctx) {
5         console.info('Initializing Ledger');
6     }
7
8     async createCitizenRecord(ctx, citizenId, name, address) {
9         const citizenRecord = {
10             name,
11             address,
12             timestamp: new Date(),
13         };
14
15         await ctx.stub.putState(citizenId, Buffer.from(JSON.stringify(
    citizenRecord)));
16         console.info('Citizen record created:', citizenRecord);
17     }
18
19     async queryCitizenRecord(ctx, citizenId) {
20         const recordBytes = await ctx.stub.getState(citizenId);
```

```
21      if (!recordBytes || recordBytes.length === 0) {
22          throw new Error('Citizen record for ID ${citizenId} not found');
23      }
24
25      const citizenRecord = JSON.parse(recordBytes.toString());
26      return citizenRecord;
27    }
28 }
29
30 module.exports = GovernmentContract;
```

Code Listing 5-5   Smart Contract – government.js

5.9.3   Program to Demonstrate the Implementation of a Basic Government Application Using Hyperledger Fabric

```
1  const { Gateway, Wallets } = require('fabric-network');
2  const fs = require('fs');
3  const path = require('path');
4
5  async function main() {
6      try {
7          const ccpPath = path.resolve(__dirname, 'connection.json');
8          const ccpJSON = fs.readFileSync(ccpPath, 'utf8');
9          const ccp = JSON.parse(ccpJSON);
10
11         const walletPath = path.join(process.cwd(), 'wallet');
12         const wallet = await Wallets.newFileSystemWallet(walletPath);
13
14         const identity = await wallet.get('user1');
15         if (!identity) {
16             console.log('\textcolor{red}{An identity for the user "user1"
    does not exist in the wallet}');
17             return;
18         }
19
20         const gateway = new Gateway();
21         await gateway.connect(ccp, { wallet, identity: 'user1', discovery: {
    enabled: true, asLocalhost: true } });
22
23         const network = await gateway.getNetwork('mychannel');
24         const contract = network.getContract('government');
25
26         // Create a citizen record
27         await contract.submitTransaction('createCitizenRecord', 'citizen123',
    'John Doe', '123 Main St');
28
29         // Query a citizen record
30         const record = await contract.evaluateTransaction('queryCitizenRecord
    ', 'citizen123');
31         console.log('Citizen Record:', record.toString());
32
33         gateway.disconnect();
34     } catch (error) {
35         console.error('\textcolor{red}{Error:}', error);
36         process.exit(1);
```

```
37         }
38 }
39
40 main();
```

Code Listing 5-6   Interaction Code – interact.js

Sample Input and Output

Creating a Citizen Record

```
1 createCitizenRecord('citizen123', 'Jane Smith', '456 Oak St');
```

Querying a Citizen Record

```
1 {
2     "name": "Jane Smith",
3     "address": "456 Oak St",
4     "timestamp": "2023-08-17T12:34:56Z"
5 }
```

5.9.4   Program to Demonstrate Finance Application Using Hyperledger Fabric

```
1 const { Contract } = require('fabric-contract-api');
2
3 class FinanceContract extends Contract {
4     async initLedger(ctx) {
5         console.info('Initializing Ledger');
6     }
7
8     async createAccount(ctx, accountId, balance) {
9         const account = {
10             balance: parseFloat(balance),
11             transactions: [],
12         };
13
14         await ctx.stub.putState(accountId, Buffer.from(JSON.stringify(account
    )));
15         console.info('Account created:', account);
16     }
17
18     async deposit(ctx, accountId, amount) {
19         const accountBytes = await ctx.stub.getState(accountId);
20         if (!accountBytes || accountBytes.length === 0) {
21             throw new Error('Account ${accountId} not found');
22         }
23
24         const account = JSON.parse(accountBytes.toString());
25         account.balance += parseFloat(amount);
```

```
26        account.transactions.push({ type: 'Deposit', amount: parseFloat(
    amount), timestamp: new Date() });
27
28        await ctx.stub.putState(accountId, Buffer.from(JSON.stringify(account
    )));
29        console.info('Deposit completed:', account);
30    }
31
32    async withdraw(ctx, accountId, amount) {
33        const accountBytes = await ctx.stub.getState(accountId);
34        if (!accountBytes || accountBytes.length === 0) {
35            throw new Error('Account ${accountId} not found');
36        }
37
38        const account = JSON.parse(accountBytes.toString());
39        if (account.balance < parseFloat(amount)) {
40            throw new Error('Insufficient balance for account ${accountId}');
41        }
42
43        account.balance -= parseFloat(amount);
44        account.transactions.push({ type: 'Withdrawal', amount: parseFloat(
    amount), timestamp: new Date() });
45
46        await ctx.stub.putState(accountId, Buffer.from(JSON.stringify(account
    )));
47        console.info('Withdrawal completed:', account);
48    }
49
50    async queryAccount(ctx, accountId) {
51        const accountBytes = await ctx.stub.getState(accountId);
52        if (!accountBytes || accountBytes.length === 0) {
53            throw new Error('Account ${accountId} not found');
54        }
55
56        const account = JSON.parse(accountBytes.toString());
57        return account;
58    }
59 }
60
61 module.exports = FinanceContract;
```

Code Listing 5-7 Smart Contract – finance.js

Interaction Code – `interact.js`

```
1 const { Gateway, Wallets } = require('fabric-network');
2 const fs = require('fs');
3 const path = require('path');
4
5 async function main() {
6     try {
7         const ccpPath = path.resolve(__dirname, 'connection.json');
8         const ccpJSON = fs.readFileSync(ccpPath, 'utf8');
9         const ccp = JSON.parse(ccpJSON);
10
11        const walletPath = path.join(process.cwd(), 'wallet');
```

```
12      const wallet = await Wallets.newFileSystemWallet(walletPath);
13
14      const identity = await wallet.get('user1');
15      if (!identity) {
16          console.log('An identity for the user "user1" does not exist in
    the wallet');
17          return;
18      }
19
20      const gateway = new Gateway();
21      await gateway.connect(ccp, { wallet, identity: 'user1', discovery: {
    enabled: true, asLocalhost: true } });
22
23      const network = await gateway.getNetwork('mychannel');
24      const contract = network.getContract('finance');
25
26      // Create an account
27      await contract.submitTransaction('createAccount', 'account123', '
    1000.00');
28
29      // Deposit funds
30      await contract.submitTransaction('deposit', 'account123', '500.00');
31
32      // Withdraw funds
33      await contract.submitTransaction('withdraw', 'account123', '300.00');
34
35      // Query account balance
36      const account = await contract.evaluateTransaction('queryAccount', '
    account123');
37      console.log('Account:', account.toString());
38
39      gateway.disconnect();
40  } catch (error) {
41      console.error(`Error: ${error}`);
42      process.exit(1);
43  }
44 }
45
46 main();
```

Code Listing 5-8 Interaction Code – interact.js

5.9.5   Program to Demonstrate the Implementation of a Finance and Payments System Using Hyperledger Fabric

```
1 const { Contract } = require('fabric-contract-api');
2
3 class FinanceContract extends Contract {
4     async initLedger(ctx) {
5         console.info('Initializing Ledger');
6     }
7
8     async createAccount(ctx, accountId, balance) {
9         const account = {
10            balance: parseFloat(balance),
11            transactions: [],
```

```
12          };
13
14          await ctx.stub.putState(accountId, Buffer.from(JSON.stringify(account
       )));
15          console.info('Account created:', account);
16      }
17
18      async deposit(ctx, accountId, amount) {
19          const accountBytes = await ctx.stub.getState(accountId);
20          if (!accountBytes || accountBytes.length === 0) {
21              throw new Error('Account ${accountId} not found');
22          }
23
24          const account = JSON.parse(accountBytes.toString());
25          account.balance += parseFloat(amount);
26          account.transactions.push({ type: 'Deposit', amount: parseFloat(
       amount), timestamp: new Date() });
27
28          await ctx.stub.putState(accountId, Buffer.from(JSON.stringify(account
       )));
29          console.info('Deposit completed:', account);
30      }
31
32      async withdraw(ctx, accountId, amount) {
33          const accountBytes = await ctx.stub.getState(accountId);
34          if (!accountBytes || accountBytes.length === 0) {
35              throw new Error('Account ${accountId} not found');
36          }
37
38          const account = JSON.parse(accountBytes.toString());
39          if (account.balance < parseFloat(amount)) {
40              throw new Error('Insufficient balance for account ${accountId}');
41          }
42
43          account.balance -= parseFloat(amount);
44          account.transactions.push({ type: 'Withdrawal', amount: parseFloat(
       amount), timestamp: new Date() });
45
46          await ctx.stub.putState(accountId, Buffer.from(JSON.stringify(account
       )));
47          console.info('Withdrawal completed:', account);
48      }
49
50      async queryAccount(ctx, accountId) {
51          const accountBytes = await ctx.stub.getState(accountId);
52          if (!accountBytes || accountBytes.length === 0) {
53              throw new Error('Account ${accountId} not found');
54          }
55
56          const account = JSON.parse(accountBytes.toString());
57          return account;
58      }
59 }
60
61 module.exports = FinanceContract;
```

Code Listing 5-9 Smart Contract – finance.js

Interaction Code – `interact.js`

```
const { Gateway, Wallets } = require('fabric-network');
const fs = require('fs');
const path = require('path');

async function main() {
    try {
        const ccpPath = path.resolve(__dirname, 'connection.json');
        const ccpJSON = fs.readFileSync(ccpPath, 'utf8');
        const ccp = JSON.parse(ccpJSON);

        const walletPath = path.join(process.cwd(), 'wallet');
        const wallet = await Wallets.newFileSystemWallet(walletPath);

        const identity = await wallet.get('user1');
        if (!identity) {
            console.log('An identity for the user "user1" does not exist in
    the wallet');
            return;
        }

        const gateway = new Gateway();
        await gateway.connect(ccp, { wallet, identity: 'user1', discovery: {
    enabled: true, asLocalhost: true } });

        const network = await gateway.getNetwork('mychannel');
        const contract = network.getContract('finance');

        // Create an account
        await contract.submitTransaction('createAccount', 'account123', '
    1000.00');

        // Deposit funds
        await contract.submitTransaction('deposit', 'account123', '500.00');

        // Withdraw funds
        await contract.submitTransaction('withdraw', 'account123', '300.00');

        // Query account balance
        const account = await contract.evaluateTransaction('queryAccount', '
    account123');
        console.log('Account:', account.toString());

        gateway.disconnect();
    } catch (error) {
        console.error(`Error: ${error}`);
        process.exit(1);
    }
}

main();
```

Code Listing 5-10 Interaction Code – interact.js

Sample Input and Output

Creating an Account

```
createAccount('account567', '1000.00');
```

Depositing Funds

```
deposit('account567', '300.00');
```

Withdrawing Funds

```
withdraw('account567', '150.00');
```

Querying Account Balance

```
{
    "balance": 1150.00,
    "transactions": [
        { "type": "Deposit", "amount": 300.00, "timestamp": "2023-08-17T12
:34:56Z" },
        { "type": "Withdrawal", "amount": 150.00, "timestamp": "2023-08-17T14
:45:30Z" }
    ]
}
```

5.9.6 Explanation of Code

The code for the smart contract, contained within the section "Smart Contract (Chaincode) – finance.js," illustrates the essence of financial operations within the blockchain network. It defines a `FinanceContract` class, which extends the `fabric-contract-api Contract` class. The smart contract is equipped with functions to initialize a ledger, create an account with an initial balance, deposit funds into an account, withdraw funds from an account while ensuring sufficient balance, and query account details. The interactions with the ledger are performed using cryptographic keys and stored as JSON data. Error handling is meticulously incorporated to ensure the integrity and reliability of financial transactions.

Moreover, the "Interaction Code – interact.js" section outlines the means to interact with the blockchain network and execute financial transactions. This code demonstrates the process of connecting to the network using a connection profile, managing user identities with a wallet, and utilizing a gateway to establish communication. Subsequently, it interacts with the smart contract by creating an account, depositing and withdrawing funds, and querying account details. The outcomes of these transactions are appropriately displayed, and error handling mechanisms are integrated to handle potential exceptions.

5.9.7 Program to Demonstrate Simple Interoperability Using the Hyperledger Fabric JavaScript SDK to Interact with the Network and Demonstrate How Two Different Smart Contracts Can Work Together

```javascript
const { Gateway, Wallets } = require('fabric-network');
const fs = require('fs');
const path = require('path');

async function main() {
    try {
        // Load the connection profile and wallet
        const ccpPath = path.resolve(__dirname, 'connection.json');
        const ccpJSON = fs.readFileSync(ccpPath, 'utf8');
        const ccp = JSON.parse(ccpJSON);

        const walletPath = path.join(process.cwd(), 'wallet');
        const wallet = await Wallets.newFileSystemWallet(walletPath);

        // Check if user identity exists in the wallet
        const identity = await wallet.get('user1');
        if (!identity) {
            console.log('An identity for the user "user1" does not exist in
    the wallet');
            return;
        }

        // Create a gateway connection
        const gateway = new Gateway();
        await gateway.connect(ccp, { wallet, identity: 'user1', discovery: {
    enabled: true, asLocalhost: true } });

        % Access the network
        const network = await gateway.getNetwork('mychannel');

        % Access the ContractA and ContractB instances
        const contractA = network.getContract('contracta');
        const contractB = network.getContract('contractb');

        % Interact with ContractA and ContractB
        const resultA = await contractA.submitTransaction('
    FunctionInContractA', 'Hello from ContractA');
        console.log('Result from ContractA:', resultA.toString());

        const resultB = await contractB.submitTransaction('
    FunctionInContractB', 'Hello from ContractB');
        console.log('Result from ContractB:', resultB.toString());

        % Disconnect from the gateway
        gateway.disconnect();
    } catch (error) {
        console.error(`Error: ${error}`);
        process.exit(1);
    }
```

```
46 }
47
48 main();
```

Code Listing 5-11 Interoperability Program

Sample Input and Output

```
1 Interacting with ContractA and ContractB
```

Code Listing 5-12 Sample Input

Output

```
1 Connected to Hyperledger Fabric network
2 Executing FunctionInContractA in ContractA...
3 Result from ContractA: Message received: Interacting with ContractA and
     ContractB
4
5 Executing FunctionInContractB in ContractB...
6 Result from ContractB: Modified message: Interacting with ContractA and
     ContractB
7
8 Disconnected from Hyperledger Fabric network
```

Explanation of Code

The program's main function initializes by loading the connection profile and wallet, establishes a connection to the network gateway, and checks for the existence of a user identity in the wallet. It then accesses the specified network and contracts, interacting with ContractA and ContractB by submitting transactions to their respective functions. The results of these interactions are displayed, and the program concludes by disconnecting from the gateway.

The code listings are framed for better visibility and presented with appropriate syntax highlighting. The use of custom colors, font styles, and formatting enhances the readability and clarity of the code, enabling a clear understanding of the interoperability process between Hyperledger Fabric smart contracts.

5.9.8   Program to Demonstrate Smart Contract Modeling with Composer and Docker

Composer for Smart Contract Modeling

This section will examine the process of modeling smart contracts using Hyperledger Composer, a platform that facilitates the creation, testing, and deployment of business network specifications.

```
1  /**
2   * Sample Smart Contract Definition
3   */
4  namespace org.example
5
6  asset Vehicle identified by vin {
7      o String vin
8      o String make
9      o String model
10     --> Owner owner
11 }
12
13 participant Owner identified by ownerId {
14     o String ownerId
15     o String firstName
16     o String lastName
17 }
18
19 transaction TransferOwnership {
20     --> Vehicle vehicle
21     --> Owner newOwner
22 }
23
24 event OwnershipTransferred {
25     --> Vehicle vehicle
26     --> Owner previousOwner
27     --> Owner newOwner
28 }
```

Code Listing 5-13 Example Smart Contract Model

The preceding example demonstrates a simple smart contract model using Hyperledger Composer syntax. It defines assets, participants, transactions, and events related to transferring vehicle ownership. This modeling approach provides a higher-level abstraction and allows business logic to be defined in a more intuitive manner.

Program for Docker-Based Playground for Testing and Simulating Smart Contract

Hyperledger Composer provides a Docker-based playground for testing and simulating smart contracts. Docker allows you to create isolated environments to run your business networks.

To interact with Composer Playground using Docker, follow these steps:

a. Install Docker on your system.
b. Pull the Hyperledger Composer Docker image: `docker pull hyperledger/composer-playground`.
c. Run the Composer Playground Docker container: `docker run -d -p 8080:8080 hyperledger/composer-playground`.
d. Access the Composer Playground web interface at `http://localhost:8080`.
e. Create, test, and deploy your smart contracts interactively using the playground.

Using Docker with Composer Playground provides a convenient and sandboxed environment for experimenting with smart contract models before deploying them to a production blockchain network.

5.9.9 Program for Demonstrating Hyperledger Caliper, a Benchmarking Tool That Measures the Performance of Hyperledger Blockchain Applications Under Various Conditions

Hyperledger Caliper is a benchmarking tool that measures the performance of Hyperledger blockchain applications under various conditions. It allows you to simulate and execute various workloads to assess the scalability and efficiency of your blockchain network.

```
/*
 * Sample Caliper Benchmark Configuration
 */
'use strict';

module.exports = {
    blockchain: 'fabric',
    sutOptions: {
        fabricVersion: '2.3.0',
        networkConfigPath: './path/to/network-config.yaml'
    },
    benchmark: {
        name: 'simple-benchmark',
        description: 'A simple benchmark scenario',
        workers: {
            type: 'local',
            number: 2
        },
        roundDuration: 30
    },
    round: {
        label: 'simple-round',
        description: 'A simple benchmark round',
        txNumber: 100,
        rateControl: {
            type: 'fixed-rate',
            opts: {
                tps: 10
            }
        }
    }
};
```

Code Listing 5-14 Caliper Benchmark Configuration

The preceding example demonstrates a sample benchmark configuration for Hyperledger Caliper. It defines the blockchain platform (fabric), system under test (SUT) options, benchmark scenario, number of workers, and benchmark round details. Caliper allows you to fine-tune various parameters to simulate different workloads and evaluate blockchain performance.

5.9.10 Running Caliper Benchmarks with Docker

To run benchmarks using Caliper and Docker, follow these steps:

a. Install Docker on your system.
b. Pull the Hyperledger Caliper Docker image: `docker pull hyperledger/caliper`.

c. Create a benchmark configuration file, e.g., `benchmark-config.yaml`.
d. Run the Caliper Docker container: `docker run -v /path/to/config:/config hyperledger/caliper benchmark run -caliper-benchconfig /config/benchmark-config.yaml`.
e. Monitor and analyze benchmark results to assess the performance of your Hyperledger applications.

The use of Docker in conjunction with Caliper facilitates the establishment of a standardized and segregated environment for the purpose of conducting performance evaluations on blockchain applications. This feature enables the assessment of the scalability and efficiency of the blockchain network, as well as the identification of potential bottlenecks.

5.10 Summary

The chapter provided a comprehensive examination of Hyperledger, exploring its foundational elements and many constituents. The discussion started with an introduction to Hyperledger, highlighting its primary objective as a comprehensive open-source blockchain architecture designed for the development of decentralized applications. The design of Hyperledger was subjected to thorough examination, encompassing discrete levels including infrastructure, framework, and tools. It also provided a detailed explanation of the various roles present in a Hyperledger network, specifically highlighting the distinct obligations assigned to contributors, endorsers, and consenters.

The importance of smart contracts, also known as chaincode, in the Hyperledger ecosystem was extensively analyzed, offering a comprehensive explanation of their functioning inside the framework. Then the chapter shifted focus to an examination of a variety of Hyperledger initiatives, drawing comparisons with alternative blockchain frameworks and highlighting notable projects such as Hyperledger Explorer and Hyperledger Fabric.

Next, the chapter provided a comprehensive analysis of the consensus mechanism employed in Hyperledger Fabric, with a specific focus on demystifying the PBFT algorithm that underlies it. The chapter expanded its scope to include the establishment and benefits of consortium networks, emphasizing the importance of collaboration and shared governance among participants in the network. Furthermore, the chapter explored the adoption of Hyperledger technology through BaaS platforms, providing a detailed analysis of the benefits and factors to consider when implementing Hyperledger networks using BaaS.

The chapter concluded with a series of practical laboratory experiments that served as concrete demonstrations of Hyperledger's practical relevance in real-world scenarios. These experiments offer practical opportunities for individuals to gain firsthand experience in engaging with Hyperledger Fabric networks, developing and designing smart contracts, evaluating application performance using Caliper, and exploring various practical scenarios.

5.11 Exercise

This section provides exercises based on topics covered in the chapter.

5.11.1 Multiple Choice Questions

a. What is the primary purpose of Hyperledger?
    i. To provide a decentralized cryptocurrency platform.
    ii. To develop gaming applications using blockchain.
    iii. To create an open-source blockchain framework for building decentralized applications.
    iv. To offer secure communication channels for social networking.
b. Which layer of the Hyperledger architecture is responsible for maintaining consensus on the order of transactions?
    i. Infrastructure layer
    ii. Framework layer
    iii. Tool layer
    iv. Consensus layer
c. What role is responsible for validating the correctness and executing a transaction against a smart contract in Hyperledger Fabric?
    i. Contributor
    ii. Endorser
    iii. Consenter
    iv. Validator
d. Which project provides a blockchain explorer for viewing and analyzing transactions on a Hyperledger network?
    i. Hyperledger Composer
    ii. Hyperledger Explorer
    iii. Hyperledger Caliper
    iv. Hyperledger Fabric
e. What is the primary benefit of using blockchain as a service (BaaS) for Hyperledger deployment?
    i. Reduced security and privacy.
    ii. Limited control over the blockchain network.
    iii. Lower cost of deployment and maintenance.
    iv. Incompatibility with existing infrastructure.
f. Which layer of Hyperledger technology is responsible for managing identity and access control?
    i. Identity layer
    ii. Communication layer
    iii. Consensus layer
    iv. Smart layer
g. What is the purpose of Hyperledger Fabric's ordering service?
    i. To validate transactions against a smart contract
    ii. To create a sequence of blocks containing transactions in a specified order
    iii. To provide a decentralized and fault-tolerant approach to ordering transactions
    iv. To manage identity and access control
h. What is a consortium network in Hyperledger?
    i. A private blockchain network with no external participants
    ii. A network where all participants have equal privileges and control
    iii. A network of organizations collaborating to achieve shared goals using blockchain technology
    iv. A network where transactions are validated using proof of stake (PoS) consensus

i. Which layer of Hyperledger technology is responsible for providing the API for developers to interact with the blockchain network?
   i. Infrastructure layer
   ii. Framework layer
   iii. Tool layer
   iv. Application layer
j. What does the Hyperledger Caliper tool measure?
   i. The security of Hyperledger smart contracts
   ii. The efficiency of blockchain consensus algorithms
   iii. The performance of Hyperledger blockchain applications under various conditions
   iv. The scalability of Hyperledger networks

5.11.2 Short Answer Questions

a. What is the primary purpose of Hyperledger?
b. Explain the concept of pluggable consensus in Hyperledger Fabric.
c. What is the role of the ordering service in Hyperledger Fabric?
d. Define the concept of channels in Hyperledger Fabric.
e. How does Hyperledger blockchain as a service (BaaS) adoption benefit organizations?
f. What is the key advantage of using Hyperledger Fabric's Kafka-based ordering service?
g. Name one Hyperledger project that provides a blockchain explorer and its purpose.
h. What is the role of consenters in Hyperledger Fabric's ordering service?
i. Briefly explain the significance of Hyperledger consortiums and networks.
j. How does Hyperledger Fabric achieve privacy while maintaining consensus on shared data?

5.11.3 Long Answer Questions

a. Describe the layered architecture of Hyperledger and explain the functions of each layer: infrastructure layer, framework layer, tool layer, and application layer.
b. Explain the following key roles in Hyperledger Fabric's functioning: contributor, endorser, and consenter. How do these roles contribute to maintaining the integrity of the blockchain?
c. Provide an overview of the consensus mechanism used in Hyperledger Fabric. Describe how practical Byzantine fault tolerance (PBFT) contributes to achieving consensus in Hyperledger Fabric's ordering service.
d. Discuss the concept of channels in Hyperledger Fabric. How do channels enable different parts of an organization to operate with different consensus algorithms or separate ledgers within the same network infrastructure?
e. Compare and contrast Hyperledger adoption through blockchain as a service (BaaS) platforms with traditional deployment. What are the advantages and considerations of using BaaS for Hyperledger projects?
f. Describe the purpose and functionality of Hyperledger Explorer. How does it contribute to enhancing transparency and monitoring within a Hyperledger network?
g. Explain the use of the Hyperledger Caliper benchmarking tool. How does Caliper measure the performance and scalability of Hyperledger blockchain applications? Provide an example scenario where Caliper would be useful.

h. Discuss the benefits and limitations of Hyperledger Fabric as an open-source blockchain frame-work. Highlight the scalability, privacy, and security features of Hyperledger Fabric.
i. Describe the formation and benefits of Hyperledger consortiums and networks. How does collaborating within a consortium network contribute to the adoption and growth of Hyperledger technology?
j. Walk through the process of running the Hyperledger Caliper benchmarks with Docker. Explain the steps involved and the insights that organizations can gain from benchmarking their Hyperledger applications.

5.11.4 Programming Questions

The following sections pose programming questions that can be implemented using Hyperledger.

5.11.4.1 Designing a Supply Chain Management Smart Contract
Design a smart contract using Hyperledger Fabric that can be used for supply chain management. Explain the key functionalities and data structures required to track the movement of goods across different participants in the supply chain. Consider how the contract can handle verification of product origins, ownership transfers, and transparency among participants.

5.11.4.2 Designing a Healthcare Records Management System
Outline the design of a Hyperledger Fabric-based application for managing electronic healthcare records. Describe the data model, access control mechanisms, and privacy considerations needed to securely store and share patient medical information among authorized healthcare providers while ensuring compliance with data protection regulations.

5.11.4.3 Designing a Decentralized Voting System
Propose a program design for a decentralized voting system using Hyperledger Fabric. Explain how the smart contract can ensure secure and tamper-proof voting while maintaining voter anonymity. Describe the roles of participants, the process of voter registration, ballot submission, and the final tallying of votes within the Hyperledger network.

5.11.4.4 Designing a Cross-Border Payment System
Design a Hyperledger Fabric application to facilitate cross-border payments. Define the components required for transferring and verifying payments between participants in different countries. Discuss the integration of smart contracts, identity management, and regulatory compliance to ensure seamless and secure cross-border financial transactions.

Case Studies Using Blockchain

6

6.1 Blockchain – The Technology for Document Management

This section showcases how blockchain revolutionizes document management, ensuring transparency, security, and traceability of digital assets in an immutable ledger. This case study illustrates the power of blockchain in enhancing data integrity and trust in document handling.

6.1.1 The Ownership

The Centre for Development of Advanced Computing (C-DAC) is a leading research and development agency within the Indian government's Ministry of Electronics and Information Technology (MeitY). Its primary focus is on conducting research and development in the fields of information technology, electronics, and related domains. Various sectors within C-DAC have emerged at different points in time, often in response to the recognition of potential prospects. One project under development is document management.

6.1.2 Introduction and Background

In the context of digitization, the importance of ensuring the security and effective management of documents has grown significantly due to the proliferation of digital artifacts, such as educational certificates, birth and death certificates, driver's licenses, health records, employee service records, and sale deed and property registration records, as well as memoranda of understanding and agreements. Furthermore, the lack of efficiency associated with the use of hard copies is being experienced in various industries. Currently, there is a growing trend toward the adoption of digitization. Consequently, blockchain technology has emerged as a prominent tool for the effective management and secure storage of all types of documents and records. The platform offers an innovative solution for safeguarding sensitive data within the financial sector, educational institutions, and government entities. The utilization of blockchain technology has significant ramifications in the realm of intellectual property security, since it provides notable advantages, such as tamper evidence, immutability, and transparency. The implementation of tamper evidence measures is highly effective in mitigating the risks associated with counterfeiting and document fraud.

R. S. Mangrulkar, P. Vijay Chavan, *Blockchain Essentials*,
https://doi.org/10.1007/978-1-4842-9975-3_6

The management of counterfeit digital artifacts represents a substantial obstacle, considering the ongoing proliferation of these materials. Numerous document management systems exhibit a deficiency in terms of the necessary attributes of transparency, security, and efficiency. The blockchain technology ensures the immutability of records, preventing their removal and preserving their sequential order. This is achieved by the system's inherent capability to just permit the addition of new entries without altering existing ones. Blockchain technology enables the verification of the chronological presence, genuineness, and prevention of denial in relation to various documents. Confidential documents necessitate a platform that facilitates the management of user rights, enabling restricted access to the data contained within the blockchain. The distinction between public and private blockchains is a critical aspect to consider in this context.

6.1.3   Problem Statement

This case study focuses on the unique issue of ensuring secure and transparent document management in an increasingly digitized environment. Traditional methods of storing documents face many difficulties in terms of ensuring authenticity, resistance against tampering, and transparency. The prevalence of inefficiencies associated with paper-based documentation and the heightened vulnerability to document fraud have emerged as significant concerns. The primary objective of blockchain technology is to address these difficulties through the provision of a secure and transparent platform for the management and storage of documents. The significance of tackling this issue is in the preservation of the integrity of confidential papers, the mitigation of counterfeiting risks, and the enhancement of overall efficiency in document management.

6.1.4   Use Case Description

The primary objective of this use case is to explore the application of blockchain technology in the realm of document management. The concept pertains to the systematic procedure of safely keeping and effectively managing a diverse range of digital artifacts, encompassing educational diplomas, licenses, and records. The utilization of blockchain technology is deemed appropriate for this particular scenario owing to its inherent characteristics of being resistant to tampering, immutable, and capable of facilitating transparent and secure record-keeping. The utilization of blockchain technology is intended to improve the credibility, traceability, and availability of digital documents.

6.1.5   Solution Architecture

The architectural framework of the blockchain system encompasses essential elements including nodes, consensus processes, smart contracts, and data storage. Nodes are active players within the blockchain network and are responsible for upholding and preserving multiple copies of the distributed ledger. Consensus algorithms play a crucial role in facilitating agreement among network nodes regarding the current state of the blockchain. Smart contracts are contracts that possess the ability to execute themselves, incorporating preestablished rules to automate and enforce business operations. The utilization of blockchain technology for data storage guarantees the preservation of document integrity through tamper-proof mechanisms and cryptographic security measures.

6.1.6   Implementation Steps

The implementation of the blockchain solution involves several steps:

a. Set up a permissioned blockchain network with identified participants.
b. Configure nodes and establish consensus mechanisms.
c. Define smart contracts to automate document management processes.
d. Integrate the blockchain solution into the existing document management system.
e. Develop user interfaces and applications for user interaction with the blockchain.

```python
import hashlib
import time

# Define a Document class
class Document:
    def __init__(self, content):
        self.content = content
        self.timestamp = time.time()
        self.hash = self.calculate_hash()

    def calculate_hash(self):
        return hashlib.sha256(str(self.content + str(self.timestamp)).encode
()).hexdigest()

# Define a Blockchain class
class Blockchain:
    def __init__(self):
        self.chain = [self.create_genesis_block()]

    def create_genesis_block(self):
        return Block(0, "Genesis Block", "0")

    def add_block(self, new_block):
        new_block.previous_hash = self.chain[-1].hash
        self.chain.append(new_block)

    def verify_document(self, document):
        for i in range(1, len(self.chain)):
            current_block = self.chain[i]
            if current_block.data.hash == document.hash:
                return True
        return False

# Main function
def main():
    blockchain = Blockchain()

    # Simulate document creation and verification
    document_content = "This is an important document."
    document = Document(document_content)

    # Verify document
    is_verified = blockchain.verify_document(document)

    # Print verification result
    if is_verified:
```

```
46        print("Document is verified and authentic.")
47    else:
48        print("Document verification failed.")
49
50 if __name__ == "__main__":
51    main()
```

Code Listing 6-1. Document Verification

6.1.7   Smart Contracts

Smart contracts are of paramount importance in addressing the issue at hand as they facilitate the automation and enforcement of business rules pertaining to document management. For example, a smart contract has the capability to establish regulations pertaining to the generation, verification, and authorization of document creation and access. The engagement of individuals with smart contracts facilitates the initiation and execution of transactions pertaining to documents. Smart contracts play a crucial role in promoting transparency, mitigating the necessity for intermediaries, and enhancing the efficacy of document management procedures.

6.1.8   Data Management and Security

The data that are saved on the blockchain are subject to encryption, ensuring their confidentiality, and are resistant to tampering, thereby maintaining their integrity and security. A distinct cryptographic hash is allocated to every document, serving as its exclusive digital identifier. The utilization of a hash function serves the purpose of guaranteeing the integrity of data and acts as a preventive measure against any illegal alterations. The blockchain's immutability ensures that once a document is registered, it is unable to undergo any modifications. The implementation of secure storage protocols for document-related data significantly improves the overall security and integrity of the document management process.

6.1.9   Interoperability and Integration

The blockchain solution establishes interaction with preexisting systems or databases by means of clearly specified interfaces. Interoperability is a critical factor in facilitating the smooth and efficient interchange of data between the blockchain and external systems. The resolution of challenges pertaining to interoperability is achieved by the use of standardized application programming interfaces (APIs) and integration protocols. The blockchain solution was developed with the aim of augmenting and strengthening the functionalities of the current document management infrastructure.

6.1.10 User Experience

The adoption of a blockchain-based document management solution offers numerous advantages. The benefits of implementing a document authentication system include enhanced document authenticity and traceability, a reduction in the risks associated with document fraud and counterfeiting, improved efficiency in document validation and verification processes, and an increase in transparency and confidence among stakeholders. The analysis of quantitative data demonstrates a notable enhancement in processing times and a decrease in the occurrence of unlawful document modifications.

6.1.11 Results and Benefits

The implementation of a blockchain-based document management solution yields several benefits:

- Enhanced document authenticity and traceability
- Reduction of document fraud and counterfeiting risks
- Improved efficiency in document validation and verification
- Increased transparency and trust among stakeholders

Quantitative data reveal improved processing times and reduced instances of unauthorized document alterations.

6.1.12 Challenges and Lessons Learned

Adoption of a document management system based on blockchain technology provides numerous benefits. Increased transparency and confidence among stakeholders; decreased risks associated with document fraud and counterfeiting; enhanced document authenticity and traceability; and improved efficiency in document validation and verification processes are all advantages of implementing a document authentication system. Through the examination of quantitative data, a significant improvement in processing times and a reduction in instances of unauthorized document modifications are evident.

6.1.13 Future Enhancements and Scalability

Potential future improvements could encompass the incorporation of sophisticated authentication mechanisms, additional refinement of document validation procedures, and investigation into the compatibility with other blockchain networks. Scalability considerations pertain to the ability to handle growing quantities of documents and user requirements while maintaining optimal performance levels.

6.1.14 Conclusion

The successful deployment of blockchain technology in document management effectively addresses difficulties pertaining to the authenticity, traceability, and efficiency of documents. The utilization of blockchain technology brings about a paradigm shift in the process of document management, as it offers a platform that is safe, impervious to tampering, and characterized by transparency. The potential influence of blockchain on the document management sector is underscored by the benefits it offers, such as greater document security, reduced fraud risks, and improved user experience.

6.2   Case Study 2: Blockchain in the Food Supply Chain

This study investigates the utilization of blockchain technology to bolster transparency, traceability, and overall integrity within the food supply chain. This case study presents practical applications of blockchain in revolutionizing the food industry, ensuring the safety and authenticity of products as they move from producers to consumers.

6.2.1   Introduction and Background

Blockchain technology is frequently linked to digital currencies such as Bitcoin and Ethereum. Nevertheless, the utility of blockchain technology extends well beyond the realm of digital currency, and it is being employed in diverse sectors such as supply chain management. In recent times, the utilization of blockchain technology has been embraced as a means to tackle obstacles and inadequacies inside supply chains, thereby effecting a transformation in the process of tracing and verifying items.

6.2.2   Problem Statement

The food supply chain business faces notable obstacles, such as food fraud and concerns over traceability. The occurrence of food poisoning and fraudulent activities has brought attention to the necessity of supply chains that are characterized by transparency and accountability. Blockchain technology provides a viable solution to these challenges by facilitating the establishment of a secure, unalterable, and instantaneous system for monitoring the journey of food items from their point of origin to their final destination.

6.2.3   Use Case Description

Blockchain technology is used throughout the food supply chain to effectively monitor and trace the source, processing, and distribution of food items. The decentralized nature of blockchain technology means that all participants throughout the supply chain are given access to precise and transparent information on the trajectory of the product.

6.2.4   Solution Architecture

The blockchain-based solution designed for the food supply chain encompasses many components, including nodes, a consensus mechanism, smart contracts, and data storage. The Hyperledger Fabric framework is widely employed in facilitating smooth collaboration and efficient data sharing among participants. The integration of supplementary technologies, such as Internet of Things (IoT) devices, has the potential to facilitate the acquisition of real-time data.

6.2.5   Implementation Steps

The process of implementation includes the establishment of a permissioned blockchain network and the configuration of individual nodes. Smart contracts are designed for the purpose of automating and ensuring the enforcement of traceability procedures. The process of integrating blockchain technology with preexisting systems facilitates the seamless interchange of data between the blockchain and traditional legacy systems.

```python
import hashlib
import time

class Block:
    def __init__(self, index, timestamp, data, previous_hash):
        self.index = index
        self.timestamp = timestamp
        self.data = data
        self.previous_hash = previous_hash
        self.hash = self.calculate_hash()

    def calculate_hash(self):
        sha = hashlib.sha256()
        sha.update(
            str(self.index).encode() +
            str(self.timestamp).encode() +
            str(self.data).encode() +
            str(self.previous_hash).encode()
        )
        return sha.hexdigest()

class Blockchain:
    def __init__(self):
        self.chain = [self.create_genesis_block()]

    def create_genesis_block(self):
        return Block(0, time.time(), "Genesis Block", "0")

    def add_block(self, new_block):
        new_block.previous_hash = self.chain[-1].hash
        self.chain.append(new_block)

def main():
    blockchain = Blockchain()

    # Simulate food supply chain steps
    products = [
        "Farm -> Processing",
        "Processing -> Distribution Center",
        "Distribution Center -> Store",
        "Store -> Consumer"
    ]

    for index, product in enumerate(products):
        block = Block(index + 1, time.time(), product, "")
        blockchain.add_block(block)
        print(f"Block {block.index} added to the blockchain.")

    # Print blockchain contents
    print("\nBlockchain Contents:")
```

```
51    for block in blockchain.chain:
52        print(f"Block {block.index}:")
53        print(f"Timestamp: {block.timestamp}")
54        print(f"Data: {block.data}")
55        print(f"Previous Hash: {block.previous_hash}")
56        print(f"Hash: {block.hash}")
57        print()
58
59 if __name__ == "__main__":
60    main()
```

Code Listing 6-2. Food Chain Implementation

6.2.6   Smart Contracts

Smart contracts play a crucial role in the automation and optimization of supply chain activities. Rules and conditions are established to govern transactions, thereby guaranteeing that all participants will comply with mutually agreed-upon standards.

6.2.7   Data Management and Security

The inherent immutability of blockchain technology guarantees the integrity and confidentiality of data contained within the distributed ledger. Cryptographic hashing and encryption methods serve to augment the integrity of data, thereby mitigating the risk of illegal access.

6.2.8   Interoperability and Integration

The integration of blockchain technology with external systems and databases is facilitated through APIs, which allow for smooth and efficient interchange of data. The resolution of interoperability difficulties is achieved by implementing standardized communication protocols.

6.2.9   User experience

User interfaces and applications are designed and implemented for the purpose of offering stakeholders convenient and intuitive means of accessing blockchain data. QR codes and mobile applications enable consumers to conveniently scan products and retrieve comprehensive information regarding their whole life cycle.

6.2.10   Results and Benefits

The integration of blockchain technology into the food supply chain has been found to result in substantial advantages. Enhanced traceability practices have been shown to have a positive impact on various aspects of the food industry, including the reduction of response times during recalls, the prevention of foodborne illnesses, and the minimization of food waste. The implementation of enhanced transparency within business practices fosters consumer trust and facilitates the promotion of ethical sourcing.

6.2.11 Challenges and Lessons Learned

The implementation of blockchain technology presents various hurdles, encompassing intricate technical aspects and the need for effective change management. The acquired insights encompass the significance of collaborative efforts, effective communication, and continuous monitoring.

6.2.12 Future Enhancements and Scalability

To ensure future enhancements and scalability of blockchain technology, it is crucial to address the challenges faced during implementation. This includes investing in research and development to improve technical aspects, such as enhancing the speed and efficiency of transactions. Additionally, establishing clear governance frameworks and standards will facilitate interoperability between different blockchain networks, enabling seamless scalability across industries.

6.2.13 Conclusion

The implementation of blockchain technology has had a significant impact on the food supply chain sector, as it has effectively improved traceability, transparency, and accountability within the industry. The effective integration of blockchain solutions in enterprises such as Walmart exemplifies the capacity to establish a food ecosystem that is more secure, streamlined, and environmentally friendly.

6.3   Case Study 3: Blokchain in the Insurance Industry

This case study explores the transformative potential of blockchain technology in the insurance sector, addressing challenges, improving efficiency, and enhancing trust within the industry. This case study delves into the practical applications of blockchain in insurance, highlighting its role in revolutionizing traditional processes and data management.

6.3.1   Introduction and Background

Blockchain technology has attracted the attention of industries around the world, promising dramatic improvements in how data are stored, exchanged, and safeguarded. The potential applications of this disruptive technology go far beyond cryptocurrencies. In this section, we look at how blockchain can be used to address significant issues in the health and life insurance industries. Rising expenses, changing customer expectations, and the looming danger of disruptive innovators necessitate fresh solutions. Blockchain, with its unique characteristics, has the potential to revolutionize several industries.

6.3.2 Problem Statement

Health and life insurance firms face a variety of issues. Administrative costs are rising, increasing automation is required, and an aging workforce demands modernization. Furthermore, changing client expectations necessitate personalized services, increased privacy, innovative products, and competitive pricing. Blockchain technology has surfaced as a prospective remedy in this context. However, there are still numerous unresolved issues concerning the potential applications of blockchain technology in terms of cost reduction, risk management, customer service enhancement, and ultimately, financial gain.

6.3.3 Use Case Description

Deloitte's Center for Health Solutions and Center for Financial Services collaborated on a crowd-sourcing research project to investigate the revolutionary potential of blockchain in health and life insurance. The goal was to determine how blockchain and similar technologies could improve the value propositions of insurers over the next 5 to 10 years. Six important use cases emerged from this exercise, providing insurers with practical and potential routes to leverage blockchain's capabilities.

6.3.4 Solution Architecture

These use cases go into the underlying procedures and business structures of life and health insurers. They include enhancements to operational functions, interactions with stakeholders, and customer experiences. The ultimate goal is to cut expenses, improve operational efficiency, and develop connections with policyholders.

6.3.5 Implementation Steps

Blockchain usage in insurance demands careful planning and smart deployment. Insurers must recognize the promise of technology to upgrade outdated IT systems, increase efficiency, and enhance competitiveness. Engaging cutting-edge blockchain technology partners and engaging with a variety of experts may be necessary. The entire potential of blockchain will be realized only when it is combined with powerful analytics, artificial intelligence, and IoT technologies. Insurers should also aggressively cooperate with healthcare consortiums to develop standards for interoperable blockchain-enabled data repositories.

6.3.6 Smart Contracts

Smart contracts are at the heart of blockchain's transformational power. These digitally signed, computable contracts allow for the automated implementation and enforcement of terms and conditions. They serve as the foundation of secure and autonomous transactions. Smart contracts, for example, can automate claims processing in insurance, minimizing the need for human interaction and administrative expenses.

An Example

```
// SPDX-License-Identifier: MIT
pragma solidity ^0.8.0;

contract InsuranceContract {
    address public insurer;
    address public policyholder;
    uint256 public premiumAmount;
    bool public policyActive;
    bool public claimSubmitted;
    bool public claimApproved;
    uint256 public claimAmount;

    constructor(address _policyholder, uint256 _premiumAmount) {
        insurer = msg.sender;
        policyholder = _policyholder;
        premiumAmount = _premiumAmount;
        policyActive = true;
        claimSubmitted = false;
        claimApproved = false;
    }

    modifier onlyInsurer() {
        require(msg.sender == insurer, "Only insurer can call this function")
;
        _;
    }

    modifier onlyPolicyholder() {
        require(msg.sender == policyholder, "Only policyholder can call this
function");
        _;
    }

    function payPremium() external payable onlyPolicyholder {
        require(msg.value == premiumAmount, "Premium amount must match");
        // Transfer premium to insurer's address
        payable(insurer).transfer(msg.value);
    }

    function submitClaim(uint256 _claimAmount) external onlyPolicyholder {
        require(policyActive, "Policy is not active");
        require(!claimSubmitted, "Claim has already been submitted");
        claimSubmitted = true;
        claimAmount = _claimAmount;
    }

    function approveClaim() external onlyInsurer {
        require(claimSubmitted, "No claim has been submitted");
        require(!claimApproved, "Claim has already been approved");
        claimApproved = true;
        // Transfer the approved claim amount to the policyholder
        payable(policyholder).transfer(claimAmount);
        policyActive = false;
    }

    function cancelPolicy() external onlyPolicyholder {
        require(policyActive, "Policy is not active");
        require(!claimSubmitted, "Claim has been submitted, cannot cancel");
```

```
57      policyActive = false;
58   }
59
60   function getContractBalance() public view returns (uint256) {
61      return address(this).balance;
62   }
63 }
```

Deploying the InsuranceContract Smart Contract

```
1 // Deploy the contract with the following parameters:
2 // Policyholder address: 0x1234567890abcdef...
3 // Premium amount: 1 ether
```

Paying the Premium by the Policyholder

```
1 // Policyholder address: 0x1234567890abcdef...
2 // Premium amount: 1 ether
3
4 InsuranceContract.payPremium({ from: 0x1234567890abcdef..., value: web3.utils
     .toWei("1", "ether") })
```

Submitting a Claim by the Policyholder

```
1 // Policyholder address: 0x1234567890abcdef...
2 // Claim amount: 0.5 ether
3
4 InsuranceContract.submitClaim(web3.utils.toWei("0.5", "ether"), { from: 0
     x1234567890abcdef... })
```

Approving the Claim by the Insurer

```
1 // Insurer address: 0xabcdef123456...
2 InsuranceContract.approveClaim({ from: 0xabcdef123456... })
```

Cancelling the Policy by the Policyholder

```
1 // Policyholder address: 0x1234567890abcdef...
2 InsuranceContract.cancelPolicy({ from: 0x1234567890abcdef... })
```

6.3.7   Data Management and Security

The data management capabilities of blockchain are unrivaled. The blockchain encrypts and stores data as a chain of blocks, ensuring their security and immutability. This powerful data security feature boosts user trust, which is crucial in the insurance market.

6.3.8   Interoperability and Integration

The potential of blockchain to establish trust between institutions makes it an appealing alternative for addressing interoperability issues in the healthcare sector. A blockchain-based comprehensive health record can help to bridge gaps between disparate health information systems and foster collaboration among healthcare providers.

6.3.9 User Experience

Blockchain technology has the potential to transform the user experience in health and life insurance. Insurers can expedite application processes by integrating secure and readily available medical records on the blockchain, bringing comfort and peace of mind to what has previously been a laborious and intrusive experience.

6.3.10 Analysis

Blockchain holds enormous promise in the insurance industry, notably in health and life insurance. Through event-triggered smart contracts, enhanced backend efficiency, disintermediation, better pricing and risk assessment, the creation of new insurance products, and reaching underserved markets, blockchain promises to bring about revolutionary changes. Blockchain's cost-cutting potential is clear, notably in claims processing, administration, underwriting, and product development.

6.3.11 Conclusion

Blockchain is more than a buzzword; it is a transformative force that has the potential to revolutionize the health and life insurance sectors. Insurers can boost efficiency, improve consumer experience, and facilitate experimentation with whole new sorts of interactive insurance and innovative services by leveraging blockchain's unique properties. Bold plans, experimentation, and engagement with emerging technology are required for the road ahead. Blockchain-driven innovation will define the future of health and life insurance, paving the way to a dynamic and customer-centric market landscape.

6.4 Case Study 4: India's Income Tax Department's Simplification of Tax Procedures

This case study explores how blockchain technology is leveraged to streamline and simplify tax procedures within the Indian Income Tax Department (ITD). It demonstrates how blockchain can optimize complex governmental processes, improve data management, and enhance overall efficiency in tax-related activities.

6.4.1 Introduction and Background

India's ITD embarked on a comprehensive digital transformation journey to satisfy rising public demand and increase the efficiency of tax operations. This strategic action aligns precisely with the government's overarching goal of increasing the accessibility and efficiency of public services through digitalization. By adopting blockchain technology and other digital tools, the ITD intends to simplify complex tax procedures, increase transparency, and provide a more user-friendly and streamlined experience for taxpayers. This initiative demonstrates India's dedication to utilizing cutting-edge technology to create a more effective and responsive government ecosystem.

6.4.2   Problem Statement

The ITD faced challenges in digitizing its operations to accommodate the growing number of taxpayers in India. It had to keep up with changing citizen expectations while also meeting major government priorities such as decreasing corruption, enhancing transparency, and promoting ease of doing business.

6.4.3   Use Case Description

In response to these challenges, the ITD decided to employ a blockchain-based strategy. This forward-thinking decision allowed the ITD to focus on specific use cases where blockchain technology could provide substantial benefits. Notably, the ITD focused on the automation of Form 15G/H and Form 26AS. These use cases were selected with a view to simplifying and automating tax-related processes for the benefit of both taxpayers and financial institutions.

Implementing blockchain technology to automate the processing of Forms 15G/H and 26AS represents a fundamental transition toward efficiency and openness in tax operations. It enables taxpayers to submit and administer these forms with minimal manual intervention and error risk. In addition, financial institutions can utilize blockchain to gain access to real-time and accurate tax information, thereby streamlining their compliance processes.

This strategic step by the ITD demonstrates the government's dedication to adopting innovative technologies such as blockchain to improve the tax ecosystem as a whole. It not only simplifies tax-related procedures but also paves the way to a more digitized and efficient tax administration system, in line with the overarching objective of enhancing government services and nurturing a business-friendly environment in India.

6.4.4   Solution Architecture

For its trust-based institutional cooperation features, ITD and its technology partner, Infosys, chose a permissioned blockchain. To maintain data privacy and security, the solution design involved the development of a secure, permission-controlled ledger. The blockchain technology also enabled the development of smart contracts for automating operations and enforcing regulations.

6.4.5   Implementation Steps

The implementation was done in stages. ITD and Infosys began testing blockchain-based use cases such as Form 15G/H and Form 26AS. These experiments were designed to assess the viability and efficacy of blockchain in expediting tax processes.

6.4.6 Smart Contracts

Smart contracts were essential in automating many tax-related activities. When certain conditions were met, they allowed for the execution of predetermined actions. Smart contracts, for example, were utilized to automate the verification of Form 15G/H submission and the generation of tax statements.

An Example

```solidity
// SPDX-License-Identifier: MIT
pragma solidity ^0.8.0;

contract IncomeTaxContract {
    address public taxpayer;
    address public taxAuthority;
    uint256 public taxAmount;
    bool public taxPaid;

    event TaxPaid(address indexed payer, uint256 amount);

    constructor(address _taxAuthority) {
        taxpayer = msg.sender;
        taxAuthority = _taxAuthority;
        taxPaid = false;
    }

    modifier onlyTaxpayer() {
        require(msg.sender == taxpayer, "Only the taxpayer can call this function");
        _;
    }

    modifier onlyTaxAuthority() {
        require(msg.sender == taxAuthority, "Only the tax authority can call this function");
        _;
    }

    function payTax(uint256 _amount) external onlyTaxpayer {
        require(!taxPaid, "Tax has already been paid");
        require(_amount > 0, "Tax amount must be greater than zero");
        taxAmount = _amount;
        taxPaid = true;
        emit TaxPaid(msg.sender, _amount);
    }

    function checkTaxStatus() external view returns (bool) {
        return taxPaid;
    }
}
```

Sample Input and Output
Taxpayer deploys the contract and indicates the tax authority's address:

```solidity
// Deployed by the taxpayer
IncomeTaxContract taxContract = new IncomeTaxContract(
    address_of_tax_authority);
```

Paying Tax

The taxpayer pays a certain amount:

```
// Taxpayer pays 5 Ether as tax
taxContract.payTax{value: 5 ether}(5 ether);
```

Checking Tax Status

All taxpayers can check their tax status:

```
bool isTaxPaid = taxContract.checkTaxStatus();
// The value of isTaxPaid will be 'true' indicating that the tax has been
    paid.
```

Attempting to Pay Tax Again

If the taxpayer tries to pay the tax again, the attempt will fail since the tax has already been paid:

```
// Attempting to pay tax again (will fail)
taxContract.payTax{value: 3 ether}(3 ether);
```

6.4.7   Tax Authority Interaction (Not Implemented in This Simplified Example)

The tax authority would have functions for verifying and processing tax payments. However, these functions are not included in this basic example.

6.4.8   Event Log

When taxpayers pay their taxes, an event is triggered, which can be captured off-chain:

```
event TaxPaid(address indexed payer, uint256 amount);
```

This event can be used to track tax payments made by different taxpayers.

6.4.9   Data Management and Security

Data security and privacy were critical considerations in the blockchain system. The immutability and cryptographic properties of the blockchain ensured that data would remain secure and tamper-proof. Permission restrictions limited data access, while smart contracts enforced data validation rules.

6.4.10 Interoperability and Integration

Multiple players, including banks, financial institutions, and government organizations, must be included in the solution. Interoperability was a critical aspect, allowing diverse groups to smoothly transmit data while ensuring data integrity.

6.4.11 User Experience

The blockchain initiative's purpose was to provide taxpayers with a smooth and user-friendly tax filing experience. The goal of process automation, such as prefilling tax forms, was to make tax compliance more accessible and easier for citizens. This organized summary summarizes the case study's essential sections and material. You can expand on each part as needed by providing additional details and analysis.

6.4.12 Analysis

The case study of India's ITD using blockchain to improve tax processes is an illustrative example of how new technology can transform complex bureaucratic operations. Given the sensitivity of financial data involved in tax operations, ITD's deployment of a permissioned blockchain system is a wise choice. This method ensures data security and transparency and prevents tampering. Furthermore, ITD's dedication to meeting changing citizen expectations by simplifying tax filing and exploring solutions such as prefilling tax statements demonstrates a user-centric approach, ultimately encouraging voluntary tax compliance.

Importantly, ITD recognized the need for a collaborative ecosystem that would include a diverse range of stakeholders, including banks, financial institutions, and government bureaus. ITD efficiently supported real-time, secure data sharing across various entities by developing a permissioned blockchain network, optimizing coordination and combatting tax evasion. Another commendable component is the introduction of smart contracts to the blockchain architecture, which promises automation and error reduction in procedures such as verification and reporting.

One of the most promising characteristics is ITD's willingness to broaden the scope of the blockchain network, allowing for additional use cases and stakeholders. Because of its adaptability, the platform is positioned as a flexible instrument capable of meeting future tax requirements. Furthermore, proactive engagement with regulators by ITD to adapt existing legislation to the blockchain concept is critical. This regulatory foresight ensures that the effort will remain legally compliant while pushing the frontiers of tax digitization.

6.4.13 Conclusion

Finally, the use of blockchain technology by India's ITD to simplify tax processes demonstrates the revolutionary potential of distributed ledger technology in government operations. This case study focused on the department's proactive strategy to meet the changing expectations of digitally savvy residents while addressing difficult tax compliance challenges. The use of a permissioned blockchain system emphasizes the significance of data security, transparency, and collaboration among multiple stakeholders.

ITD's dedication to user-centricity, as evidenced by its objective of simplifying tax filing and fostering voluntary compliance, holds great promise for improving the broader tax environment. The incorporation of smart contracts into the blockchain architecture represents a forward-thinking approach that has the potential to automate procedures and decrease errors in data verification and reporting.

Furthermore, ITD's readiness to broaden the scope of the network and its engagement with other stakeholders, including banks, financial institutions, and government agencies, demonstrates a flexible and adaptable strategy. Because of its elasticity, the blockchain platform may change in response to changing tax laws and legislation.

Overall, the Indian ITD's blockchain effort establishes a precedent for modernizing government operations while increasing efficiency, openness, and confidence. It shows how emerging technology can be used to improve user experiences and streamline key government tasks.

6.5   Case Study 5: Retail Banking

The transformative potential of blockchain technology within the retail banking sector has been investigated. The retail banking sector has historically operated in a competitive and saturated market, with banks competing through incremental enhancements. However, the emergence of blockchain technology presents a unique opportunity to develop a blue ocean strategy – a market space with less competition and greater value for both customers and institutions.

6.5.1   Introduction and Background

The retail banking industry is on the verge of a transformational breakthrough as it explores the vast potential of blockchain technology. As of 2021, the global market for blockchain in retail banking was valued at USD 0.64 billion, and it is poised for rapid expansion, with a projected compound annual growth rate of 83.9% from 2022 to 2030. This extraordinary growth trajectory is primarily attributable to blockchain's ability to eliminate intermediaries, enhance trust, and revolutionize retail banking data management.

Retail banks, which are renowned for the active development of digital business models and the expansion of service offerings to meet the needs of millions of consumers, have adopted blockchain technology with caution. Their reluctance to plunge headfirst into this promising environment stands in stark contrast to the zeal and creativity observed in other industries. Governments, investment institutions, and infrastructure providers have enthusiastically adopted blockchain because they recognize its potential to reduce operational costs and improve transparency. For example, investment banks foresee a future in which execution, post-trade processing, and settlement are instantaneous, rendering many middle- and back-office processes obsolete. They are interested in smart contracts because of their potential to revolutionize automation.

6.5.2   Problem Statement

This problem statement highlights a significant obstacle confronting the retail banking industry in the context of the adoption of blockchain technology. While various entities, such as governments, investment banks, and infrastructure providers, have been actively engaging in blockchain experiments to reduce costs and increase transparency, retail banks have adopted a significantly more cautious stance, largely avoiding active participation.

This issue is representative of a larger trend in the industry, whereby retail institutions have opted to observe the blockchain revolution rather than actively participate in it. Unlike their counterparts in other industries, retail banks have not fully tapped blockchain technology's potential benefits. This problem statement identifies this reluctance as an urgent issue in retail banking.

6.5.3   Use Case Description

In the context of blockchain technology adoption, this problem statement highlights a significant obstacle confronting the retail banking sector. While various entities, such as governments, investment banks, and infrastructure providers, have been proactively engaging in blockchain experiments to reduce costs and increase transparency, retail banks have adopted a significantly more cautious stance, largely avoiding active participation.

This issue exemplifies a larger trend in the industry, in which retail banks have opted to observe rather than actively participate in the blockchain revolution. Unlike their counterparts in other industries, retail banks have not completely exploited the potential benefits offered by blockchain technology. This problem statement identifies such hesitation as a pressing concern within the retail banking environment.

6.5.4   Solution Architecture

The solution architecture designed to encourage retail banks to adopt blockchain technology is a comprehensive framework that integrates various elements, spanning from organizational strategies to technology and regulatory compliance. This multifaceted approach seeks to provide retail banks with a clear and structured path for adopting blockchain technology, while effectively managing associated risks and capitalizing on opportunities.

Blockchain Infrastructure
At the heart of this architecture is the selection of a blockchain platform suited to the particular requirements of retail institutions. This decision could entail selecting a public, private, or consortium blockchain, with popular options including Ethereum, Hyperledger Fabric, Corda, and Quorum. Moreover, integrating blockchain nodes into the bank's infrastructure is essential. These nodes serve a variety of purposes, such as validation and mining in public blockchains or as permissioned nodes in private networks.

Regulatory Compliance
Retail banks must engage actively with regulatory authorities to ensure seamless integration with existing regulatory frameworks. Establishing a collaborative relationship with regulators enables banks to shape blockchain-related regulations and proactively resolve concerns. In addition, integrating know-your-customer (KYC) and anti-money laundering (AML) compliance solutions with blockchain is necessary for effectively meeting regulatory requirements.

6.5.5   Implementation

To encourage retail banks to adopt blockchain technology, defining clear objectives and identifying pertinent use cases is an essential first step. This initial phase establishes the overall course of the adoption procedure. Retail banks must delineate the specific objectives they intend to meet through blockchain implementation. These objectives may include augmenting transaction efficiency, lowering operational expenses, bolstering security, and providing innovative customer services. Alongside these objectives, it is essential to identify pertinent use cases. Retail banks must identify operational areas where blockchain technology can have a significant impact. These may include cross-border remittances, KYC procedures, fraud prevention, and financing for the supply chain. By defining these objectives and use cases, retail banks can establish a strategic basis for their blockchain adventure, which will guide subsequent decisions and actions.

After establishing objectives and use cases, the next stage is to select the blockchain platform that will best meet a retail bank's unique requirements. The capabilities, scalability, and organizational structures of blockchain platforms vary. Retail banks must thoroughly evaluate available options such as Ethereum, Hyperledger, Corda, and Quorum, taking into account operational scale, privacy requirements, and system compatibility. The choice of blockchain platform is crucial to the success of the implementation, as it determines the bank's operational technical framework. Therefore, this decision-making process requires a comprehensive evaluation of both immediate and future needs.

Collaboration with regulatory bodies is essential to promoting the adoption of blockchain technology by retail institutions. As blockchain operates in a regulatory landscape that is largely uncharted, retail banks must proactively engage regulators to influence the evolving regulatory framework. Concerns regarding security, data privacy, and compliance with AML and KYC regulations will be addressed in an open dialogue. Through strategic partnerships with regulatory bodies, retail banks have the potential to aid in the development of pragmatic and unambiguous protocols that not only streamline the implementation of blockchain technology but also safeguard the ethical standards of the financial sector. Establishing this collaborative relationship fosters an environment conducive to blockchain innovation in retail banking by reducing regulatory uncertainties.

6.5.6   Data Management and Security

In the context of enticing retail banks to adopt blockchain technology, this chapter concentrates on the critical data management and security issues within blockchain systems. This section outlines the strategies and considerations retail banks should employ to ensure the integrity, privacy, and resiliency of data as they migrate to blockchain-based solutions.

Data management in blockchain incorporates a number of crucial aspects, as given below:

Data Integrity
It is crucial to ensure the veracity and consistency of data stored on the blockchain. The blockchain's immutable ledger is designed to prevent illicit changes to recorded data. To maintain data integrity, retail institutions must implement robust data validation and consensus mechanisms.

It is essential to determine how and where data are stored on the blockchain network. This includes on-chain versus off-chain storage considerations for various categories of data, particularly sensitive customer information.

Data Migration
If retail banks are to transition from legacy systems to blockchain, they must have a well-defined data migration strategy. This will ensure that historical data will be transferred to the blockchain in a secure manner that does not compromise its integrity.

On the other hand, security is a multifaceted aspect.

Smart Contract Auditing
Smart contracts, which automate processes on the blockchain, must be subjected to stringent auditing to identify vulnerabilities or defects that could be exploited by malicious actors. To ensure the dependability of these contracts, routine security audits and code evaluations are required.

Access Control

Access control to blockchain networks is crucial. To prevent unauthorized access to critical data and functions, banks should employ robust identity and access management systems.

6.5.7 Network Security

Protecting the blockchain network as a whole from external attacks is essential. To protect against cyberattacks, retail banks should implement robust security measures such as firewalls, intrusion detection systems, and encryption.

6.5.8 Incident Response

In the ever-changing landscape of cybersecurity, preparation serves as an impregnable fortress, particularly in the financial industry. In a digital age rife with looming threats and cybercriminals persistently refining their tactics, it cannot be overstated how important it is to have robust incident response plans. These meticulously constructed blueprints are comparable to impregnable armor for banks in their never-ending battle against the unrelenting tide of cyberattacks.

First and foremost among these plans is the requirement for hyper-responsive detection mechanisms. Banks must invest in cutting-edge cybersecurity solutions capable of detecting even the most elusive intrusion indicators. The incorporation of machine learning algorithms and artificial intelligence becomes paramount, enabling real-time analysis of enormous datasets to detect anomalies and potential threats with unprecedented speed and accuracy.

Adaptable and effective mitigation strategies are of equal importance. Once an incident is discovered, the immediate deployment of actions to contain the threat and prevent its spread takes center stage. Banks must meticulously outline procedures for isolating compromised systems or networks while simultaneously preserving vital evidence for in-depth forensic analysis. In addition, establishing predefined communication channels with law enforcement agencies and regulatory bodies can expedite mitigation efforts, thereby increasing the likelihood of capturing cybercriminals.

Recovery procedures should be, not an afterthought, but rather an integral component of the response plan. Banks must diligently develop strategies to expedite the restoration of affected systems and services, thereby minimizing customer and internal business disruptions. This frequently requires the deployment of robust backup systems, rigorous validation of data integrity, and the implementation of fortified security measures to prevent recurrence.

6.5.9 Interoperability and Integration

This section of the solution architecture for enticing retail banks to implement blockchain technology is crucial to the widespread adoption of blockchain in the banking industry. It outlines the strategies and considerations required to ensure that blockchain systems integrate seamlessly with existing banking infrastructure, such as legacy systems, third-party partners, and regulatory frameworks.

The establishment of interoperability standards and cross-blockchain compatibility is a primary focus of this section. By adhering to industry-standard protocols and designing blockchain solutions that are compatible with multiple blockchain platforms, retail banks can ensure technological flexibility and adaptability. This section also emphasizes the significance of integrating blockchain technology with legacy systems, including data migration strategies and smart contract integration.

This integration facilitates a seamless transition to blockchain technology while preserving core banking functions. In addition, it highlights the importance of collaborating with external partners and regulatory entities to ensure secure data sharing and transaction processing. Overall, interoperability and integration entail devising a detailed road map for retail banks to seamlessly integrate blockchain technology into their operations, thereby improving efficiency and transparency while maintaining compliance with industry standards and regulations.

6.5.10 User Experience

This section emphasizes the importance of designing user-friendly interfaces and experiences to facilitate a seamless transition to blockchain technology. For retail banking customers, this entails developing platforms that are user-friendly, secure, and easily accessible for blockchain-based transactions such as cross-border payments and account administration. The objective is to make customers' adoption of blockchain technology transparent and uncomplicated, thereby enhancing their overall banking experience.

This section emphasizes the significance of providing comprehensive training and support for the effective use of blockchain systems to bank employees and staff. This includes creating educational materials, conducting training sessions, and establishing a helpdesk to address any inquiries or concerns that may arise during the adoption process. By ensuring that employees are adequately trained to navigate and manage blockchain technology, retail institutions can improve operational efficiency and reduce disruptions.

In addition, the concern with user experience recognizes the value of feedback loops and continuous refinement. Retail banks should actively solicit feedback from both customers and employees in order to identify pain points, solicit suggestions for improvements, and modify their blockchain systems accordingly. This iterative approach will enable banks to refine their blockchain solutions over time, making them more user-friendly and aligning them with the requirements and expectations of customers and employees.

6.5.11 Analysis

This section on retail banks' use of blockchain technology and cryptocurrencies reveals a dynamic landscape in which traditional banking services face the challenges of digital transformation. From early online banking services to the current era of mobile banking, the retail banking industry has undergone significant evolution. However, the vast majority of retail banks have operated in the "red ocean," a domain characterized by intense competition and limited innovation.

In this context, blockchain technology arises as a transformative force that could propel the industry toward a "blue ocean" strategy, offering both differentiation and cost benefits. Blockchain's secure and transparent distributed ledger system has the potential to revolutionize the way retail banking handles transactions and data.

The analysis also emphasizes the need for widespread industry adoption of blockchain and cryptocurrencies to fully realize the benefits. To accomplish this, the industry must overcome regulatory and standardization obstacles. The success of blockchain in retail banking is contingent upon the establishment of a formal network that facilitates global access and payment clearing, thereby fostering cooperation between banks and other stakeholders.

In addition, the analysis focuses on the current landscape of retail banking, where traditional products and services such as checking and savings accounts, mortgages, and personal loans predominate.

The analysis emphasizes the pioneers' role in creating a blue ocean through "value innovation." Collaboration between the Nasdaq stock market and Citibank demonstrates the capacity of blockchain technology to streamline payments and create real-time digital solutions. The transformative power of blockchain resides in its capacity to automate processes, improve security, and enable ecosystem-based transactions.

6.5.12 Conclusion

In conclusion, the case study on retail banking and blockchain technology demonstrates the immense transformative potential of the financial sector. The findings emphasize the central role of blockchain in disrupting traditional banking practices, particularly in cross-border remittances, KYC processes, and fraud prevention. It emphasizes the need for retail banks to adopt a proactive approach to blockchain adoption in order to access benefits such as reduced costs, increased efficiency, and a more secure banking ecosystem.

In addition, the case study provides a comprehensive solution architecture that incorporates technological, regulatory, and organizational elements to assist retail banks in adopting blockchain technology. This architecture comprises essential stages such as platform selection, regulatory engagement, talent acquisition, proof-of-concept projects, collaboration with fintech partners, customer education, scalability planning, and security measures.

In addition, the study evaluates the current state of retail banking and outlines a strategy canvas, highlighting the significance of consumer value creation. It differentiates between settler, migrant, and pioneer offerings within the industry, demonstrating the potential for blockchain innovation to create a "blue ocean" of uncontested market space.

6.6   Summary

In this chapter, numerous case studies illustrated the practical applications of blockchain technology across industries. These case studies illuminated how blockchain has evolved into a powerful instrument for a variety of purposes, including document management, enhancing transparency and security in supply chains, and even simplifying complex processes within government agencies.

The first case study, titled "Blockchain – The Technology for Document Management," examined blockchain's application in document management. It described the history and ownership of the technology and the issue it solves and provided an overview of blockchain technology. The case study further investigated a use case, solution architecture, implementation stages, smart contracts, data management, and security.

The emphasis of the second case study, titled "Blockchain in the Food Supply Chain," shifted to how blockchain could revolutionize the food industry. Beginning with a background and problem statement, the section illustrated how blockchain could improve agricultural supply chain management, transparency, and traceability.

The third case study, "Blockchain in Insurance Industries," examined the prospective applications of blockchain technology in the insurance industry. The case study examined use case descriptions, solution architecture, implementation stages, smart contracts, data management, security, interoperability, and user experience in depth. The analysis section of the case study analyzed the impact of blockchain technology on the insurance industry, and the study concluded with key takeaways.

The fourth case study, "India's Income Tax Department's Simplification of Tax Procedures," examined blockchain's potential to simplify tax processes. It outlined the problem statement and described the use case for simplifying tax procedures in India. The case study analyzed the solution architecture, implementation stages, smart contracts, interaction with tax authorities, event logging, data management, security, interoperability, and user experience, as well as the solution's implementation.

The concluding case study, "Retail Banking," examined the use of blockchain in the banking industry. It began with an introduction, a problem statement for retail banking, and a use case for blockchain adoption. The case study examined solution architecture, implementation procedures, data management, security, network security, incident response, interoperability, and user experience.

Throughout the chapter, the authors provided insightful commentary on the obstacles faced in blockchain implementation, lessons learned, and potential scalability and efficiency enhancements. These real-world case studies illustrated the adaptability and potential of blockchain technology across multiple industries and provided a comprehensive overview of its practical applications and advantages.

6.7   Exercise

This section presents exercises based on topics covered in this chapter.

6.7.1   Multiple Choice Questions

a. Which industry has implemented blockchain technology to enhance the transparency and traceability of the supply chain?
   i. Healthcare
   ii. Fashion
   iii. Agriculture
   iv. Entertainment
b. In the case of the "Walmart Food Safety" blockchain project, what is the primary goal of using blockchain?
   i. Reducing operational costs
   ii. Improving food safety
   iii. Enhancing customer experience
   iv. Expanding the product line
c. Which cryptocurrency was created as a result of the Ethereum blockchain's smart contract capabilities?
   i. Bitcoin
   ii. Ripple (XRP)
   iii. Litecoin
   iv. Ether (ETH)
d. Which industry is most likely to benefit from the use of blockchain in reducing fraud and counterfeiting?
   i. Automotive
   ii. Real estate
   iii. Banking
   iv. Gaming

e. Which blockchain consortium is known for its focus on enhancing the interoperability of different blockchain networks?
   i. R3 Corda
   ii. Hyperledger
   iii. Enterprise Ethereum Alliance
   iv. Binance Smart Chain
f. The "IBM Food Trust" blockchain platform is primarily used for what purpose in the food industry?
   i. Tracking and tracing food products
   ii. Online food delivery
   iii. Restaurant management
   iv. Food packaging design
g. Which blockchain use case involves recording property ownership and land titles to prevent fraud and disputes?
   i. Healthcare records
   ii. Supply chain management
   iii. Identity verification
   iv. Real estate and land registry

6.7.2 Short/Long Answer Questions

a. Explain what blockchain technology is and, in simple terms, how it works.
b. Explain the concept of decentralization in the context of blockchain.
c. What are the key components of a blockchain network?
d. Describe the role of consensus mechanisms in maintaining the integrity of a blockchain.
e. How does blockchain technology enhance security and trust in data transactions?
f. Name two industries besides finance that have adopted blockchain technology and briefly explain their use cases.
g. What is a smart contract, and how does it automate processes on a blockchain?
h. How do public and private blockchains differ, and what are their respective advantages?
i. What challenges or limitations are associated with blockchain technology adoption?

Beyond Blockchain

7

The metaverse is an innovative technology that aims to revolutionize the way we interact and engage with virtual worlds. By leveraging the decentralized nature of blockchain, it provides a secure and transparent platform for users to create, own, and trade digital assets within the metaverse. This technology has the potential to empower users by giving them true ownership and control over their virtual identities and possessions, fostering a new era of immersive and interconnected virtual experiences.

7.1   Blockchain for the Metaverse

The utilization of blockchain technology holds significant potential in facilitating the establishment of trust, security, and decentralization within the metaverse. This section examines the potential of blockchain technology in addressing the distinct issues and specific requirements of the immersive digital reality.

7.2   Emergence of the Metaverse

Imagine a virtual world where billions of people live, work, trade, learn, and interact while sitting on their couches in the real world.

In this world, the computer screens we use to connect to the worldwide web of information have become portals to a palpable, three-dimensional (3D) virtual world – just like real life, but superior. Avatars, which are digital representations of ourselves, move freely from one experience to the next, carrying our identities and money with them. This is known as the metaverse, and, contrary to popular belief, it does not currently exist.

What should business leaders make of an overhyped, swiftly evolving concept that has the potential to drastically transform the way humans live? The comprehensive guide to the metaverse by TechTarget describes the current state and future trajectory of this emergent technological revolution. It addresses the metaverse's supporting technologies and platforms, as well as its advantages and disadvantages, investment strategies, historical background, significance, and implications for the future of labor.

There are links throughout the guide to in-depth analyses of these and other pertinent topics, as well as definitions of key metaverse concepts such as interoperability, digital siblings, spatial computing, and Web 3.0.

© The Author(s), under exclusive license to APress Media, LLC, part of Springer Nature 2024
R. S. Mangrulkar, P. Vijay Chavan, *Blockchain Essentials*,
https://doi.org/10.1007/978-1-4842-9975-3_7

Figure 7-1 Layer
structure in Metaverse

7.3   Understanding the Metaverse

The metaverse is an emerging 3D-enabled digital space that employs virtual reality (VR), augmented reality (AR), and advanced Internet and semiconductor technologies to facilitate lifelike online personal and commercial experiences. Interest in the metaverse has skyrocketed in recent years, with Internet queries for the term "metaverse" increasing by an astounding 7,200% in 2021.

This interest surge is not limited to individuals; private capital is also investing significantly in the metaverse. In 2021, companies associated with the metaverse raised over $10 billion, more than doubling their funding from the previous year. This trend persisted in 2022, with over $120 billion invested in metaverse-related endeavors. According to McKinsey's most recent research, the metaverse has the potential to generate up to $5 trillion in value by 2030, making it an unmissable opportunity.

The concept of the metaverse is interpreted differently by different individuals. Some see it as a commercial space for businesses to interact with consumers.The perspective of McKinsey includes both of these interpretations. According to the firm's June 2022 report, "Value Creation in the Metaverse," the metaverse is best characterized as an evolution of the Internet that people are profoundly immersed in as opposed to merely observing. It represents the convergence of numerous digital technologies, such as cryptocurrencies, artificial intelligence (AI), AR, VR, and spatial computing, among others. The "enterprise metaverse" may be more than just a virtual space for interactions; it may also unleash new opportunities.

7.4   Metaverse Layers

The metaverse can be conceptualized as a multifaceted ecosystem that includes seven foundational layers, each of which assumes a pivotal function in defining the whole metaverse encounter. The layered structure of the metaverse is given in Figure 7-1:

Experience
This layer signifies the fundamental essence of the metaverse, wherein individuals actively participate in immersive and synchronous encounters. The objective of this approach extends beyond mere passive observation, since it strives to create a digital environment that is both highly participatory

and authentic. Individuals might anticipate encounters that replicate the tangible realm, thereby enhancing the immersion and authenticity of activities such as gaming, social interactions, e-commerce, entertainment, and e-sports.

Discovery
The concept of the discovery layer refers to a user interface that provides a simplified and unified access point to various information resources within a library or other information system.

The primary objective of the discovery layer is to examine the mechanisms through which users locate and investigate novel experiences, platforms, technologies, and communities inside the metaverse. This encompasses a range of channels, such as application shops, search engines, review platforms, and advertising displays. The presence of efficient discovery techniques is crucial in enabling users to navigate the expansive metaverse with proficiency.

Creator Economy
The scope of this layer comprises the various tools and applications utilized by developers and content creators for the purpose of generating digital assets, immersive experiences, and other resources within the metaverse. The focal point lies in the promotion of content creation democratization, facilitating the transition of individuals into creators, developers, or designers through the utilization of user-friendly platforms and drag-and-drop functionalities.

7.4.1 Spatial Computing

Spatial computing refers to an information technology solution that combines augmented and virtual reality. Spatial computing, according to Radoff, enables us to access and manipulate three-dimensional spaces. It empowers users to digitize objects via cloud computing, integrate sensors with actuators for responsive functionality, and digitize the physical environment via spatial mapping. This stratum comprises critical components, including 3D engines like Unity and Unreal. In addition, Niantic Planet-Scale AR, Cesium, and Descartes Labs' geospatial mapping contribute to the interpretation and mapping of the interior and exterior of the planet.

Decentralization
From an idealistic perspective, the metaverse should exhibit decentralization and openness, with governance entrusted to decentralized autonomous organizations (DAOs) in order to uphold transparency and prevent central ownership. Blockchain technology and decentralized applications (DApps) play a pivotal role in this layer by effectively addressing problems related to privacy and security. Prominent instances encompass Decentraland, an exemplar of a decentralized virtual realm that operates under the governance of a DAO. The Human Interface layer refers to the component of a system that facilitates interaction between humans and the underlying technology.

Human Interface
The human interface layer primarily concentrates on the technological aspects that facilitate users' engagement with the metaverse through the utilization of sophisticated human–computer interaction (HCI) techniques. The aforementioned technologies encompass VR headsets, smart glasses, haptic feedback devices, and AR technologies such as Google Glass. These interfaces serve as a means of connecting the physical and digital realms, facilitating smooth and uninterrupted movement.

Infrastructure

The infrastructure layer is a crucial component within the context of a system or network. It encompasses the foundational technologies and components that provide support for the entirety of the metaverse ecosystem. This includes several technological advancements such as high-speed networks like 5G for the purpose of minimizing latency and congestion, semiconductors, microelectromechanical systems (MEMS), durable batteries, blockchain technology, AI, cloud architecture, and graphics processing units. These technologies are responsible for ensuring the seamless and effective functioning of the metaverse.

7.4.2   Metaverse Components

The metaverse is an emerging digital space that extends the capabilities of the Internet by facilitating immersive and interactive experiences through technologies such as VR, AR, blockchain, and others. It is a shared, interconnected virtual universe where users can interact in real time with each other and digital environments. The metaverse consists of numerous components, as discussed in what follows.

Virtual Worlds

These are digital environments that simulate physical spaces or wholly fictitious worlds. Virtual worlds can be recreations of real-world locations or wholly fabricated landscapes. Using avatars, users can investigate and interact with these worlds.

Avatars

Avatars are digital representations of metaverse users. They can be modified to reflect the appearances, identities, and preferences of the user. Avatars enable users to navigate and interact with the virtual environment; they are essentially users' digital personas.

Digital Assets

Digital assets are digital objects or products that possess value in the metaverse. These assets can include virtual real estate, avatar apparel, digital collectibles, virtual currency (typically represented by nonfungible tokens or NFTs), and more. Within the metaverse, digital assets can be possessed, traded, and utilized.

Spatial Computing

Technologies of spatial computing, such as AR and VR, play a crucial role in the creation of immersive experiences within the metaverse. AR superimposes digital information onto the real world, whereas VR generates entirely virtual environments for users to inhabit.

Interactivity

Interactivity is a fundamental characteristic of the metaverse, allowing users to interact with the digital environment and other users. This includes social interactions, recreation, commerce, education, and other activities. Communication and collaboration in real time are essential features.

Blockchain Technology

Blockchain technology is frequently used to support the metaverse, as it provides a secure and transparent method for managing digital assets, verifying ownership, and facilitating transactions. Unique digital items or assets are represented by NFTs, which are frequently associated with blockchain technology.

Decentralization

The metaverse frequently operates under decentralized principles, reducing its dependence on central authorities. This decentralization may include distributed servers, governance based on blockchain technology, and user-driven content creation and curation.

Cross-Platform Compatibility

One of the primary objectives of the metaverse is to facilitate cross-platform compatibility, allowing users to access and interact with the metaverse from a variety of devices, such as personal computers, VR headsets, AR glasses, smartphones, and more.

User-Generated Content

Users are encouraged to contribute to the metaverse by generating their own content, be it virtual spaces, digital art, or interactive experiences. User-generated content is the primary force behind the metaverse's richness and diversity.

7.5 Metaverse Through Immersive Technologies

The use of immersive technology, specifically VR, as a means to access the metaverse has emerged as a crucial approach for a multitude of organizations. This technological advancement enables access to a computer-simulated realm that facilitates worldwide interactions. Numerous enterprises are integrating VR technology into their operational frameworks as a strategic measure to adapt to an anticipated future characterized by computer-simulated environments.

What follows is a comprehensive sequential manual aimed at assisting enterprises in embarking upon the metaverse through the use of VR technology.

Identify High-Impact VR Use Cases
The initial step involves the identification of high-impact VR use cases.

Begin by assessing the ways in which VR might augment and optimize your organizational workflows. VR has the potential to be utilized in several applications, ranging from strengthening training and onboarding initiatives to augmenting digital advertising through the incorporation of VR components. To commence, it is advisable to launch a modest-scale initiative within the confines of your institution. It is recommended to develop a proof of concept in order to substantiate one's ideas prior to making significant financial commitments.

Find an Experienced VR Partner
When considering the prospect of engaging in a collaborative effort with an external technology partner for the purpose of developing a VR solution, it is of utmost importance to carefully choose a software development business that possesses a high level of proficiency and specialization in the field of VR. Seek out partners who provide extensive VR application development services, encompassing the validation of ideas, 3D design, user acceptability testing, and continuous support. Conduct an analysis of the prospective vendor's VR project portfolio, with a specific emphasis on their prior involvement within your sector. It is recommended to solicit client testimonials and case studies in order to acquire a more comprehensive understanding of the vendor's skills. In addition, it is advisable to take into account media coverage, awards, and customer ratings as part of the assessment process for possible partners. Conducting comprehensive research and considering one's options carefully are crucial when selecting an appropriate partner for VR software development.

Choose a Suitable VR Platform
There exist multiple VR platforms, each possessing distinct advantages and disadvantages. Engage in a collaborative effort with a proficient VR vendor to carefully evaluate and choose the platform that best corresponds to the specific requirements of your organization. The commonly available choices include Oculus Rift, HTC Vive, and Google Cardboard.

Develop VR Content and Set Up VR System
The fourth step entails the creation of VR content and the establishment of the VR system.

After selecting a platform, the next stage is to create or acquire VR content for use with the selected platform. The VR technology partner can provide guidance in selecting the optimal content format, which encompasses interactive scenery, photos, movies, animation, 3D models, or complete virtual environments. The process of establishing a VR system commonly involves the installation of VR software on a computer and the subsequent connection of that computer to a VR headset.

Continuously Improve with Feedback
Following the initiation of a VR project, it is imperative to solicit feedback from both the internal team and external clients. Such feedback will be of great use in improving ongoing initiatives and strategizing for future endeavors. The technological landscape is undergoing continuous evolution, necessitating the imperative to remain abreast of the most recent breakthroughs and trends. Incorporating feedback into projects will ensure that initiatives will maintain a leading edge in the realm of technology.

7.5.1 Challenges in Metaverse Implementation

Building a seamless, interconnected metaverse poses several significant challenges, as this endeavor requires overcoming technical, social, and economic hurdles. The following discussion touches on some of the key challenges.

Interoperability

Achieving interoperability between diverse metaverse platforms, devices, and technologies is one of the greatest obstacles. Different companies and developers construct their own metaverse ecosystems, making it challenging for users to navigate between them seamlessly. A lack of standardized protocols and formats can hinder communication and data exchange across platforms.

Scalability

As the metaverse seeks to simultaneously accommodate millions, if not billions, of users, scalability represents a significant challenge. It is essential to ensure that the infrastructure can manage the massive data flows, computational demands, and user interactions that occur in virtual worlds.

Content Standards

Establishing content standards and moderation mechanisms is essential for sustaining a safe and inclusive metaverse. It can be difficult to strike a balance between creative license and the need to prevent harassment, hate speech, and inappropriate content.

Digital Identity and Privacy

Protecting the digital identities of metaverse users and assuring their privacy is a complex issue. Users must have control over their personal data and digital assets, while retaining the ability interact with others and conduct transactions.

Security and Trust

Establishing confidence in the metaverse is crucial to its viability. Remaining constantly vigilant to prevent fraud, hacking, and cyberattacks poses a formidable challenge. Security measures must protect not only user information but also the virtual economy and digital assets.

Digital Asset Ownership

Defining and enforcing ownership rights for digital assets such as virtual real estate, NFTs, and other items can be legally and technically complex. Smart contracts based on blockchain technology can be beneficial, but disagreements may still arise.

Economic Models

The establishment of enduring economic models for the metaverse can be difficult. It requires a delicate balance to determine how creators, developers, and platform providers will be compensated while ensuring that virtual experiences will remain accessible to a large audience.

Inclusivity and Diversity

It is a social challenge to ensure that the metaverse is inclusive and representative of diverse populations. Developers and content creators must take proactive measures to avoid discrimination, bias, and inequality within the digital space.

User Experience

It is essential to provide a seamless and enjoyable user experience. Reducing latency, enhancing the quality of graphics, and enhancing user interfaces are ongoing technical challenges. Additionally, motion sickness and discomfort within virtual environments must be addressed.

Legal and Regulatory Frameworks

The metaverse operates within a legal and regulatory gray area. Governments and policymakers are still adjusting to the concept, which can create ambiguity regarding taxation, intellectual property rights, and jurisdiction.

Community Governance

Establishing governance mechanisms for metaverse communities can be difficult. Decisions regarding norms, standards, and dispute resolution procedures must incorporate community input and account for potential power imbalances.

Education and Digital Literacy

It is essential to promote digital literacy and educate users on the metaverse's capabilities, dangers, and benefits. Many users may be unfamiliar with immersive technologies and their implications.

7.6   Blockchain's Role in the Metaverse

Blockchain technology plays a crucial role in shaping the metaverse, providing solutions to a number of the challenges and requirements inherent in the creation of a seamless and secure digital environment.

7.6.1   Why Blockchain Technology Is Crucial for the Metaverse

Blockchain introduces the concept of digital scarcity, enabling virtual assets to have unique, verifiable ownership. NFTs allow users to genuinely own digital assets, such as virtual real estate, in-game items, and digital art, in the metaverse. NFTs, which are indivisible and cannot be replicated, provide a transparent and immutable ownership record. This is necessary for establishing the worth of virtual assets and facilitating secure transactions.

7.6.2 Interoperability and Standards

Blockchain technology provides a standard method for representing and trading virtual assets across various metaverse platforms. This interoperability means that users can transport their assets between different virtual environments. Developers of the metaverse can establish a unified ecosystem where assets are universally recognized and transferable by adhering to common blockchain standards.

7.6.3 Security and Trust

Blockchain's decentralized ledgers increase security and trust within the metaverse. On a distributed network, transactions are recorded, making it exceedingly difficult for malicious actors to manipulate data or pilfer assets. Smart contracts facilitate trustless interactions on blockchain networks, automating transactions and ensuring parties fulfill their obligations without the need for intermediaries.

7.6.4 Monetization and Incentives

Blockchain enables the development of new economic models in the metaverse. Without relying on centralized platforms, creators and developers are able to monetise their content and creations directly. For their participation and contributions to the virtual ecosystem, users can receive tokens. These economic incentives promote a thriving, self-sustaining metaverse economy in which value is more equitably distributed among participants.

7.7 Digital Scarcity and Ownership of Virtual Assets

The concept of digital scarcity represents a fundamental shift in how we perceive and value virtual assets within the metaverse. Traditional digital items can be endlessly copied, leading to a lack of uniqueness and ownership. Blockchain technology changes this by enabling the creation of NFTs, which represent true ownership of virtual assets.

The concept of digital scarcity signifies a major shift in our understanding and evaluation of virtual goods within the metaverse. The proliferation of conventional digital artifacts has led to a scarcity of uniqueness and ownership. The utilization of blockchain technology brings about a significant transformation in the existing environment by enabling the introduction of NFTs, which function as a mechanism to create indisputable ownership over virtual assets.

NFTs offer several notable benefits:

Provenance

This refers to the capacity of users to trace the origin and ownership history of assets backed by NFTs, thereby ensuring their authenticity and establishing a transparent record of their origin.

Ownership Rights

NFTs provide users with transparent and verifiable ownership rights to digital assets, such as the ability to transfer, trade, or exhibit them.

Scarcity

NFTs are intended to be scarce, generating uniqueness and scarcity that can stimulate demand and increase value.

This allows users to confidently purchase, sell, and trade virtual assets in the metaverse, as their ownership is recorded on an immutable blockchain.

7.8   Building Trust and Security in the Decentralized Metaverse

In the dynamic and ever-changing realm of the metaverse, trust and safety are of utmost importance. In light of the ongoing expansion of the digital sphere, it is crucial to establish a decentralized environment that effectively protects users' security and inspires their trust.

7.8.1   Trustless Nature of the Metaverse

The metaverse, as conceptualized within the framework of Web 3.0, possesses an intrinsic characteristic of trustlessness. The system is predicated around decentralization, wherein a lack of central authority ensures that the entire ecosystem remains unregulated. This characteristic is in accordance with the fundamental principles of blockchain technology, wherein transactions may be verified and remain unchangeable without the involvement of intermediaries.

7.8.2   Zero Trust Security in the Metaverse

To cultivate trust within the context of decentralization, it is imperative to adopt a zero trust security architecture that is built upon foundational principles. The underlying assumption of this paradigm posits that, irrespective of their position within the metaverse ecosystem, no entity, user, or device should be granted inherent trust. The following subsections represent the major concerns in connection with metaverse security:

Hardware Security

The preservation of tamper resistance and security against attacks on user devices, including VR headsets and AR glasses, is of utmost importance in safeguarding the overall security of the metaverse.

Authentication and Authorization

To mitigate the risk of unwanted access to metaverse spaces and assets, it is imperative to employ robust authentication techniques and implement precise authorization rules.

Protection Against Deep Fakes

The prevention of the misuse of deep fakes in the metaverse poses a substantial security problem due to the rapid progress of AI. The implementation of AI-based detection and verification systems can aid in the mitigation of this risk.

7.9   Data Hub for Crypto, DeFi, NFT, Metaverse

Apache Kafka plays a crucial role in facilitating real-time data streaming, enabling enterprises to efficiently acquire, process, and disseminate data in real time across diverse applications and systems.

7.9.1   Real-Time Data Streaming

Within the domain of data ingestion in a cryptocurrency exchange platform, Apache Kafka assumes a crucial role in the efficient aggregation and administration of live market data originating from diverse cryptocurrency exchanges. The aforementioned procedure is of utmost importance in guaranteeing that the platform offers traders and investors with real-time data on cryptocurrency prices and trading volumes.

The Kafka producers play a vital role in facilitating the data import process. The role of these producers is to serve as intermediaries between various cryptocurrency exchanges, facilitating the retrieval of up-to-date market data. Each exchange may possess distinct characteristics in terms of data format, update frequency, and application programming interfaces. However, Kafka producers simplify these difficulties by establishing connections with the exchanges and gathering data in a consistent fashion.

After the collection of data, the Kafka producers proceed to push the acquired data into designated Kafka topics. Within the described framework, Kafka topics can be conceptualized as structured channels or data streams within the Kafka ecosystem, devised to effectively manage distinct categories of data. For example, many Kafka topics can be utilized to represent discrete cryptocurrency pairs, like BTC/USD, ETH/BTC, and others.

By categorizing data into several distinct themes, the cryptocurrency exchange platform provides numerous benefits, discussed in the next few subsections.

7.9.1.1 Data Organization
The term "data organization" pertains to the systematic administration of the extensive volume of data produced by several cryptocurrency exchanges. The dataset encompasses up-to-date market data, including cryptocurrency prices and trading volumes, which holds significant importance for traders and investors in facilitating well-informed decision-making. Apache Kafka, a widely adopted data streaming platform, plays a crucial role in effectively managing this dataset.

7.9.1.2 Parallel Processing

Kafka facilitates the execution of parallel processing on data across different topics, thereby enabling the simultaneous ingestion of data from diverse exchanges. This concurrent approach enhances the overall throughput of the system.

7.9.1.3 Scalability

Scalability is a crucial aspect in the context of exchanges or cryptocurrency pairs. Kafka's scalability facilitates the platform's ability to effectively manage the expanding data volume as the number of exchanges or cryptocurrency pairs grows.

7.9.1.4 Data Isolation

Data isolation refers to the practice of maintaining the separation of data originating from distinct sources, ensuring that each dataset remains confined within its specific domain. This approach serves to mitigate the potential hazards associated with data contamination or interference.

7.10 Digital Trust Networks

The concept of a digital trust network goes beyond the realm of blockchain technology and plays a pivotal role in the establishment of trust among diverse digital interactions. In this discussion, we will examine the concept of a delay-tolerant network, its relevance within the domain of blockchain technology, and its broader implications extending beyond the scope of blockchain applications.

The DTN assumes a crucial function inside the digital domain by effectively tackling trust-related obstacles encountered in transactions and interactions. In contrast to blockchain technology, which largely centers on the recording of transactions, delay-tolerant networks incorporate a wider range of digital protocols and activities. Trust is strengthened by the implementation of digital technologies that streamline transaction processes from start to finish. This is achieved by integrating many components such as standards, Internet of Things (IoT), oracles, and smart contracts. This practice enhances the likelihood of the veracity of claims made during transactions, as well as the adherence to obligations, thereby cultivating a sense of trust among parties involved.

Distributed temporal networks surpass the capabilities of blockchain technology by organizing interactions via standardized interfaces and facilitating secure and trustworthy transactions. Frequently, a prevalent virtual database is incorporated, functioning as a reliable repository of information. Blockchain technology plays a significant role in enhancing trust between intermediaries, whereas delay-tolerant networks primarily focus on establishing trust in digital exchanges. Modern technologies decrease reliance on conventional intermediaries, granting counterparties enhanced authority and transparency in managing their transactions. Digital transformation networks play a crucial role in reconfiguring the digital environment by emphasizing trust as a basic component in transactions and interactions, thereby augmenting security and dependability.

7.10.1 Diverse Applications of Digital Trust Networks

DTNs cover a diverse range of applications within the digital domain, each fulfilling specific objectives in establishing trust or handling distrust among entities engaged in interactions. These applications exemplify the adaptability and importance of delay-tolerant networks in several environments.

7.10.2 Peer-to-Peer Marketplaces

Services such as Uber, Airbnb, and Amazon Marketplace utilize disruption-tolerant networks to foster trust and allay skepticism among buyers and sellers. These platforms enable secure transactions in the sharing economy by providing transparent ratings, reviews, and secure payment mechanisms.

7.10.3 Platform Ecosystems

The Apple iOS ecosystem exemplifies the implementation of digital technology networks within platform ecosystems. Apple upholds trust by engaging in the curation of app content and exercising control over developer conduct via rigorous regulations and code review procedures. This measure guarantees a secure and dependable user experience.

7.10.4 Zero Trust Security Systems

Zero trust security systems are implemented in corporate environments to effectively manage and regulate employee and external access, while also monitoring and controlling their actions. These systems rely on the use of dynamic trust negotiations to ensure a comprehensive security framework. These solutions aim to mitigate the potential for unwanted access and security breaches.

7.10.5 Digital Identity Platforms

The Aadhaar architecture in India exemplifies the efficacy of DTNs in establishing a robust framework for the provision of secure digital identification services. Aadhaar, with its enrollment of about 1.4 billion individuals, facilitates the provision of trust-dependent services, including but not limited to financial inclusion and the delivery of government benefits.

7.10.6 Decentralized Autonomous Organizations

DAOs are novel systems that utilize smart contracts executed on blockchains to emulate some corporate capabilities. DAOs make use of blockchain technology, although their decision-making and trust management are primarily facilitated by distributed trust networks.

7.11   Beyond Cryptocurrency: Transforming ESG, Digital Assets, and Financial Markets

The emergence of blockchain technology coincided with the introduction of Bitcoin in 2008. Since then, this technology has undergone substantial advancements and is anticipated to undergo further notable progress in the future. Its potential extends well beyond the domain of cryptocurrencies. This discourse provides a brief overview of the future trajectory of blockchain technology.

7.11.1 Environmental, Social, and Governance (ESG)

ESG investing has emerged as a crucial factor for institutional investors and individuals with a strong social conscience. It encompasses the issues that play a major role in investment decisions. The potential of blockchain technology resides in its ability to augment transparency in corporate governance, thereby providing investors with comprehensive visibility into a company's ESG activities. The promotion of openness in the ESG-driven investment landscape is crucial for cultivating trust and credibility. Furthermore, the implementation of blockchain technology has the potential to bring about a significant transformation in the voluntary carbon credit markets. This can be achieved by enhancing transparency and eradicating fraudulent activities through the utilization of distinct metadata records for each carbon credit. As a result, a trustworthy marketplace can be established, ensuring credibility in the trading of carbon credits.

7.11.2 Digital Assets and Currency

Digital assets, such as NFTs and other assets like them, are becoming increasingly significant due to the utilization of blockchain technology on platforms like Ethereum, which ensures the secure ownership of these digital assets. In addition to artistic works, NFTs encompass a diverse range of digital assets, including essays and domain names, which derive advantages from the immutable record-keeping facilitated by blockchain technology. The financial services sector acknowledges digital assets as a prospective development, with a significant majority of companies envisioning digital assets supplanting fiat currency during the next decade. Stablecoins, which are supported by reserve assets like the United States Dollar (USD) or gold, are gaining traction due to their capacity to augment the advantages of cryptocurrencies while ensuring a stable value.

7.11.3 Central Bank Digital Currencies

Central bank digital currencies (CBDCs) are now being explored by many governments globally, including the United States, United Kingdom, Japan, and the European Union (EU). Although not all CBDCs are dependent on blockchain technology, there is ongoing experimentation with distributed ledger technology (DLT) for facilitating cross-border interbank transactions. These trials highlight the potential of DLT in augmenting international financial institutions.

7.11.4 Blockchain Modernizing Financial Markets

Blockchain technology is facilitating the modernization of conventional financial markets, thereby enhancing their operational efficiency. Bonds, which have traditionally been traded through complex processes, can now be traded electronically on platforms utilizing blockchain technology. The process of digitization improves transparency, liquidity, and settlement speed, thereby optimizing the efficiency of bond market operations.

7.11.5 Blockchain and AI: A Synergy for Trust and Intelligence

AI has significant prospects for augmenting and propelling blockchain technology across diverse industries, fields, and markets.

7.11.6 Data Analysis and Predictive Insights

AI exhibits unique skills in efficiently processing and accurately interpreting large volumes of data, thereby enabling the generation of predictive insights. In the context of blockchain technology, AI exhibits superior performance in analyzing transaction data and patterns, surpassing the capabilities of human agents. Examination of these data can provide significant observations regarding market patterns, user actions, and the identification of irregularities that may suggest possible instances of fraudulent behavior. By utilizing past blockchain data, AI has the capability to generate predictions based on data analysis, thereby equipping users with decision-making tools that are grounded in information.

7.11.7 Smart Contract Automation

Smart contract automation is a fundamental aspect of blockchain technology, wherein predetermined actions are executed automatically upon the fulfillment of specific conditions. AI has the potential to enhance smart contracts by facilitating their ability to adapt and react in real time to real-world events and incoming data streams. In a supply chain context, AI has the capacity to observe and analyze data obtained from IoT sensors. It can then independently initiate smart contracts to modify orders or logistics routes based on dynamic factors such as variations in weather conditions or fluctuations in demand.

7.11.8 Enhanced Security

Security is a fundamental aspect of blockchain technology, and the integration of AI can provide additional reinforcement to its protective measures. AI algorithms demonstrate proficiency in the ongoing surveillance of blockchain networks to detect atypical or questionable behaviors, such as unauthorized access attempts and hacking operations. AI has the ability to identify complex behavioral patterns that could indicate a security breach. In such instances, AI promptly reacts to protect the overall integrity of blockchain networks.

7.11.9 Scalability and Performance

Scalability and performance pose significant issues for numerous blockchain networks, particularly those of a public nature such as Bitcoin and Ethereum. AI interventions have the potential to optimize these networks, thereby improving their performance and scalability. Machine learning algorithms have the capacity to evaluate network traffic and usage patterns, thereby facilitating the optimization of resource allocation for increased efficiency. This enhancement improves the speed of transaction processing and addresses congestion issues.

7.12   The Future of Banks

The potential for a revolution in the financial industry lies in the forthcoming acceptance and incorporation of blockchain technology. Blockchain, a decentralized ledger technology that serves as the foundation for digital currencies such as Bitcoin, presents numerous benefits and prospects for financial institutions to transform their activities and offerings. This presentation offers an overview of the potential ways in which banks of the future may utilize blockchain technology.

7.12.1 Instant and Efficient Cross-Border Payments

Traditional cross-border payments frequently require the involvement of numerous intermediaries, leading to significant delays and exorbitant expenses. Blockchain technology has the potential to be leveraged by future financial institutions to facilitate international transactions that are both expeditious and economically efficient. This technological advancement will obviate the need for correspondent banks and reduce settlement durations, thereby conferring advantages upon both customers and financial institutions.

7.12.2 Streamlined Trade Finance

Trade financing is a multifaceted process that encompasses intricate documentation and the involvement of numerous stakeholders. The utilization of blockchain technology streamlines this procedure through the conversion of physical papers into digital format, the automation of various activities, and the provision of instantaneous access to up-to-date information regarding transaction progress. Banks are in a position to enhance the efficiency of trade finance operations, diminish reliance on physical documentation, and mitigate the likelihood of errors and conflicts.

7.12.3 Innovative Revenue Streams

Blockchain technology has the potential to create novel avenues for generating revenue inside the banking industry. Users have the opportunity to investigate various services pertaining to digital assets, custody solutions specifically designed for cryptocurrencies, and investment products that are based on blockchain technology. These solutions have the potential to appeal to a wider range of customers and enhance the diversification of income sources.

7.13   Blockchain and Sustainable Technologies

Blockchain technology holds promise with respect to facilitating the progression of sustainable technologies and effectively tackling environmental and societal issues. There exist several aspects of blockchain technology's potential contributions to the promotion of sustainability.

7.13.1 Renewable Energy Trading

Blockchain technology has the capacity to transform renewable energy trading, presenting novel and inventive resolutions to the urgent predicaments encountered within the energy industry. One of the primary prospects exists within the domain of peer-to-peer energy trading, where blockchain technology facilitates the establishment of a decentralized, transparent, and efficient platform for energy trading. Solar panel owners and others who generate renewable energy have the ability to establish direct connections with their neighbors or the wider electrical grid, thereby obviating the need for intermediaries and promoting a collective sense of belonging to an energy community. The facilitation of energy transactions is achieved through the use of smart contracts, which effectively automate the process and guarantee equitable remuneration for the involved participants.

Moreover, the incorporation of blockchain technology has the potential to be applied in the advancement of microgrids, which are decentralized energy systems capable of functioning autonomously or in conjunction with the primary energy grid. Blockchain's decentralized ledger functionalities have the potential to augment the administration of microgrids through the secure documentation and validation of transactions occurring between producers and consumers within the network. This invention not only enhances energy resilience in the presence of disturbances but also optimizes the allocation of renewable energy resources, thereby making a significant contribution to a more sustainable and efficient energy ecosystem.

Furthermore, blockchain technology has the potential to bring about a transformation in carbon offset markets. The implementation of a tamper-proof ledger system facilitates the tracking and verification of carbon offset credits, thereby instilling in enterprises more confidence regarding their investments in renewable energy projects and sustainable activities. The implementation of transparency measures not only facilitates process efficiency but also guarantees the credibility and veracity of claims made with respect to the environment. Blockchain technology enables enhanced monitoring and auditing of carbon offset projects, advancing worldwide efforts to mitigate climate change and foster sustainable environmental practices.

7.13.2 Environmental Conservation

Blockchain technology has the potential to make significant contributions to the protection of endangered species and effectively overcome the various obstacles encountered in the realm of wildlife conservation. The application of blockchain technology enables the secure recording and tracking of vital data pertaining to the environment, population, and movements of endangered animals. Such data function as a digital ledger, offering visible and unalterable documentation of crucial information pertaining to conservation efforts.

One of the key benefits of implementing blockchain technology in the field of wildlife conservation is its capacity to address the issue of poaching. Blockchain technology enables the storage of comprehensive information pertaining to the geographical location and well-being of endangered fauna. These data may be readily disseminated among various entities such as conservation groups, governmental bodies, and other relevant parties. The availability of real-time information facilitates prompt action in addressing possible risks and illicit behaviors, such as the act of poaching or the degradation of habitats. In addition, blockchain technology has the potential to enable the verification of wildlife products, such as ivory or exotic animal skins, thereby confirming their lawful origin and deterring illicit activities associated with the trading of endangered species.

The field of forestry and land conservation encompasses the study and management of forests and natural landscapes with the aim of preserving their ecological integrity and promoting the sustainable use of resources.

The use of blockchain technology can be applied to the domains of forestry and land conservation, effectively addressing pressing concerns pertaining to the implementation of sustainable forestry methods and the preservation of natural landscapes.

A notable application involves the authentication of lumber that has been harvested in a sustainable manner. Global commerce in timber and wood products is considerable, with illicit logging presenting a substantial peril to forests and ecosystems. Blockchain technology enables the establishment of a verifiable and immutable ledger pertaining to the production and distribution of timber, thereby ensuring transparency. Blockchain can be used to record and document every stage of a supply chain, including activities such as harvesting, processing, and transportation. This practice can help to guarantee that timber products will be obtained from forestry operations that adhere to legal and sustainable practices, thereby mitigating the negative impacts of deforestation and habitat damage.

7.14   Tangle

Tangle is a blockchain alternative that emerged around 2014. It is built upon directed acyclic graph (DAG) technology, which gives rise to a distinctive tangle-shaped architecture wherein transactions are coupled via nodes. In contrast to conventional blockchain systems, this alternative approach obviates the need for mining and proof of work, instead relying on distributed validators inside the network to authenticate transactions. This novel methodology presents a number of significant benefits, discussed in the following subsections.

Parallel Verification

Transactions on the Tangle network undergo parallel verification, as opposed to the sequential block processing characteristic of conventional blockchain networks. As a consequence of this, the process of validating transactions is expedited, obviating the need for miners to authenticate transactions.

Speed and Efficiency

The transaction approval process on Tangle is characterized by its rapidity and efficiency, as it requires users to authenticate the two preceding transactions within the network. This feature effectively reduces the latency associated with achieving consensus among network participants, as observed in the context of blockchain technology. Tangle has the capability to perform a range of 500–800 transactions per second, which means enhanced scalability and speed in comparison to some blockchain platforms.

Scalability

The Tangle protocol possesses the theoretical advantage of unlimited transaction scalability. As the quantity of transactions incorporated into the network expands, there is a corresponding rise in the number of verifiers, guaranteeing effective validation even in the presence of a substantial volume of transactions.

Feeless Transactions

IOTA (Internet of Things Crypto Platform) is a notable crypto project focusing on IoT, aiming to revolutionize the ecosystem with its distributed ledger technology. In contrast to blockchain networks, which rely on transaction fees as rewards for miners, Tangle, specifically in the context of IOTA, operates without any transaction costs. Transaction costs are affected by various parameters, such as the amount of the transaction, the level of network activity, and the desired speed of confirmation. This makes it economically advantageous, particularly for small-scale payments.

Ecosystem Building

The work of developing a full ecosystem for emerging technologies such as Tangle and IOTA, both in India and on a global scale, is ongoing. Continuing efforts are being made to cultivate awareness and acceptance that extend beyond the mere act of purchasing and selling coins.

Coexistence with Traditional Blockchains

The coexistence of diverse blockchain technologies is expected, as they are projected to meet distinct objectives. As an illustration, Bitcoin has the potential to persist as a means of preserving wealth, whereas IOTA is specifically designed to cater to the requirements of IoT applications. It is anticipated that conventional blockchain methodologies will coexist with these nascent technologies.

Future Development

Although Tangle and DAG-based technologies exhibit promise in terms of scalability and efficiency compared to blockchain, a comprehensive understanding of their performance and acceptance is expected to take several more years. Tangle and Hashgraph, two DAG-based technologies, are perceived as viable substitutes for conventional blockchains, each possessing distinct advantages and applications.

7.15   Summary

This chapter introduced the metaverse, highlighting implementation challenges and the need for innovative solutions. Blockchain technology plays a crucial role by enabling interoperability, enhancing security and trust, and supporting monetization. It ensures digital asset ownership and security in the decentralized metaverse, serving as a data hub. DTNs facilitate various applications, while blockchain is transforming ESG, digital assets, financial markets, and AI integration. Smart contracts automate processes, and blockchain ensures scalability and data integrity in the metaverse. Tangle serves as an alternative to traditional blockchain technology. It relies on DAG architecture, forming a distinctive tangle-shaped structure where transactions are interconnected via nodes.

7.16   Short/Long Answer Questions

a. What are some potential challenges that blockchain technology may face in the future, and how might researchers address them?

b. Explain the concept of blockchain scalability, and discuss possible solutions to improve the scalability of blockchain networks.

c. Describe how blockchain technology can impact traditional financial systems, and provide examples of ongoing research in this area.

d. What role can blockchain play in enhancing cybersecurity, and what research initiatives are focusing on blockchain's security applications?

e. Briefly explain the concept of blockchain interoperability and its significance in the blockchain ecosystem. Provide examples of current research addressing interoperability issues.

f. How can blockchain technology contribute to supply chain management, and what are some research directions aimed at optimizing supply chain processes using blockchain?

g. Discuss the potential environmental concerns associated with blockchain technology, and elaborate on research efforts aimed at making blockchain more sustainable.

Bibliography

1. Dannen, C. (2017). Introducing Ethereum and Solidity: Foundations of Cryptocurrency and Blockchain Programming for Beginners.
2. Çulha, D. (2023). A gamification model for teaching blockchain programming. International Journal of Technology Enhanced Learning.
3. Jurgelaitis, M., Čeponienė, L., Butkus, K., Butkienė, R., & Drungilas, V. (2022). MDA-Based Approach for Blockchain Smart Contract Development. Applied Sciences.
4. Brünjes, L., & Gabbay, M.J. (2020). UTxO- vs account-based smart contract blockchain programming paradigms. ArXiv, abs/2003.14271.
5. Sguanci, C., Spatafora, R., & Vergani, A. (2021). Layer 2 Blockchain Scaling: a Survey. ArXiv, abs/2107.10881.
6. Ahlawat, S., & Tripathi, A. (2021). Chapter 2 Blockchain: implications for accounting and audit practice. Blockchain 3.0 for Sustainable Development.
7. Faustino, S., Faria, I., & Marques, R. (2021). The myths and legends of king Satoshi and the knights of blockchain. Journal of Cultural Economy, 15, 67–80.
8. Ahmad, S.S., Khan, S., & Kamal, M.A. (2019). What is Blockchain Technology and its Significance in the Current Healthcare System? A brief Insight. Current pharmaceutical design.
9. Ismail, A., Toohey, M., Lee, Y.C., Dong, Z., & Zomaya, A.Y. (2022). Cost and Performance Analysis on Decentralized File Systems for Blockchain-Based Applications: State-of-the-Art Report. 2022 IEEE International Conference on Blockchain (Blockchain), 230–237.
10. Millar, C.C., Lockett, M., & Ladd, T. (2017). Disruption : Technology, innovation and society. Technological Forecasting and Social Change, 129, 254–260.
11. Semenzin, S., Rozas, D., & Hassan, S. (2022). Blockchain-based application at a governmental level: disruption or illusion? The case of Estonia. Policy and Society.
12. Nakamoto, S. (2022). Charting the Bitcoin Universe (and other New Research).
13. Kumar, A., & Kumar, S. (2022). Secured Ethereum Transactions using Smart Contracts & Solidity. YMER Digital.
14. El-Abbasy, E.M. (2023). The Impact of Distinctive Features of Blockchain Technology on the Customer's Agility: The Modified Role of the Requirements for the Implementation of Blockchain Technology-Applied Study in the Egyptian Pharmaceutical Companies. Jordan Journal of Business Administration
15. Cahyadi, F.A., Owen, A.I., Ricardo, F., & Gunawan, A.A. (2021). Blockchain Technology behind Cryptocurrency and Bitcoin for Commercial Transactions. 2021 1st International Conference on Computer Science and Artificial Intelligence (ICCSAI), 1, 115–119.
16. Antonopoulos, A.M. (2014). Mastering Bitcoin: Unlocking Digital Crypto-Currencies.
17. Bowler, R.D., Speed, C., Goodell, G., & Revans, J. (2023). A Non-Custodial Wallet for CBDC: Design Challenges and Opportunities. ArXiv, abs/2307.05167.
18. Noor Sayuti, M., Hasnita, & Munfaridah, F. (2023). ZIS Payment Interest on LAZ Nurul Fikri in Palangka Raya: The Impact of Digital Wallet Service Features. Proceeding of International Conference on Islamic Philantrophy.
19. Ilieva, G., Yankova, T., Dzhabarova, Y., Ruseva, M., Angelov, D., & Klisarova-Belcheva, S. (2023). Customer Attitude toward Digital Wallet Services. Syst., 11, 185.
20. Buccafurri, F., Lax, G., Russo, A., & Zunino, G. (2018). Integrating Digital Identity and Blockchain. OTM Conferences.
21. Rodwald, P. (2021). An Analysis of Data Hidden in Bitcoin Addresses.
22. Jovic, Z. (2016). Bitcoin - Banking and Technological Challenges.

23. Laborde, P., Lebanoff, L., Peterson, C.L., Zhang, D., & Dechev, D. (2019). Wait-free Dynamic Transactions for Linked Data Structures. Proceedings of the 10th International Workshop on Programming Models and Applications for Multicores and Manycores.

24. Bisheh-Niasar, M., Azarderakhsh, R., & Mozaffari-Kermani, M. (2021). Cryptographic Accelerators for Digital Signature Based on Ed25519. IEEE Transactions on Very Large Scale Integration (VLSI) Systems, 29, 1297–1305.

25. Lamriji, Y., Kasri, M., Makkaoui, K.E., & Beni-Hssane, A. (2023). A Comparative Study of Consensus Algorithms for Blockchain. 2023 3rd International Conference on Innovative Research in Applied Science, Engineering and Technology (IRASET), 1–8.

26. Sun, Z., Zhang, S., & Liu, M. (2021). Speed racing industry information management system based on machine learning and data mining. Journal of Intelligent and Fuzzy Systems, 1–13.

27. Yang, J., & Li, Z. (2020). Impact of Bitcoin's Distributed Structure on the Construction of the Central Bank's Digital Currency System. 2020 Fourth International Conference on Inventive Systems and Control (ICISC), 829–832.

28. Kushwaha, S.S., Joshi, S., Singh, D., Kaur, M., & Lee, H. (2022). Systematic Review of Security Vulnerabilities in Ethereum Blockchain Smart Contract. IEEE Access, PP, 1–1.

29. Omar, I.A., Jayaraman, R., Debe, M.S., Hasan, H.R., Salah, K., & Omar, M.A. (2022). Supply Chain Inventory Sharing Using Ethereum Blockchain and Smart Contracts. IEEE Access, 10, 2345–2356.

30. Nakamoto, S. (2020). International Journal of Innovative Technology and Exploring Engineering (IJITEE).

31. Chishti, M.S., Sufyan, F., & Banerjee, A. (2022). Decentralized On-Chain Data Access via Smart Contracts in Ethereum Blockchain. IEEE Transactions on Network and Service Management, 19, 174–187.

32. Bragadeesh, S.A., & Arumugam, U. (2022). Secured Vehicle Life Cycle Tracking Using Blockchain and Smart Contract. Comput. Syst. Sci. Eng., 41, 1–18.

33. Peng, G., Ai, S., Zhang, L., Rong, C., & Markeset, T. (2018). Equipment Life-cycle Management based on Private Blockchain and Smart Contract. EasyChair Preprints.

34. Precht, H., Schwarm, F., & Gómez, J.M. (2022). Enhancing Smart Contract Quality by Introducing a Continuous Integration Pipeline for Solidity Based Smart Contracts. International Congress on Blockchain and Applications.

35. Gümüş, C. (2019). Effects of the contracts and construction of Istanbul-Baghdad railway on Anatolian forests. Journal of Sustainable Forestry, 38, 572–590.

36. Liao, Z., Hao, S., Nan, Y., & Zheng, Z. (2023). SmartState: Detecting State-Reverting Vulnerabilities in Smart Contracts via Fine-Grained State-Dependency Analysis. Proceedings of the 32nd ACM SIGSOFT International Symposium on Software Testing and Analysis.

37. Jurgelaitis, M., Čeponienė, L., & Butkienė, R. (2022). Solidity Code Generation from UML State Machines in Model-Driven Smart Contract Development. IEEE Access, PP, 1–1.

38. Zhang, S., Tang, M.C., Li, X., Liu, B., Zhang, B., Hu, F., Ni, S., & Cheng, J. (2022). ROS-Ethereum: A Convenient Tool to Bridge ROS and Blockchain (Ethereum). Security and Communication Networks.

39. Tikhomirov, S., Voskresenskaya, E., Ivanitskiy, I., Takhaviev, R., Marchenko, E., & Alexandrov, Y. (2018). SmartCheck: Static Analysis of Ethereum Smart Contracts. 2018 IEEE/ACM 1st International Workshop on Emerging Trends in Software Engineering for Blockchain (WETSEB), 9–16.

40. Omonayajo, B., Mubarak, A.S., Al-turjman, F.M., & Ameen, Z.S. (2022). Ethereum Gas Price Prediction Using Facebook Prophet Model. 2022 International Conference on Artificial Intelligence in Everything (AIE), 455–459.

41. Srikant, S., & Kolodziejski, L.A. (2020). Vulcan: Classifying Vulnerabilities in Solidity Smart Contracts Using Dependency-Based Deep Program Representations.

42. Saingre, D., Ledoux, T., & Menaud, J. (2020). BCTMark: a Framework for Benchmarking Blockchain Technologies. 2020 IEEE/ACS 17th International Conference on Computer Systems and Applications (AICCSA), 1–8.

43. Ray, V., Singh, A., Singh, M., Singh, R., & Palwe, S. (2021). The Study of Usage of Hyperledger Fabric in Agricultural Ecommerce. Recent Trends in Intensive Computing.

44. Shaikh, Z.A., Khan, A.A., Baitenova, L., Zambinova, G., Yegina, N., Ivolgina, N., Laghari, A., & Barykin, S.E. (2022). A Blockchain Hyperledger and Non-Linear Machine Learning: A Novel and Secure Educational Accreditation Registration and Distributed Ledger Preservation Architecture. Applied Sciences.

45. Androulaki, E., Barger, A., Bortnikov, V., Cachin, C., Christidis, K., Caro, A.D., Enyeart, D., Ferris, C., Laventman, G., Manevich, Y., Muralidharan, S., Murthy, C., Nguyen, B., Sethi, M., Singh, G., Smith, K.A., Sorniotti, A., Stathakopoulou, C., Vukolic, M., Cocco, S.W., & Yellick, J. (2018). Hyperledger fabric: a distributed operating system for permissioned blockchains. Proceedings of the Thirteenth EuroSys Conference.

46. Gaba, P., Raw, R.S., Mohammed, M.A., Nedoma, J., & Martínek, R. (2022). Impact of Block Data Components on the Performance of Blockchain-Based VANET Implemented on Hyperledger Fabric. IEEE Access, 10, 71003–71018.

47. Klaokliang, N., Teawtim, P., Aimtongkham, P., So-In, C., & Niruntasukrat, A. (2018). A Novel IoT Authorization Architecture on Hyperledger Fabric With Optimal Consensus Using Genetic Algorithm. 2018 Seventh ICT International Student Project Conference (ICT-ISPC), 1–5.

48. Wu, O., Li, S., Zhang, H., Liu, L., Wang, Y., & Li, H. (2022). An Optimized Scheduling Algorithm for the Multi-channel Hyperledger Fabric. 2022 IEEE Intl Conf on Parallel & Distributed Processing with Applications, Big Data & Cloud Computing, Sustainable Computing & Communications, Social Computing & Networking (ISPA/BDCloud/SocialCom/SustainCom), 636–643.

49. Weerasinghe, N., Hewa, T.M., Liyanage, M., Kanhere, S.S., & Ylianttila, M. (2021). A Novel Blockchain-as-a-Service (BaaS) Platform for Local 5G Operators. IEEE Open Journal of the Communications Society, 2, 575–601.

50. Kim, J.J., Lingga, P., Jeong, J.P., Choi, Y., & Park, J. (2022). A Web-Based Monitoring System of Network Security Functions in Blockchain-Based Cloud Security Systems. 2022 International Conference on Information Networking (ICOIN), 454–459.

51. Choi, W., & Hong, J.W. (2021). Performance Evaluation of Ethereum Private and Testnet Networks Using Hyperledger Caliper. 2021 22nd Asia-Pacific Network Operations and Management Symposium (APNOMS), 325–329.

52. Lee, J.,& Yeol, C.H. (2018). A Case Study of Using Hyperledger Composer based on Docker Container for Implementing Block Chain Distributed Ledger. Korean Association Of Computers And Accounting.

53. Azzam, F., Jaber, M., Saies, A., Kirresh, T., Awadallah, R., Karakra, A., Barghouthi, H., & Amarneh, S. (2023). The Use of Blockchain Technology and OCR in E-Government for Document Management: Inbound Invoice Management as an Example. Applied Sciences.

54. Zhao, X., Zhang, Z., Hu, R., Liu, J., Yang, X., Zhang, R., & Gao, H. (2022). Blockchain Technology Based Digital Document Management System Design. 2022 7th Asia Conference on Power and Electrical Engineering (ACPEE), 440–446.

55. Wang, Z., Liffman, D.Y., Karunamoorthy, D., & Abebe, E. (2018). Distributed Ledger Technology for Document and Workflow Management in Trade and Logistics. Proceedings of the 27th ACM International Conference on Information and Knowledge Management.

56. Vikram, A., Kumar, S., & Mohana (2022). Blockchain Technology and its Impact on Future of Internet of Things (IoT) and Cyber Security. 2022 6th International Conference on Electronics, Communication and Aerospace Technology, 444–447.

57. Spain, T., & Turner, D.A. (2022). Food for thought: Transport within the food supply chain. The Journal of Transport History, 43, 194–213.

58. MacDonald, A.J. (2019). Minimizing Terminal Food Waste within the Food Supply Chain. Ardra, S., & Barua, M.K. (2022). Inclusion of circular economy practices in the food supply chain: Challenges and possibilities for reducing food wastage in emerging economies like India. Environment, Development and Sustainability, 1–34.

59. Song, Hao, Wenfei Ge, Pan Gao, and Wei Xu. 2023. "A Novel Blockchain-Enabled Supply-Chain Management Framework for Xinjiang Jujube: Research on Optimized Blockchain Considering Private Transactions" Foods 12, no. 3: 587. https://doi.org/10.3390/foods12030587

60. Getahun, M. (2016). Capital Structure and Financial Performance of Insurance Industries in Ethiopia. Global Journal of Management and Business Research, 16.

61. Flückiger, I., & Duygun, M. (2022). New technologies and data in insurance. The Geneva Papers on Risk and Insurance. Issues and Practice, 47, 495–498.

62. Trivedi, S. (2022). A Risk Management Framework for Life Insurance Companies. Journal of corporate governance, insurance and risk management.

63. Bhasin , R. (2022). Digitization of Income Tax Administration in India. VISION: Journal of Indian Taxation.

64. Mohapatra , M.R., & Mohapatra, S. (2016). AN APPRAISAL OF CORPORATE TAX IN INDIA: A SELF ASSESSMENT. Abhinav-International Monthly Refereed Journal Of Research In Management & Technology, 5, 40–48.

65. Alwedyan, A. (2021). The Impact of Training Sessions on Job Performance of Employees at Income Tax and Sales Department in Irbid Province. Academic Journal of Interdisciplinary Studies, 10, 22–22.

66. Amelia, A., Mathies, C., & Patterson, P.G. (2021). Customer acceptance of frontline service robots in retail banking: A qualitative approach. Journal of Service Management.

67. Haralayya, D.B. (2021). Retail Banking Trends in India. PSN: Financial Institutions (Topic).

68. Mukerjee, K. (2020). Impact of self-service technologies in retail banking on cross-buying and word-of-mouth. International Journal of Retail & Distribution Management, 48, 485–500. Mukerjee, K. (2020). Impact of self-service technologies in retail banking on cross-buying and word-of-mouth. International Journal of Retail & Distribution Management, 48, 485–500.

69. Wang, D., Deng, Y., Oudich, M., Benalcazar, W.A., Ma, G., Physics, Y.J., University, H.K., Tong, K., Kong, H., China, Acoustics, G.P., University, T.P., Park, U., 16802, P., USA., Physics, D.O., University, E., Atlanta, & 30322, G. (2023). Realization of a Z classified chiral-symmetric higher-order topological insulator in a coupling-inversion acoustic crystal.

70. Gadekallu, T.R., Huynh-The, T., Wang, W., Yenduri, G., Ranaweera, P.S., Pham, Q., Costa, D.B., & Liyanage, M. (2022). Blockchain for the Metaverse: A Review. ArXiv, abs/2203.09738.
71. Bouachir, O., Aloqaily, M., Karray, F., & El Saddik, A. (2022). AI-based Blockchain for the Metaverse: Approaches and Challenges. 2022 Fourth International Conference on Blockchain Computing and Applications (BCCA), 231–236.
72. Setiawan, K.D., Anthony, A., Meyliana, & Surjandy (2022). The Essential Factor of Metaverse for Business Based on 7 Layers of Metaverse – Systematic Literature Review. 2022 International Conference on Information Management and Technology (ICIMTech), 687–692.
73. Ramesh, U.V., Harini, A., Gowri, C.S., Durga, K.V., Druvitha, P., & Kumar, K.S. (2022). Metaverse: Future of the Internet.
74. Park, S., & Kim, Y. (2022). A Metaverse: Taxonomy, Components, Applications, and Open Challenges. IEEE Access, 10, 4209–4251.
75. Jung, S., & Jeon, I. (2022). A study on the components of the Metaverse ecosystem.
76. Xu, M., Ng, W.C., Lim, W.Y., Kang, J., Xiong, Z., Niyato, D.T., Yang, Q., Shen, X.S., & Miao, C. (2022). A Full Dive Into Realizing the Edge-Enabled Metaverse: Visions, Enabling Technologies, and Challenges. IEEE Communications Surveys & Tutorials, 25, 656–700.
77. Soni, L., Kaur, A., & Sharma, A. (2023). A Review on Metaverse and Immersive Technologies. 2023 Third International Conference on Artificial Intelligence and Smart Energy (ICAIS), 924–928.
78. Gonçalves, G., Melo, M., Barbosa, L., Vasconcelos-Raposo, J., & Bessa, M. (2021). Evaluation of the impact of different levels of self-representation and body tracking on the sense of presence and embodiment in immersive VR. Virtual Reality, 26, 1–14.
79. Meepung, T., & Kannikar, P. (2022). Metaverse; Virtual World Challenges and Opportunities for Digital Business. Journal of Economics, Business and Management.
80. Brekke, J.K., & Fischer, A. (2021). Digital scarcity. Internet Policy Rev., 10.
81. Arewa, O.B. (2022). Scarcity amidst plenty: Regulating digital transformation. Frontiers in Research Metrics and Analytics, 7.
82. Cheng, R., Chen, S., & Han, B. (2023). Towards Zero-trust Security for the Metaverse. ArXiv, abs/2302.08885.
83. He, Y., Li, W., Liu, L., & He, W. (2023). NFTs – A Game Changer or a Bubble in the Digital Market? Journal of Global Information Technology Management, 26, 1–8.
84. McDonald, L., & Adcock, L. (2017). Intersecting Dialogues in Health and Aging: Developing Digital Trust Networks in Regional Australia. The International Journal of Aging and Society, 7, 91–100.
85. Pietrzak, P., & Takala, J.A. (2021). Digital trust – asystematic literature review.
86. Jacbs, G. (2018). Cryptocurrencies & the Challenge of Global Governance.
87. Sadiq, M., Ngo, T.Q., Pantamee, A.A., Khudoykulov, K., Thi Ngan, T., & Tan, L.P. (2022). The role of environmental social and governance in achieving sustainable development goals: evidence from ASEAN countries. Economic Research-Ekonomska Istraživanja.
88. Pai, R.Y., Shetty, A., Shetty, A.D., Bhandary, R., Shetty, J., Nayak, S., Dinesh, T.K., & D'souza, K.J. (2022). Integrating artificial intelligence for knowledge management systems – synergy among people and technology: a systematic review of the evidence. Economic Research-Ekonomska Istraživanja, 35, 7043–7065.
89. Stulz, R.M. (2019). Fintech, Bigtech, and the Future of Banks. Corporate Finance: Capital Structure & Payout Policies eJournal.
90. Kregel, J.A. (2018). The past and future of banks 1. Financial Stability, Systems and Regulation.
91. Tang, Y., Huo, W., Liu, M., & Jiang, Y. (2022). Renewable energy trading mechanism based on blockchain technology. Other Conferences.
92. Bramas, Q. (2018). The Stability and the Security of the Tangle. International Conference on Blockchain Economics, Security and Protocols.
93. Núñez, R., & Cooperrider, K. (2013). The tangle of space and time in human cognition. Trends in Cognitive Sciences, 17, 220–229.

Index

© The Author(s), under exclusive license to APress Media, LLC, part of Springer Nature 2024
R. S. Mangrulkar, P. Vijay Chavan, *Blockchain Essentials*,
https://doi.org/10.1007/978-1-4842-9975-3

Printed in the United States
by Baker & Taylor Publisher Services